CHASING THE EPHEMERAL

50 Routes for a Successful SCOTTISH WINTER

Simon Richardson is one of Scotland's most prolific winter climbers with more than 600 new routes to his credit.

As well as developing classic climbing areas such as Aonach Mòr, he helped introduce the Scottish two-tier winter grading system, pioneered modern mixed climbing on Ben Nevis and is author of the Scottish Mountaineering Club's climbers' guide to Ben Nevis, The Aonachs & Creag Meagaidh. During the winter he reports on the Scottish Winter Climbing scene via his popular blog *www.scottishwinter.com*

He lives in Aberdeen with his wife Christine and has a son and daughter.

CHASING THE EPHEMERAL

50 Routes for a Successful SCOTTISH WINTER

Simon Richardson

mica

ISBN: 978-0-9560367-9-7
A catalogue record for this book is available from the British Library

Front Cover: Cumming-Crofton Route (IV,6), Beinn a' Bhuird. Climber Robbie Miller (photo Henning Wackerhage)

WARNING

The British Mountaineering Council and Mountaineering Council of Scotland state that climbing and mountaineering are activities with a danger of personal injury or death.

In winter, Scotland's mountains take on a seriousness out of proportion to their size, and both weather and climbing conditions can change with little warning.

Winter climbers should be aware of and accept these risks and be responsible for their own actions and involvement.

While every effort has been made to check the accuracy of the information contained within this book, neither Mica Publishing, nor the author accept liability for personal or third party injury or death, or damage to property, arising from its use.

Published by **Mica Publishing**, Glasgow & Edinburgh

Printed & bound by Bell & Bain Ltd, Glasgow, Scotland

Distributed by Cordee, 11 Jacknell Road, Dodwells Industrial Estate, Hinkley, LE10 3BS
(t) 01455 61185   (e) sales@cordee.co.uk   (w) www.cordee.co.uk

CONTENTS

THE ROUTES

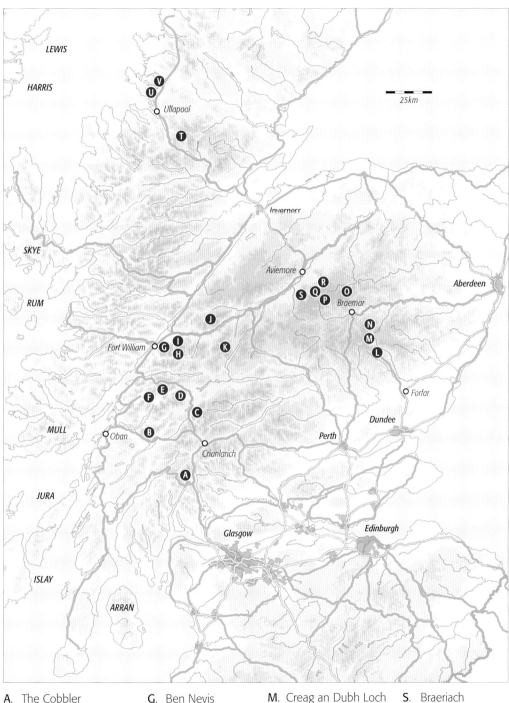

A. The Cobbler
B. Ben Cruachan
C. Ben Dorain
D. Buachaille Etive Mòr
E. Stob Coire nan Lochan
F. Beinn Fhionnlaidh
G. Ben Nevis
H. Aonach Beag
I. Aonach Mòr
J. Creag Meagaidh
K. Ben Alder
L. Glen Clova
M. Creag an Dubh Loch
N. Lochnagar
O. Beinn a' Bhuird
P. Shelter Stone Crag
Q. Hell's Lum Crag
R. Cairn Gorm
S. Braeriach
T. Beinn Dearg
U. Sgùrr an Fhidhleir
V. Cùl Beag

Solving the frozen puzzle of finding protection while leading a pitch is a key aspect of Scottish winter climbing, but the underlying challenge is predicting the conditions and selecting an appropriate route

Simon Richardson

INTRODUCTION

I consider myself a lucky man. As a hopelessly addicted winter climber, Scotland is one of the few places in the world where I can get up in the morning, have a full mountain adventure and return home the same evening. The Scottish mountains are exactly the right scale to be approached, climbed and descended within a full winter's day.

During the winter months, the Scottish Highlands take on a seriousness out of proportion to their size. Snow collects in huge quantities on the summit plateaux, from where the prevailing winds sweep it into deep glacier-scoured corries, whose cliffs are typically fractured, vegetated and perfect for on-sight climbing. Cracks take protection readily and frozen turf has the consistency of plastic ice. When conditions are good, gullies choke with ice and snow, ice dribbles down corners, powder snow drapes steep walls, and rime ice transforms buttresses into frosted fantasy castles towering into the sky.

Many routes are a race against time and the short winter day. The wind blows frequently, it is often raining in the glens and snowing on the tops, and

despite modern clothing and materials, you are often damp. On longer routes, a single push is far more effective than a multi-day ascent as the weather is too poor to consider bivouacking. The sub-arctic climate is unforgiving, and it is always better to keep moving than to stop.

Bolts are shunned and there is very little fixed gear on Scottish cliffs. Many routes can feel like a first ascent, particularly on less frequented crags. Protection has to be placed on the lead and belays can sometimes be difficult to find. It is this mental dimension that makes Scottish winter climbing so compelling. Solving the frozen puzzle of finding protection and leading a pitch is one aspect, but long approaches, short winter days, wild and unpredictable weather, and difficult navigation all add to the experience.

However, predicting conditions and selecting an appropriate route is the underlying challenge. Conditions change daily, and while many Scottish climbs are reliably in condition at some point during the season, others require a particular sequence of snowfall, wind, thaw and freeze to form, and it may take several years for this combination to occur. Historically, many of the most successful Scottish winter climbers have not been the strongest or most technically gifted, but those with the knack of being in the right place at the right time.

Like many climbers I juggle my family and a job with my climbing. For many years, my work commitments constrained me to climbing at weekends, and to fit in with family activities I chose to go climbing on Sundays. Selecting a route that fitted the conditions was critical. If I made a poor call there was no second chance – I would have to wait until the following weekend to try again.

However, unlike summer when it has to be warm and dry to climb in the mountains, winter climbing is less dependent on really favourable conditions. With careful thought about where to go and what to climb,

I believe it is possible to climb winter routes in the Scottish mountains nine weekends out of ten from November through to April.

By their very nature, Scottish winter climbs are transitory and elusive. Catching that fleeting moment in time is the essence of the winter experience and the key Scottish winter climbing skill is route choice. This is made up from three elements – **where to go, when to go** and **what to climb**. There is little point training hard to climb Grade VII if you keep going to the wrong place and finding your chosen routes out of condition.

This book is more than a selected guide. It is about strategy and tactics – how to select your route and then go and climb it. If *Chasing The Ephemeral* prompts you to think more widely about those critical factors, then it will have achieved its aim.

WHY THIS BOOK?

Several years ago George McEwan, chief instructor at Glenmore Lodge, invited Chris Cartwright and I to talk at a Winter Climbing Performance Seminar. Chris and I had climbed together for ten years and had a strong winter track record, so there was a gentle air of anticipation when we started to talk. Our presentation described the tactics, skills and knowledge required to consistently climb challenging routes, but when we finished the audience was a little subdued. That evening in the bar the reason became apparent – our message appeared too simple. We must have kept some cards close to our chest. Surely for Chris and I to succeed on a good route every weekend there had to be a magic bullet?

A year later I was in the bar again and a Lodge instructor came up to me. "You know Simon," he said quietly, "the talk you and Chris gave at last year's seminar has completely transformed my winter climbing. I'm climbing harder and have a higher success rate, because I'm making better route choices. When I'm at the crag I can concentrate on the climbing itself. I've already thought through the other factors and know what to do, so there are no distractions." I was thrilled when I heard this and delighted that the message had landed. The genesis of this book is the philosophy that Chris and I presented at that original seminar.

At first sight, this book might appear to be just a selection of 50 Scottish winter routes. But it is intended to be more than that. The objective is to explain how to choose your route and find it in winter condition. To do this, I believe it is helpful to

understand firstly the types of Scottish winter Mountain Conditions, secondly the five Styles of Winter Route, and finally the process of pre-route planning needed to merge the two. The key to successful Scottish winter climbing is to choose a route to fit the prevailing conditions, rather than forcing the conditions to fit the climb or vice versa. This requires flexibility and an understanding of how the Style of winter route and Mountain Conditions interplay with each other.

The routes described in this book are all excellent climbs, but they are not meant to represent the very best winter routes in Scotland. Many of Scotland's 'best' routes require optimum conditions that may only occur once every few years. And frustratingly, when good conditions finally arrive, many of these routes are in condition all at the same time.

The Scottish winter can be up to six months long, so this book contains a varied selection of objectives to keep you climbing throughout the season. This will allow you to choose a venue and routes that are likely to be in condition at any point in the winter.

This book focuses on technical winter climbing in the Scottish mountains. Mountain icefalls are included but valley icefalls, which are a speciality unto themselves are not, and nor are ridge traverses such as the Aonach Eagach, which are more mountaineering outings than technical climbs. Neither is this book about climbing technique or equipment – there are far better qualified people to write about these aspects. But similar to the finest guidebooks, my hope is that this book will inspire as well as inform.

MOUNTAIN CONDITIONS

Most winter seasons follow a similar pattern, although the very changeable Scottish weather makes it impossible to predict the exact timing and sequence. The first stage when choosing a route is to recognise the prevailing Mountain Conditions:

1. **Early** season means anything from the first snowfalls in October through to the end of December. Routes climbed in this period are typically Snowed-Up Rock or Mixed routes that have sufficient altitude to come into condition early.

2. **Cold** represents a period that normally occurs in the depth of winter (often in January) when Polar air sets in and it is bitterly cold. The cold air is often accompanied by huge falls of snow. This can be a frustrating time, because the mountains may be completely white and look like a picture postcard, but approaching them and finding routes in condition is a different story. Alternatively, it can be bitterly cold and the mountains bare of snow.

3. **Lean** conditions follow a deep thaw and can occur at any time during the season. Thaws are an essential part of the cycle needed to build Top Nick winter climbing conditions, but they can appear to completely strip the hills. Fortunately, winter still lingers high in the cold north facing corries, and as soon as the freezing level drops below summit level, specific routes rapidly come back into condition.

4. **Top Nick** conditions are what we all look forward to and typically take place in February and March. The combination of snowfall and freeze-thaw earlier in the season sets up the famous Gullies, the mountain Icefalls and the long icy Mixed climbs that make Scottish winter climbing famous the world over.

5. **Late** season conditions typically occur from mid-March and can last until early May. On high north facing cliffs, snow banks ooze ice that grows with the regular freeze-thaw cycles of spring. This is when many of the famous Ben Nevis mountain Icefalls and Thin Face routes are best climbed.

STYLES OF WINTER ROUTE

One of the great attractions of Scottish winter climbing is the huge variety available. There are five Styles of winter route in Scotland:

1. **Snowed-Up Rock** routes tend to follow the lines of summer climbs and need to be covered in snow, rime ice or hoar frost to turn them into genuine winter ascents. The climbing relies on underlying rock features, so ice and frozen turf are not required for upward progress. Key techniques involve hooking edges, torquing picks, and jamming shafts in cracks.

2. **Mixed** routes involve a combination of ice, frozen turf, and snowed-covered rock. Many of these routes take steep, wet and vegetated terrain that would be very unpleasant in summer and are typically 'winter-only' routes.

3. **Icefalls** form when steep drainage lines freeze in sustained cold weather. Although Scottish icefalls lack the length and stature of the great pillars in the Alps, Norway and Canada, they are often composed of soft plastic ice that is a pleasure to climb.

4. **Gullies** are synonymous with winter climbing in Scotland. Wet and vegetated in summer, they provide natural lines of weakness when choked with snow and ice. Gullies were sought out by the pioneers of Scottish climbing and many are recognised as the country's finest winter climbs.

5. **Thin Face** routes embrace a style of winter climbing that is almost unique to Ben Nevis. Here, the altitude and exposure to continuously changing Atlantic weather allows a thin layer of snow-ice to build on steep slabs and walls high on the mountain. The climbing is bold, delicate and always memorable.

Icefalls, Gullies and Thin Face routes are the more traditional types of Scottish winter climbs. Deciding when these routes are in winter condition is relatively easy as they all need ice, névé or snow. Clearly there is little sense climbing Point Five Gully when it's bare, or venturing onto an Icefall such as Mega Route X when it's unformed. Likewise, attempting a Ben Nevis Thin Face route such as Albatross would be extremely bold and challenging if there was an insufficient thickness of snow-ice plating the lower blank slabs.

Convention dictates that Snowed-Up Rock routes should be covered in powder snow, hoar frost or rime ice to be in winter condition. Climbing bare rock is not very rewarding from an aesthetic point of view – a major attraction of winter climbing is the beauty of the snow and ice and its various forms. If there is one underlying ground rule however, it is to try to look after the environment in which we climb. As winter climbers we have a collective responsibility to keep axe scratches, crampon scrapes and peg scars to the absolute minimum, and this is particularly important for winter ascents of summer rock routes. It should be remembered the convention across the UK is that it is unacceptable to hammer equipment into summer

Henning Wackerhage

Steep, narrow, and choked with ice, Point Five Gully on Ben Nevis is the perfect example of a Scottish Gully climb

Styles Of Winter Route In Scotland –
Examples
Snowed-Up Rock – Savage Slit, Gargoyle Wall
Mixed – Invernookie, Tower Face Of The Comb
Icefalls – Smith's Route, Mega Route X
Gullies – Raeburn's Gully, Point Five Gully
Thin Face - Orion Direct, Albatross

climbs (largely to maintain their pristine nature).

Acceptable conditions for climbing Mixed routes have evolved in recent years, and it is worth reviewing a little history at this point. During the lean 1981 winter season, Andy Nisbet made some experimental mixed ascents on Càrn Etchachan in the Cairngorms. At the time people commented that these routes were not real winter climbs. They just had a thin layer

of powder covering the rock and were climbed on frozen turf. But by recording these routes, Nisbet not only upset the status quo, but ushered in a new dimension for winter climbing. Until this point, Scottish mixed had largely progressed by making increasingly difficult winter ascents of summer climbs, but this alternative direction led to the concept of 'winter-only' climbs that tackle wet or vegetated ground that would be unimaginable in summer.

Nowadays, it is recognised that the most enjoyable mixed climbing occurs when frozen rock and turf is overlain by a thin covering of snow or frost. Logically climbs that are winter-only lines do not have to look white, but most believe that they should. (This is a point worth bearing in mind if you wish to record a new route). Again it is important not to damage the mountain, so please do not attempt Mixed routes when the turf is unfrozen.

HOW TO USE THIS BOOK

The book is divided into five chapters, each relevant to a particular set of Mountain Conditions. The routes selected for each chapter match the conditions, but a key critereon for their inclusion is that I have climbed and enjoyed each of them. I've included some of the finest winter routes in Scotland such as Orion Direct and Point Five Gully, but also selected many less well-known climbs that are off the beaten track. Clearly, Wobble Block Chimney is not in the same class as Orion Direct, but it may be the best possible route that you can climb on a particular day. Taking this more opportunistic approach will open up Scottish winter climbing to a full six month-long season rather than just limiting it to a number of 'perfect conditions' days.

The broad selection of climbs described in this book should allow you to choose a route to fit the prevailing weather and conditions at any point in the season. I've included several of my own, not to highlight my achievements, but simply because I know that they are good climbs that fit specific conditions criteria. During the course of my climbing I've deliberately sought out previously unclimbed crags on mountains such as Aonach Mòr, Cairn Gorm, Ben Cruachan and Lochnagar in order to expand my repertoire of places to visit under a wide variety of conditions.

Although I've climbed extensively across Scotland, there are some areas that I know better than others. Other authors may have included a quartzite route from Beinn Eighe in the Early Bird chapter for example, but I don't feel I know the mountain well enough to make an informed choice. In short, this book is a synthesis of my own experience and what has worked for me during 35 years of climbing in the Scottish mountains.

Of course, many of the selected routes can be climbed in Mountain Conditions different to their allocated chapter. Some climbs are remarkably resilient and can be ascended across the full spectrum of winter conditions, whilst others require more specific criteria. The **Route Suitability Table** opposite compares the routes in this book against their suitability for different conditions.

The selected routes span the five different Styles of winter route and cover a full spread of venues in mainland Scotland from the Southern to the Northern Highlands, including the Cairngorms, Ben Nevis and Glen Coe. Climbs vary from Grade III to Grade VI, which is the grade range in which the majority of winter climbers operate. I have also included a couple of Grade VIIs to aspire to. Both of these are low in their grade and should be accessible to many keen and committed winter climbers.

Grades

The Scottish two-tier winter grading system has been used where the first (Roman) numeral describes the overall difficulty of the route, and the second (Arabic) numeral conveys the difficulty of the hardest section.

A well protected Grade V Mixed route may be rated V,6 for example, whilst a technically easier, but bolder and poorer protected Thin Face route may be given a grade of V,4.

Each route description is prefaced with an introduction to add some background and colour. This may be more detail about the climb itself and why it fits the conditions, or a vignette from personal experience. Sometimes I have included some historical context or have acknowledged the contributions of influential climbers. The route descriptions are accompanied by details of the approach and descent along with a Top Tip (or two).

Finally, and most importantly, there is a section suggesting nearby Alternative Routes that can be climbed in similar conditions. Flexibility is key, so *Chasing The Ephemeral* should be viewed as a complement to the definitive guidebooks that provide detailed descriptions of the venues and Alternative Routes.

A Note On Gaelic Pronunciation

An accent on a vowel in a Gaelic name in this book indicates that it is a long vowel when spoken. Thus Cùl would be pronounced *kool* (not *kul*), while Aonach Mòr would be pronounced *oenach more* (not *oenach mawr*).

Key For Maps & Diagrams

———	**12**	Active Numbered Route
	43	Inactive Numbered Route
- - - - - - -	**RH**	Alternative Route
	P	Car Park
	P	Other parking

Key For Route Suitability Table

Route likely to be in climbable condition
Route possibly in climbable condition
Route unlikely to be in climbable condition

Route Suitability Table

Route	Grade	Style	Early Bird	Cold Snaps	Lean Times	Top Nick	Late Season
1 Savage Slit	V,6	Snowed-Up Rock					■
2 The Hoarmaster	VI,6	Snowed-Up Rock					■
3 The Message	IV,6	Snowed-Up Rock					■
4 Fingers Ridge	IV,5	Snowed-Up Rock					
5 Gargoyle Wall	VI,6	Snowed-Up Rock					
6 Number Three Gully Buttress	III,4	Snowed-Up Rock					■
7 Grooved Arete	V,6	Mixed					■
8 Magic Pillar	IV,5	Mixed					■
9 First Light	IV,5	Mixed					■
10 Jenga Buttress	III,4	Mixed					■
11 Tainted Elixir	V,6	Mixed					
12 The Sting	VI,6	Mixed			■		■
13 Cul Of The Wild	V,6	Mixed	■		■		
14 Fhidhleir's Nose Direct	VII,7	Mixed	■				
15 South-West Ridge	IV,5	Mixed					
16 Right-Angled Gully Direct	V,6	Snowed-Up Rock					
17 Silver Threads Among The Gold	IV,5	Mixed					
18 Mega Route X	VI,6	Icefall	■				
19 Rapunzel	IV,4	Gully					
20 Wobble Block Chimney	IV,5	Mixed			■		
21 Cherokee Chimney	V,6	Mixed		■			
22 Alderwand	III	Mixed	■				
23 Western Rib	III	Mixed	■				
24 Tower Ridge	IV,3	Mixed					
25 Green Gully	IV,3	Gully					
26 Left Twin	III,4	Gully					■
27 Raeburn's Gully	III	Gully					
28 Deep Cut Chimney	IV,4	Mixed					■
29 Top Gun	V,6	Mixed					
30 Darth Vader	VII,7	Mixed					■
31 North-East Ridge	III	Mixed	■				■
32 North-East Buttress	IV,5	Mixed					
33 South Post Direct	V,4	Gully	■				
34 Smith's Gully	VI,5	Gully	■				
35 Crowberry Gully	IV,4	Gully					
36 Hanging Garden Route	V,4	Gully					
37 Royal Pardon	VI,5	Icefall					
38 Black Spout Buttress	III,5	Mixed					
39 Raeburn's Route	IV,4	Mixed					
40 Tower Face Of The Comb	VI,6	Mixed					
41 Postern	VI,6	Mixed					
42 Archway	IV,4	Mixed					
43 Invernookie	III,4	Mixed					
44 Mitre Ridge	V,6	Mixed		■			
45 Point Five Gully	V,5	Gully	■				
46 Orion Direct	V,5	Thin Face					
47 Albatross	VI,5	Thin Face					
48 The White Line	IV,4	Icefall	■				
49 Hadrian's Wall Direct	V,5	Icefall	■				
50 Smith's Route	V,5	Icefall	■				

Try to choose a route to fit the forecasted conditions. If the weather deteriorates, a classic climb like Tower Ridge on Ben Nevis can become unexpectedly arduous and time-consuming. The climber is belayed in Tower Gap (see also p125)

Mike Pescod

STRATEGY
Winter Strategy Guidelines

Scottish winter climbing strategy is all about being on the right route, in the right place at the right time. This of course, is far easier said than done, however the following Strategy Guidelines provide a good starting point:

1. **Choose A Route To Fit The Conditions**. If you have a particular objective in mind it is very tempting to have a crack at it regardless of the weather and conditions. Single-minded focus is a key attribute for climbers, but for Scottish winter climbing flexibility is just as important. Select a venue and a route that matches the conditions of the day rather than the other way around. Having a long list of routes you aspire to do is a simple way of circumventing the single-minded approach. Include climbs with a variety of styles and locations. I have a wish list several hundred routes long, with a simple note for each climb listing altitude of the cliff base, aspect and any specific conditions required for an ascent.

2. **Climb Routes When Frozen.** This may appear an obvious statement as nobody wants to climb a Mixed route when the turf is unfrozen, or start up a Snowed-Up Rock route with water running down the rock. However, the situation is often more complicated than it first appears. A sub-zero air temperature is no guarantee that the turf will be frozen or ice will be found. Neither will it provide protection against the sun that can quickly strip exposed routes. Although Mixed routes can sometimes be climbed on the immediate onset of a thaw, Snowed-Up Rock routes

do not stay in condition very long because rime ice, hoar frost and powder snow melt fast. Similarly, Thin Face routes quickly turn to unclimbable mush once the temperature rises above zero. However, Icefalls and Gullies can sometimes be climbable in above-freezing temperatures, although careful route choice is required to avoid objective dangers from collapsing cornices or avalanches.

3. **Consider Wind Direction As Well As Temperature.** It is natural to first look at freezing levels when choosing a venue, but the wind direction is just as important. Wind dictates which aspect has cooled (or warmed) quickest, and also indicates whether snow transport may have led to the generation of windslab or cornices. It will also determine whether a route has a wintry appearance, as aspects in the lee of the wind typically collect more wind-blown snow. This can be helpful when conditions are frozen and lean, but can be a problem early in the season, or after a thaw, as snow-covered ground can insulate the vegetation and prevent it freezing. In stormy weather, climbing on the opposite side of the country to the prevailing wind is an excellent rule of thumb.

4. **Select Mixed Routes Just Above The Snowline.** In general, technical Mixed routes become more difficult as the depth of snow covering them increases. If routes are buried it can be very difficult to determine the underlying features to find placements and place protection. Progress can be very slow as the route has to be laboriously cleared with a tool. Choosing Mixed routes that are a couple of hundred metres above the snowline (so long as they are

frozen) provides the best of both worlds – good frozen conditions but not too much snow. This is clearly not a hard and fast rule as the Mixed routes in the Northern Corries of Cairn Gorm and on Ben Nevis typically lie well above the snowline, but if it is very snowy on these cliffs the climbing will be very arduous. On Ben Nevis, many climbers resort to climbing on lower crags such as the Douglas Boulder in heavy snow conditions.

5. Always Have A Back Up Route. Few winter climbers succeed on their primary objective every time they go out. Your route may not be in condition, the weather is poor, or someone else may have arrived there first. Having a couple of well thought through back up options will allow you to quickly transfer to another route. For each selected climb, the Alternative Routes section provides examples of back up routes that are similar in style and grade.

Weather Forecasts

The accuracy of mountain forecasts has improved enormously in recent years. The Met Office states that they can predict the weather four days ahead as accurately as they could forecast a day ahead 30 years ago. Gone are the days when winter climbers had to piece together a weather chart from listening to the Shipping Forecast on the car radio. The Met Office <www.metoffice.gov.uk> and the Mountain Weather Information Service (MWIS) <www.mwis.org.uk> provide the most popular mountain weather forecasts. Although they are derived from similar forecasting models, it is worth looking at both, and noting any discrepancies, as this suggests more uncertainty in the overall prediction.

Perhaps the biggest limitation with the specialist weather forecasts is that they are issued the afternoon prior to the forecasting period. This could be 24 hours before you reach the crux of your route the following day. Currently, the Met Office provides an update to its Mountain forecast in the early hours of the morning and this may be worth checking before you set out. Having established the pattern of weather, and the likely freezing level and wind speeds from the specialist forecasts, I then refer to the general BBC weather forecasts <www.bbc.co.uk/weather>. These are updated more frequently and can be useful if the weather situation is unstable and rapidly changing. Both the Met Office and MWIS provide a five-day forecast. This is excellent for planning, but the key trick is not to make any hard and fast decisions about where to go and what to do until the last possible moment.

A helpful feature of the Met Office website is the availability of forecasts for specific places and many mountain summits. This is interpolated data, but will provide a good indication of the wind direction and temperature at your chosen venue. Another excellent tool is the observed data section that lists the actual weather over the last 24 hours. This can be particularly useful to find out where and when it has snowed, and since it is based on satellite data combined with temperature measurements, it is reasonably accurate.

It is worth reviewing the weather forecast at least once a day through the winter season. This will allow you to build up a mental picture of the ongoing weather pattern and see how it translates into Mountain Conditions. Try to visualise how the weather is changing conditions on the mountains. Is it freezing or thawing? Is it dry, raining or snowing? Which direction is the wind coming from? How mobile is the snow and is it being transported by the wind? How does this affect avalanche conditions and the formation of wind-slab? Which winter cliffs are likely to be in the best condition? When you are next in the mountains, make a mental note to check how your perception of the conditions matches reality.

Water has some unusual physical properties, and its high latent heat means that it does not change state instantly. As a result, it takes time for turf to freeze and ice to melt. Therefore, ambient temperature is not a direct indication of winter conditions because there is a time delay. Experienced Scottish winter climbers implicitly understand this and use it to their advantage to expand their repertoire of potential routes as Mountain Conditions change. Temperatures are frequently passing through the freezing point in the Scottish mountains, and learning how to effectively use this transition period greatly extends the window available for winter climbing.

Another curious phenomenon is the Wet Bulb Effect that takes place when the air is dry and the snow remains frozen on shaded slopes, even though the freezing level is above the summits. These conditions cause sublimation, where the snow rapidly evaporates rather than melting first, and the resulting energy loss keeps the snow's temperature below freezing point. So in clear weather, don't be misled by a forecast that implies a temperature a few degrees above zero will make everything soggy and melting. These conditions can be a delightful time to climb classic snow and ice routes.

Early season hoar frost on Savage Slit, Coire an Lochain, Cairn Gorm – a classic Snowed-Up Rock route

Dave Riley

Rime Ice, Hoar Frost & Verglas

The white frosted cliffs of early winter are covered in rime ice or hoar frost, although these two terms are often confused and interchanged. Rime ice is composed of large ice crystals which form feathers facing into the wind and is the most common form of frosting. It is created by cloud transported supercooled droplets freezing instantly when they come into contact with an obstacle, which is why rime ice accumulates on exposed features during a storm. Hoar frost on the other hand is comprised of more delicate ice crystals that form under clear frosty nights when the surface temperature of the rock drops below zero due to radiant cooling. The creation of hoar frost is similar to the formation of dew, except the temperature is below zero.

When a few centimetres thick, rime ice and hoar frost provide excellent Mixed and Snowed-Up Rock climbing conditions. The cliffs are spectacularly white, but the cracks are free of ice and provide solid protection for nuts and cams.

Verglas is a thin coating of ice formed by freezing rain landing on frozen rock. The droplets have time to spread out before they freeze which creates a thin layer of hard transparent ice. Verglas also forms after a short thaw and re-freeze and results in icy cracks that are very difficult to protect. Cams are close to useless in verglassed cracks, and nuts are very difficult to seat securely. As a general rule, verglas does not result in good Snowed-Up Rock climbing, and in these conditions it may be best to focus on Mixed routes that rely more on frozen vegetation for upward progress.

Using The Internet

The Internet has revolutionised winter climbing by providing (almost) real time information; gold dust for climbers seeking out the latest data on winter conditions. The simplest way of using the web is to keep an eye on logbooks and forums on climbing websites. When someone has climbed a route you want to do, rush out and climb it the following day. Assuming the weather has not changed, and the report was accurate, this is a viable way of finding routes in condition.

But there are several points to bear in mind with this approach. Firstly, few people have the flexibility to drop everything and go, and many will have to wait until the following weekend when conditions may have changed. Secondly, hundreds of other climbers will have read the same report, and it is highly likely that several will have the same idea as you, and the route may be crowded. Thirdly, you need to ensure the report has come from a reliable source and someone has not logged a route that is out of condition. Finally, successfully predicting when a route is in condition is extremely satisfying and removing this aspect takes away an important dimension from the Scottish winter climbing experience. However, this information can still be extremely useful. For example, if an Internet report reveals that Route X is in condition, Route Y nearby, with a similar route base, aspect and route Style, is likely to be in condition too.

Photographs posted online provide the most accurate real time information, and mountain webcams are a very effective way of assessing the height of the snow line and the depth of snow across the country. For example, as a result of the typical east-west temperature gradient, the snow line can be considerably higher in the North-West than the Cairngorms, and this understanding can be easily confirmed by looking at a variety of webcams in conjunction with a map. The well illustrated blogs accompanying the Scottish Avalanche Information Service (SAIS) <*www.sais.gov.uk*> are particularly useful to gauge snow conditions across the popular winter climbing areas.

Websites hosted by guides and mountaineering instructors are another excellent source of real time information as they are often updated every day and contain many photos. These sites are refreshingly upbeat, and typically provide an enthusiastic view on current conditions and future options in their local area.

When the weather is good but you are unable to go winter climbing, it can be very frustrating viewing picture after picture of perfect mountain conditions and crystal blue skies on your computer screen. And frustration levels will rise even higher if the weather is set to break at the end of the week before you have a chance to get out. A constructive exercise in these circumstances is to consult the weather forecasts and ongoing conditions and decide what route you would go and do if you were free the following day. You can later check the logbooks and see if anyone actually climbed your route and what the conditions were like. This may appear a little masochistic, but it is a good way of practicing your conditions prediction skills!

Henning Wackerhage

Exposed turf freezes quickly, but it can stay soft if insulated by a layer of snow at the beginning of the season. In this situation it is best to choose a Snowed-Up Rock route that does not rely on frozen vegetation

Avalanches are the most serious objective danger facing Scottish winter climbers. Be sure to study the avalanche report before you set off

Mike Pescod

Avalanches

The only time I have been avalanched was in Coire an Lochain in the Northern Corries of Cairn Gorm. It was a poor day at the start of the season, and Roger Everett and I were approaching the foot of No.4 Buttress with our hoods down to shelter from the wind. Without warning the snow began to gently move under my feet. It was in slow motion at first, but it was impossible to step off the now moving slope. Soon, I was tumbling down towards the lochan, very surprised at the speed I was travelling. Fortunately I landed on top of a heap of snow at the bottom and was none the worse for wear except for a snapped crampon. Roger, who was just to my side when the slope started sliding was completely unaware that there had been an avalanche at all, and was very surprised when I shouted up to him from the base of the corrie, that I was OK. The avalanche had been completely silent, and the most frightening aspect of

the experience is that if I had been buried, Roger would have had little idea where to look. Avalanches in Scotland may appear benign compared to bigger mountains elsewhere in the world but they can be a silent killer. You want to do everything you possibly can to avoid being caught up in one.

The simplest way of staying away from avalanches is to avoid going out into avalanche territory at all. The conventional advice is not to go into the mountains for 24 hours following a heavy snowfall. This is the time when the snow may be at its most unstable, but instabilities in the snowpack may still remain after this period.

Following the Strategy Guidelines and selecting a Mixed route not far above the snow line is a good tactic in snowy conditions, but you will still need to consider the avalanche potential of the descent. Wind-slab, which often forms in the lee of the wind on convex slopes at the tops of climbs, is a common cause

18

of avalanche incidents among winter climbers. Take time to learn how it is formed and how to recognise the tell-tale chalky appearance of the surface of the snow. In late season, avalanches caused by cornice collapse are another significant objective danger.

The Scottish Avalanche Information Service (SAIS) <*www.sais.gov.uk*> provides excellent up to date reports on the six key climbing areas (Northern Cairngorms, Southern Cairngorms, Lochaber, Glen Coe, Creag Meagaidh and Torridon). Checking these reports is an essential part of the route planning process. Take avalanche information very seriously, and consider in advance the danger points on the approach and descent as well as the climb itself.

An important point to remember is that an avalanche does not need to be big to be fatal. A slab a few centimetres thick and only a few metres wide may be substantial enough to knock you off your feet, and if that happens above a big drop the consequences may be disastrous. An overall moderate risk (Level 2) does not mean relatively safe conditions everywhere, as there may well be patches of much more dangerous snow just where you don't want them. This is a key point to remember when interpreting avalanche risk forecasts.

Approaches & Descents

Avalanches are the main objective danger likely to be encountered when approaching a route. Beware of smooth slab aprons below crags (i.e. Coire an Lochain on Cairn Gorm) or unstable conditions on steep unbroken slopes below the cliff (i.e. Coire an Lochain on Aonach Mòr).

The descent, however, can be the most dangerous part of the day. You may be tired after a long and demanding climb, the weather bad, visibility poor and it is getting dark. And quite frequently it is all of these things. This is no time to start studying the map to work out the best way down. Ensure you have done this as part of your pre-route planning and have discussed the descent with your partner so that you both know exactly where to go when you reach the top of the route.

Always have an alternative descent in mind, should conditions force you to change your plans. In some circumstances it may be safest and more expedient to abseil the route you have just climbed. This is more likely to work on a short climb in the Northern Corries, but is unlikely to be a sensible option after a long multi-pitch route on Ben Nevis or Creag Meagaidh.

The Process of Choosing a Route

These are my steps when selecting an objective, assuming I plan to go climbing on Sunday, leaving home early in the morning and returning that evening.

Mon – Thu: Follow the weather forecasts on the BBC, Met Office and MWIS. Build up a mental picture of the conditions across the Highlands taking particular note of any thaws. Check by looking at the SAIS Avalanche conditions and blogs. Look at blogs, websites and log-books to keep up to date with recent climbing activity.

Fri: Based on the above information, combined with observations of conditions when last climbing in the mountains (preferably the previous weekend), decide on the likely Mountain Conditions. Is it Early, Cold, Lean, Top Nick or Late? Match this to the appropriate style of winter route – Snowed-Up Rock, Mixed, Icefall, Gully or Thin Face. Consult your wish list of climbs and match route aspect and cliff base to the forecast wind direction and temperature. Discuss the options with your climbing partner. Listen very carefully to their thoughts as this is not an exact science, and two brains are better than one. Agree a short list of possible objectives.

Sat: Review weather forecasts on the BBC, Met Office and MWIS early in the evening. Check SAIS Avalanche observations and prediction for Sunday. Review blogs, websites and logbooks for any real time climbing information from routes climbed that day. Check Traffic Scotland for driving conditions if roads are likely to be snowy. Agree venue and objective with your climbing partner. Confirm approach, descent and back up routes. Clarify alternative descent options. Leave a note of where you are going in the event of a late return. Check BBC forecast before going to sleep.

Sun: Check the Met Office early morning forecast. Travel to venue and walk up to cliff. Assess approach and climbing conditions on primary objective. If circumstances are poor, choose an appropriate back up. Climb route and return safely.

This process appears very mechanical when written down, but in practice it is natural and intuitive. The key point is to maintain maximum flexibility and only make a decision on where to go at the last possible moment. An important part of the cycle is to learn from experience. On the Monday evening following the climb, I will review Sunday's SAIS Avalanche conditions and compare their observations to my personal experience on the mountain. I will look at blogs, websites and logbooks to see what climbs were done that day. Almost certainly others will have made more optimum choices. The aim is to continually build a bank of experience. Did my partner and I choose the most appropriate venue and route, and what learnings can we apply next time we go out?

Climbing in bad weather is an unavoidable aspect of winter climbing and warm and weather-proof clothing is essential

Henning Wackerhage

TACTICS – BEFORE YOU GO
Training & Fitness
Even in the most favourable conditions, Scottish winter climbing can be arduous, and hill fitness is essential. If you've found the walk-in tiring, climbing the route itself will feel physically and psychologically tough. You may also need strength in reserve for the descent and return, battling into a headwind through deep snow, all with a heavy rucksack. A good level of fitness for safe and enjoyable winter climbing can be gained by plenty of hill walking in the autumn. Such trips can also be used to familiarise yourself with the regions where your winter objectives lie, and to scout out the approaches and descents. Take the opportunity to add some 'ballast' to the rucksack, so that the first climbing sack of the winter, replete with ropes and heavy hardware, does not feel too much of a shock.

Climbing fitness is also important, but perhaps less so for most routes in this book. Climbers operating in the upper grades train specifically for winter climbing by doing regular gym work and developing their strength and technique at dry tooling venues. For many of the routes described here this is not necessary, and even for the harder climbs that are included, some regular stamina training at an indoor wall will suffice.

Clothing & Footwear
The first time I went winter climbing more than 30 years ago, I wore a football shirt, a woolen jumper my auntie had knitted me and a Neoprene-proofed cagoule. Not surprisingly, I spent most of my time shivering on stances. Since then, clothing has improved enormously, and I now wear a modern system of inner and mid-layers complete with a Gore-tex shell. Some climbers have success with soft shell garments, but I am frequently climbing in poor weather and find I require the protection of a hard shell. A good breathable hard shell jacket is an expensive item, but it is money well spent. Having a jacket with armpit zips is useful to prevent overheating on the approach, but the most important design aspect is a deep hood that goes over your helmet without restricting visibility or movement. Overtrousers with full-length zips that can be put on over your boots and crampons complete the set up.

Over the years boots have progressed from leather (cold feet) to plastic (warm and wet) to composite (warm light and nimble). It is very important to find a pair of boots that you're comfortable walking in for long distances, as you will be wearing them for many hours each time you go climbing.

Gloves
Well fitting thin climbing gloves work best for leading hard mixed pitches and placing gear. A medium thickness pair is better for climbing ice. A warm pair of thicker gloves or mitts is useful when belaying the leader on the next pitch. Unless conditions are perfect it is unlikely that your gloves will remain dry throughout the route, so take more than one pair. If

the weather is particularly poor, or you are climbing an icefall in above freezing temperatures, plan on using one pair per pitch – I have taken up to seven pairs on some routes! Boot proofing wax keeps leather palms waterproof and makes the gloves sticky for holding on to tools.

Belay Jacket

Although it is a simple idea, taking a warm jacket for the belayer to wear is a relatively new concept. The advantage is that the leader can climb with less clothes and is light and unencumbered whilst the second stays warm and cosy. As a result, the belayer consumes less energy on the stance, and is ready to go when it is time to second the pitch. The trick is to take one jacket between two and ensure that it is big enough to go over the outer layer of the largest person. A deep hood to keep out the weather is a must, and the jacket can also serve as spare clothing in the event of an emergency. Many jackets fold up into an internal pocket and can be hung off your harness, but I find it more practical to simply loosely stuff it into a light rucksack the second is carrying containing head torches, drink, snacks, spare gloves, guidebook, map and compass and anything else you may need for the route.

Leashed Or Leashless?

It is simpler and more natural to climb with leashless tools rather than having them permanently attached to your wrists. It makes placing protection easier and rope management simpler. For technically difficult routes, leashless tools have revolutionised the sport by allowing climbers to move faster, climb more efficiently and shake out.

For easier climbs, the benefits of leashless tools are not so apparent. They are difficult to plunge in snow slopes and their bulky-shaped handles make them difficult to jam into cracks. But their biggest disadvantage is actually that they have no leash! With leashed tools you are belayed every placement and are more secure if something goes wrong. With leashless tools this is not the case, and if you release your grip on the tool you may fall. You could be on easy ground and lose consciousness when hit by a falling rock, the snow could collapse under you, or simply you could lose concentration. Either way, on easy ground you will be safer with a leashed tool. My solution to this conundrum is to carry a set of detachable leashes in my pocket. Whenever the ground becomes straightforward (Grade II), I simply attach the leash to the head of my tool. This allows me to quickly climb lower-angled ground with less protection, safe in the knowledge that if something untoward happens, I am still physically attached to my tools.

Many climbers attach their leashless tools to their harness with a tether to prevent dropping them. Tethers with swivels work best, but even so it takes a

Henning Wackerhage

Many climbers use leashes or tethers to prevent dropping their tools

Modern sharp ice screws provide reliable protection on Icefalls and Gullies when the ice is solid and well formed

Henning Wackerhage

little practice to prevent tangling the tether with the ropes, especially when clipping runners. Remember that tethers are designed to prevent you losing a tool. They are not rated to hold a fall or a slip, and can break when shock loaded. Experienced leashless users forego the tether completely, and take care never to drop their tools.

Protecting Winter Routes

The golden rule is to place protection whenever possible as you never know when you will be able to place your next piece. For the majority of Mixed and Snowed-Up Rock routes, a conventional trad rack of wires, hexes and camming devices will suffice. Harder routes (typically Grade V and above) will require a double set of wires, whilst for easier routes a lighter rack will be sufficient. Hexes are more effective than cams in icy cracks, and the new generation of tapered hexes (Wild Country Hexcentrics for example) are excellent on Ben Nevis, when placed sideways in flared slots that are notoriously difficult to protect. Don't be afraid to use your tool to seat a nut. A couple of taps with your pick is all that is required. There is no need to treat a wired nut like a copper-head and 'weld' it in. When placing a piece of gear, always think about any damage you may be doing to the rock and how easily your second will be able to remove it. You may wish to have a separate rack of nuts to your summer set, as they will soon look a little battered, and remember to check for broken strands of wire.

The number and range of camming devices to be carried will depend on route type and location. They work particularly well on Cairngorm granite and North-West sandstone, and for Snowed-Up Rock and Mixed routes a full set will probably be very useful. In contrast, they may be all but dispensable on climbs thoroughly plastered with snow and ice.

Icefalls, Gullies and Thin Face routes will normally require ice screws, but they are rarely worth taking on Mixed routes, and are completely out of place on a Snowed-Up Rock route. Ice screws work well in solid water ice but are next to useless in aerated or layered ice and snow, frequently encountered in Scotland. Unlike continental icefalls where ice screws can be placed securely over the majority of the climb, screw placements in Scottish ice have to be chosen care-fully. For this reason it is probably better to push your grade on a well protected Mixed route rather than an Icefall or Thin Face route.

Ice screws have improved enormously over the last 20 years, but it is important to keep them clean, sharp and undamaged. Store them with the thread protec-tors as well as the end cap, and carry them in a sepa-rate bag or stuff sack. Take care when placing in thin ice, as the teeth are easily damaged if the screw bottoms out on underlying rock. I normally take a couple of 'stubbies' – screws of 10 and 13cm in length – that can provide all-important confidence before a crucial move, when the ice is thin and there is no other gear in sight. Conversely, 22cm screws are normally too long to place in Scottish ice.

Drive-in ice screws, or Warthogs, are the time-honoured protection for frozen turf. When the turf is frozen rock hard they can be excellent, but nowadays ice hooks have largely superseded them. These do not penetrate quite as deep, but they are mechanically more secure. They also work well in icy or turfy cracks, but be wary about hammering them too hard as they are very difficult (and time consuming) to remove,

although some climbers grind off the teeth, which makes them easier to extract. Whenever you sink your tool into a deep solid placement in a crack, think about it as a possible ice hook protection placement. Typically I carry two ice hooks, but on some more serious Mixed routes you may need half a dozen as there may be very few other protection opportunities. It is easier to rack multiple hooks if the sewn sling is removed.

Pegs are extremely useful in winter as they are more secure in icy or vegetated cracks than nuts or cams. They can damage the rock however, and on winter routes that follow established rock climbs, they should only be placed in extremis. If I am on a winter-only line, I carry a selection of angles and kingpins, as well as Peckers in lieu of blade pegs. Peckers are the rock equivalent of an ice hook and provide surprisingly good and mechanically secure placements in very thin cracks. You can never have too many slings in winter. They are extremely useful for placing around chock-stones and for extending runners. I typically take six or so, including one made from Aramid that is stiff enough to poke through long threads. I also take a small length of abseil cord in case of retreat.

Walking Poles
Poles can be very useful and can make approaches through deep snow easier, and descents less taxing on the knees. Try not to take walking poles by default however, because if you intend to descend a different route to your approach, you will need to carry your poles up the route with you. In these circumstances, a useful compromise is to take one pole each.

Ropes
Most Scottish winter climbers use double 8.5mm ropes. Double ropes have a greater safety factor in the event of a rope being damaged or cut, and provide the ability to abseil off in case you have to retreat. All the routes in this book can be climbed with 50m ropes, however it is often more pleasant to climb ice routes with 60m ropes, as they provide the option for longer pitches when looking for a belay. Ropes designed for ice can be as thin as 7.0mm, but I would not recommend these for Mixed or Snowed-Up Rock routes. Most rope manufacturers offer a dry treatment option. This works well when the rope is new and is worth paying a little extra for. When climbing remote routes with short pitches, doubling up a 60m or 70m rope is a good option to reduce weight.

Head Torches
Always carry a head torch with you and make sure you put it in your pocket if you leave your rucksack at the foot of the route. Remember to take spare batteries. Many head torches nowadays use lithium

Navigation in poor visibility is an essential skill for Scottish winter climbing

Mike Pescod

batteries that are lighter and longer lasting than alkaline ones. Torch technology has come on in leaps and bounds in recent years. In the past it was only possible to climb ice routes by head torch, but powerful modern LED lights make it feasible to climb Mixed and Snowed-Up Rock routes at night as well.

Mobile Phones & Personal Locator Beacons

There is mobile phone reception at many winter climbing areas nowadays (such as Lochnagar, the Northern Corries of Cairn Gorm and many parts of Ben Nevis), so it makes sense to take a mobile phone in the event of an emergency. If you take one phone between two, make sure you both know the security code to turn it on.

Mobile phones can be very useful to let those waiting at home or in the valley know that everything is going OK if you are delayed. It can be extremely inconvenient to explain your situation to your loved one whilst battling a gale near the top of Ben Nevis, so a simple pre-prepared text message such as 'All OK running late' will set minds at rest. And importantly, it frees your mind to concentrate on the job at hand, rather than worrying about whether the rescue teams will be called out. If you have no signal on the climb, remember to try again from the top.

Emergency 999 calls can be picked up by any service provider even if you are contracted to one that has no signal. If you cannot make voice calls, you can contact the 999 emergency services by SMS text from your mobile phone. You will only be able to use this service if you have already registered with emergency SMS – see <*www.emergencysms.org.uk*>.

The use of Personal Locator Beacons overland in the UK became legal in 2012. When activated, this compact satellite communication device transmits your location to an International rescue centre. Although it is a piece of equipment that you hope you will never use, it could be a lifesaver in a location where there is no mobile coverage.

Rucksack Packing

The most efficient way to pack a winter rucksack is in reverse order. Place items that you are likely to need first on top. I pack my rucksack in a similar way every time I go out. At the bottom will be the rack and rope followed by my harness. I then pack my mid-layer clothes that I will change into before the start of the climb. At the top will be my waterproofs, spare gloves and also easy access to my drinking bottle. Some climbers take hydration bladders, but I find them difficult to use in winter and you run the risk of them being spiked by a crampon and leaking. Drinking plenty and hydrating well before you begin can be a practical strategy. For more remote venues like Braeriach and Beinn a' Bhuird I carry a bivouac sack or bothy bag. These could save a life in the event of an emergency.

TACTICS – GETTING THERE
Transport

Whilst it is possible to go winter climbing in places like Ben Nevis and the Cairngorms using public transport, this will considerably restrict your flexibility to respond to varying Mountain Conditions. This book assumes that you have access to a car or vehicle. Winter tyres are the simplest winter upgrade you can make to a vehicle, and offer a more significant benefit than four-wheel drive. The difference between winter and normal tyres on snowy roads is enormous, and they can easily make the difference between a successful (and safe) day out and a frustrating failure to reach the start of the walk-in. Manual transmission and front wheel drive also help when driving along wintry roads. I always carry a shovel and make sure my windscreen wash and fuel are topped up. I also carry chains but have rarely used them.

Many routes require an early start, so sleeping in the car at the beginning of the approach is a good tactic. Avoiding using a stove in the morning speeds things up and a breakfast of sandwiches with a hot drink from a thermos is a quick way to go. Alternatively, cereal ready to go in a Tupperware box complete with spoon is another good option.

Make sure you have a change of clothes for when you come off the hill (it's surprising how many first-time winter climbers forget this). You'll be hungry and thirsty, so food and drink will be very welcome too. Some people use protein recovery drinks, but sharing a tin of rice pudding with your partner is possibly just as effective. And remember, the day is not complete until you have safely driven back home.

Cycling

Approaches to several routes described in this book can be eased by cycling. Any bike capable of riding estate tracks will do, however some preparation for riding icy terrain in the dark will pay dividends. Cycling downhill in the dark with a heavy rucksack on your back can be precarious and the most dangerous part of the day. Studded tyres for riding icy surfaces are readily available nowadays and are well worth fitting. Good lights make a difference too, especially on the downhill sections, and having a two-light set up where one is angled on the track just ahead and the other set to the far distance works well. Rim brakes tend to ice up so disc brakes are best, and I find it easier to carry my rucksack on my back rather than using panniers. The ideal set up is a light hardtail mountain bike with lockable front forks to maximise energy transmission when going uphill.

Henning Wackerhage

Cycling can make long approaches easier, but make sure your bike is equipped for wintry conditions

Ten minutes checking out your route before starting climbing is time well spent and can be the most critical point of the day

Alex Messenger

Navigation

Accurate navigation is an essential mountain skill. Visibility is often poor due to bad weather or darkness, and it is easy to become disorientated and lost. All climbers should carry a map and a compass and know how to use them. I have my map folded open at the relevant area and carry it in a zip-lock plastic bag. The summit of a mountain in a raging storm is no place to start unfolding a full sized map. If you have access to digital maps, printing the relevant section and placing it in a plastic wallet is a good option that will save weight and space. It is worth printing two copies as they are easily blown away.

I am most familiar with Ordnance Survey 1:50,000 maps so I tend to use those, but others prefer the detail of the 1:25,000 series. The Harvey 1:25,000 Summit and 1:40,000 maps are also very good and often show more topographical detail than OS maps. Whichever scale you use, it is worth learning how distance on the map equates to distance on the ground and what that means to the individual in terms of pacing.

Carrying a GPS is a sensible idea especially if you are on a cliff you haven't visited before, or are climbing in a remote area. Be sure you know how to use it and make sure it is properly charged and set up. On more than one occasion I have tried to use my GPS in anger only to find it is set to the wrong coordinate system following an overseas trip. Beware

of navigating near a cliff edge that may be corniced, and if in doubt, rope up.

As part of your pre-route planning, carefully study the descent. You may wish to pre-set the initial bearing on your compass. Make sure you have fully discussed the descent route with your partner (including alternative options) before you set off.

Arriving Below The Cliff

This can be the most important point of the day. Ten minutes spent carefully reviewing conditions can make the difference between a successful or disappointing outing. Study the approach to your objective and establish that it is not avalanche prone. Check the condition of your route. Is the Snowed-Up Rock route white with hoar frost or rime? Is the turf frozen enough for Mixed climbing? Is the Icefall thick enough? Is the Gully full and complete? Has the critical amount of snow-ice formed down the crux of the Thin Face route? If the critical factors are not in place, take time to review your back up routes. With sufficient flexibility you should be able to choose an appropriate route for the conditions of the day. Don't rush this process, because once committed to a climb it may take several hours to back off and try something else and the day will be lost. Once you've settled on an objective, confirm the descent route (and alternative) with your partner.

TACTICS – DURING THE CLIMB
Timing

I came to Scottish winter climbing from an alpine climbing background where timing is everything. In Scotland, the routes may not be as long as in the Alps, but the shorter winter day puts a similar pressure on time. Understanding and embracing the time element is one of the keys to successful Scottish winter climbing. The earlier you set out, the earlier you can start your climb and this will not only give more time for the climbing itself, but will also allow for eventualities that you couldn't foresee. It also allows you to switch to a back up route.

Ideally, if you are attempting a long climb, you should plan to start your route just after daybreak. Typically this will involve an approach in the dark. You can arrive too early however. In the darkness of night or in the gloom of the pre-dawn your cliff can look very steep and also very black. It's easy to intimidate yourself and become convinced that your climb is not in condition or it is too hard. In the light of day things change. Features begin to show up, the angle eases and the true wintry nature of the cliff becomes apparent. The ideal timing is to arrive just before dawn so you have 30 minutes (it always seems to take that long) to gear up and prepare to start climbing. And by the time you are ready to go, there will be enough daylight to study the route.

Once on the climb it's important to keep track of time. It's amazing how many hours can be eaten up with a long and demanding lead. Whilst wearing winter clothes it can be difficult to look at your wrist, but one technique is to wear a digital watch and set it to beep every hour. You may not always hear it, but when you do, it will remind you that time is passing.

In mid-winter with only eight-hours of daylight you may not only start in the dark, but finish in the dark too. Being clear on your descent route will pay dividends, because once night falls, everything seems to take at least three times as long. The short winter day, and the requirement to be in the right place at exactly the right time, is one of the great challenges of Scottish winter climbing. It adds an extra dimension, enhancing the routes and mountains and increasing their stature.

Gearing Up

Some things in winter always seem to take a minimum amount of time. For example, it always takes me one hour to wake up, get dressed, eat breakfast and set off for the hill. Another universal constant is that it always takes half an hour to gear up below the climb. The process of putting on warm clothes under waterproofs, buckling on your harness, fitting crampons, having a bite to eat, repacking rucksacks, gearing up and uncoiling ropes always takes far longer than you think. If the weather is bad this can be a miserable process with fingers and toes going numb as you stand around.

One option to make this a little more pleasant is to gear up in installments. As you move towards the crag, stop to put on extra layers and your overtrousers. Putting on crampons well before you need them is also a very good idea. Everyone has made the mistake of leaving crampons off until it's almost too late, and then struggling to put them on whilst balancing on one foot on a small icy foothold. A couple of shorter stops will turn out to be far more pleasant than one single occasion where you do everything, and may even be quicker overall in the end.

One Rucksack Or Two?

It's easier to climb without a rucksack, so deciding whether to take your rucksacks with you or leave them at the foot of the route is a key decision. In almost all circumstances it's worth taking a half-empty rucksack up the route with head torches, belay jacket, map, compass, drink and food. If you leave a rucksack at the bottom, think carefully about how you're going to retrieve it. Even if you have a straightforward descent to where you think you've left it, make sure you can find it in the dark or buried under new snow. Waymarking it with your GPS can be useful, and remember to take your car keys with you!

Often the descent will take you down a different part of the mountain, so you'll need to climb with all your equipment. Using different sized rucksacks so that one fits inside the other is a good tactic, and having the second carry it will leave the leader less weighed down. Two rucksacks when combined can be quite heavy and bulky, especially if you have two sets of walking poles, so it's worth thinking through the essential equipment that you'll need, before you set out.

Partners

Your climbing partner underpins your safety in the mountains, and it is essential that you work together as a team. During the late 1990s I climbed some of my finest winter routes with Chris Cartwright, when we started experimenting with mixed climbing on Ben Nevis. Chris and I were unlikely candidates to be at the vanguard of Scottish winter climbing. Although neither of us were particularly talented rock climbers, we had developed into a strong winter team. We were similar in technical ability and Chris provided the perfect foil to my analytical approach. I would often provide the inspiration as to where to go and what to do, whilst Chris would display a stubborn determination to never give up when the going got tough. Most

The approach, especially if it is a long one, can be the most psychologically demanding part of the day. Selecting an appropriate route to match the Mountain Conditions, and identifying a back up route, is the overarching strategy for successful Scottish winter climbing

Henning Wackerhage

importantly we trusted each other's judgement implicitly and our pairing was a classic example of the sum being greater than the two parts.

Psychology

So you've finally got there. You're in position below your dream route. Conditions are perfect. The forecast is good and you've arrived on time with the full day ahead of you. But you feel nervous. The climb looks hard and it has a big reputation. It's very tempting to leave it for another day and do something easier instead.

Don't give up. You've successfully completed the hardest part of the process by being in the right place at the right time. Winter climbing is a head game and it's easy to become overwhelmed by the scale and remoteness of the situation. If you've walked in for an hour to a cliff it feels nice and friendly and not too

serious, but if it's taken you more than four hours to get there it's a different matter altogether. It can feel very lonely and exposed setting off up a climb a long way from the nearest road.

The trick with mountaineering is never give up until you absolutely have to. Start the route. Keep climbing. If it's too difficult, or the weather becomes bad, you can always abseil off. Break the climb into manageable chunks and slowly and surely tick off each section one by one. Before you know it you'll reach a point where you realise that nothing can stop you now and you will succeed. This is a fantastic feeling that will amply repay all the planning and preparation.

And remember, if you never try, you will never succeed

ACKNOWLEDGEMENTS

Chasing The Ephemeral has been seven years in the making and many people have assisted in the writing and production of this book. Firstly, I would like to thank Tom Prentice for persuading me to embark on the project and Chris Cartwright for the origin of the idea and many lengthy discussions on how to succeed at the Scottish winter game. Roger Everett, Henning Wackerhage, Dave Riley, Christine Richardson, Fran Sullivan and George McEwan reviewed the text in considerable detail and made a large number of incisive and pertinent suggestions. This book contains one of the largest collections of Scottish winter climbing photographs ever published and I am grateful to all the photographers who enthusiastically provided their work, especially Henning Wackerhage, Mike Pescod and Dave Cuthbertson who gave access to their extensive portfolios. Many other people provided key information or helped source photos. A full list of contributors follows – I thank them all.

Dave Anderson, Rab Anderson, Stewart Anderson, Andy Bain, Keith Ball, Michael Barnard, David Barratt, Andy Brown, Robin Campbell, Chris Cartwright, George Cave, Sophie Grace Chappell, Geoff Cohen, Ben Cooling, Alan Crichton, Ken Crocket, Duncan Curry, Dave Cuthbertson, Peter Duggan, James Edwards, Steve Elliott, Roger Everett, Hamish Frost, Mike Gardner, Graeme Gatherer, Alan Halewood, Lee Harrison, Paul Headland, Ian Hey, Jim Higgins, Richard Hines, Steve Holmes, Andy Inglis, Murdoch Jamieson, Rob Jarvis, Jenny Jarvis, Craig Lamb, Ruth Love, Ewan Lyons, John Mackenzie, Alastair MacLean, Chris McDaid, George McEwan, Stuart McFarlane, Colin McGregor, Ian McIntosh, Robert McMurray, Alex Messenger, Dan Moore, Dafydd Morris, Neil Morrison, Scott Muir, Tim Neill, Grahame Nicoll, Andy Nisbet, Ian Parnell, Mike Pescod, Tom Prentice, Heike Puchan, Rob Reglinski, Helen Rennard, Ben Richardson, Christine Richardson, Dave Riley, Dave Ritchie, Niall Ritchie, John Roberts, Ali Rose, Marcello Sanguineti, Viv Scott, Davie Scott, Sandy Simpson, Iain Small, Helena Smith, Ian Stennett, Guy Steven, Karl Stewart, Tony Stone, Greg Strange, Fran Sullivan, Ruth Taylor, Jim Teesdale, Alex Thomson, Alistair Todd, John Trudgill, Joris Volmer, Henning Wackerhage, Mike Watson, Roger Webb, Euan Whitaker, Brian Whitworth, Bob Wightman & Jeremy Windsor.

FURTHER READING

The Scottish Mountaineering Club publishes a set of comprehensive guidebooks that cover all of the climbing areas of Scotland. Cicerone publish a series of more selective guides to the major climbing areas.

Scottish Winter Climbs *Andy Nisbet, Rab Anderson & Simon Richardson* (Scottish Mountaineering Club 2008, 2016): A selected guidebook covering a wide selection of the finest and most popular climbs within the major Scottish winter venues. Andy Nisbet's introductory section on Venue, Winter Tactics and Risk provides a concise summary on how to play the winter game.

Scotland's Winter Mountains *Martin Moran* (David & Charles 1998): A well written and thorough textbook describing winter climate, weather and snow conditions together with instructional advice on skills and techniques.

Winter Climbing+ *Neil Gresham & Ian Parnell* (Rockfax 2009): A contemporary textbook on ice and mixed climbing equipment and technique. Also covers training and psychological aspects. Although written from a worldwide perspective it has a strong Scottish focus.

A Chance in a Million *Bob Barton & Blyth Wright* (Scottish Mountaineering Trust 2000): The definitive book on Scottish avalanches is essential reading for anyone setting out into the Scottish mountains in winter.

Cold Climbs *Ken Wilson, Dave Alcock & John Barry* (Diadem Books 1991): The classic compilation of great snow and ice climbs across the British Isles.

The Great Mountain Crags of Scotland *Guy Robertson & Adrian Crofton* (Vertebrate Publishing 2014): An inspirational large format book describing 33 of the finest mountain cliffs in Scotland with first-hand accounts of recent cutting-edge climbs.

Ben Nevis, Britain's Highest Mountain *Ken Crocket & Simon Richardson* (Scottish Mountaineering Trust 2009): This comprehensive history of mountaineering on Ben Nevis also provides a good summary of the evolution of winter climbing across Scotland.

The Cairngorms, 100 Years of Mountaineering *Greg Strange* (Scottish Mountaineering Trust 2010): The companion volume to *Ben Nevis, Britain's Highest Mountain* providing a parallel history of the other key winter climbing area in Scotland.

Scottish Hill Names *Peter Drummond* (Scottish Mountaineering Trust 2010): The origin, meaning and pronunciation of Scotland's hill names.

Scottish Mountaineering Club Journal (SMC, published annually): Obligatory reading for the keen Scottish climber, the Journal includes descriptions of all the new routes climbed in Scotland during the previous year. To ensure the record is maintained, please send details of any new routes to the New Routes Editor. Contact details can be found on the SMC website <*www.smc.org.uk*>.

APPROACHES

Throughout this book, approaches to climbs on Ben Nevis are described as starting from the CIC Hut. This is superbly situated alongside the Allt a' Mhuilinn at NN167722 and lies at an altitude of 670m. The hut was built in 1928 by William and Jane Inglis Clark in memory of their son Charles Inglis Clark who was killed in action during the First World War. The hut can sleep 24 people and is an excellent base for climbing on Ben Nevis, but it is often full during the winter season, especially at weekends. It is owned by the Scottish Mountaineering Club, and bookings should be made well in advance through the hut custodian <*www.smc.org.uk/huts/cic*>. Given the limited spaces in the hut, most climbers approach and descend from the valley the same day, and use the walls of the hut as a wind-break when gearing up and having a bite to eat.

There are two ways of reaching the CIC Hut:

North Face Car Park

The shortest and most popular approach is from the North Face Car Park. It is situated at NN144763 and signposted from the A82 at Torlundy, north-east of Fort William. Follow a track from the north end of the car park across a small bridge, and after 100m take an excellent path on the right that leads up to the line of a disused narrow gauge railway.

Cross this and follow a series of switchbacks through the forest to gain a track on the east (left looking up) side of the Allt a' Mhuilinn. Follow this to a small dam (NN147752), climb over a stile (NN148750) and continue up the east side of the Allt a' Mhuilinn to the CIC Hut (**1hr 30mins** to **2hrs**).

Ben Nevis
North-East Face

Càrn
Dearg

Trident
Buttressess

Castle
Ridge

Meall an
t-Suidhe

Càrn Dearg
Buttress

Glen Nevis

Approaching from Glen Nevis is not as quick as from the North Face Car Park, but it is more convenient for a descent down the Red Burn. From the Ben Nevis Inn at Achintee (NN125729), the Glen Nevis Youth Hostel (NN128718), or the Ben Nevis Visitor Centre (NN123730), follow the Mountain Track to the broad col between Meall an t-Suidhe and Càrn Dearg. Leave the main track above Lochan Meall an t-Suidhe (the Halfway Lochan) at NN146723, and continue north above the lochan to the far side of the col. Here a path descends 30m and bears north-east contouring under the North Wall of Càrn Dearg. Pass a large boulder, known as the Lunching Stone, on the left and continue up the west side of the Allt a' Mhuilinn to reach the CIC Hut just above its junction with the burn descending from Lochan na Ciste (**2hrs** to **2hrs 30mins**).

This and previous page Cubby Images

The CIC Hut is optimally sited below the great North-East Face of Ben Nevis

DESCENTS

The deeply-indented summit plateau of Ben Nevis is surrounded on nearly all sides by steep and difficult ground. It is a serious place, especially in winter, and many accidents have occurred in descent. There is a small shelter located 10m south-west of the summit trig point, but it is cold and cramped and should only be used in an emergency.

Red Burn

The south (left looking down) bank of the Red Burn provides the safest and easiest route off the mountain. From the summit shelter (NN167712) follow a bearing of 231º Grid for 140m to reach a point just left of Gardyloo Gully, then continue downhill on a bearing of 282º Grid for 800m to reach the middle of the 'summer' zigzags on the Mountain Track and the Red Burn area. It is important to follow the bearing exactly as many accidents have occurred when parties have fallen into the upper reaches of Five Finger Gully that lies just to the south. The initial section from the summit across the plateau is marked by a series of two-metre high navigation cairns positioned at 50m intervals, but a compass bearing will still be required in poor visibility. Continue down an easy slope for about 1km, then turn north towards Lochan Meall an t-Suidhe (the Halfway Lochan). Either descend the Mountain Track to Glen Nevis, or continue to the north end of the Halfway Lochan and follow Allt Coire an Lochain

to reach the small dam in the Allt a' Mhuilinn and follow the path to the North Face Car Park.

For the climbs that finish east of the summit, it is best to continue up to the summit shelter and descend as described above. For routes that finish west of the summit, a different initial bearing will be required to gain the main bearing of 282º Grid leading to the Red Burn.

Number Four Gully

The most commonly used descent by those returning to the CIC Hut or the Allt a' Mhuilinn is to downclimb Number Four Gully (Grade I). In good visibility this is straightforward. Follow the line of the plateau, keeping well clear of the cornices, to reach the top of the gully, which is marked by a distinctive navigation cairn (NN158717) labelled with a '4'. Descend the gully to Coire na Ciste. Sometimes the cornice is impassable, but it is often possible to gain the gully by descending steeper ground just to the north, or by making an abseil from the cairn. If this is not possible a bearing of 270º Grid leads to the Red Burn descent described above.

Càrn Mòr Dearg Arete

This is the quickest way of losing height from the summit, but it should only be used with great care. On the upper section there have been fatalities to parties who have strayed too far north (left) of the summit in poor visibility, and there have been many accidents descending the snow slope into Coire Leis, which can be extremely icy. The descent should be avoided in poor visibility and windslab conditions after a period of heavy snowfall and high winds. From the summit shelter follow a bearing of 134⁰ Grid. The ground is flat for the first 100m, and then steepens abruptly. After 200m of descent a slight col is reached on the left that lies about 500m from the summit. At this point there is a two-metre high navigation cairn (NN171710). From here descend the 150m snow slope on the west into Coire Leis (Grade I) and follow the line of the Allt a' Mhuilinn to the CIC Hut.

	Climb	Finish Point	Descent
5	Gargoyle Wall	Number Three Gully	260⁰ Grid to Red Burn
6	Number Three Gully Buttress	Number Three Gully	260⁰ Grid to Red Burn
24	Tower Ridge	Tower Ridge	214⁰ Grid for 140m then 282⁰ Grid to Red Burn
25	Green Gully	The Comb	220⁰ Grid for 180m then 282⁰ Grid to Red Burn
30	Darth Vader	Number Three Gully	260⁰ Grid to Red Burn
32	North-East Buttress	Summit Shelter	231⁰ Grid for 140m then 282⁰ Grid to Red Burn
40	Tower Face Of The Comb	The Comb	220⁰ Grid for 180m then 282⁰ Grid to Red Burn
45	Point Five Gully	Summit Shelter	231⁰ Grid for 140m then 282⁰ Grid to Red Burn
46	Orion Direct	Summit Shelter	231⁰ Grid for 140m then 282⁰ Grid to Red Burn
47	Albatross	Summit Shelter	231⁰ Grid for 140m then 282⁰ Grid to Red Burn
48	The White Line	Tower Ridge	214⁰ Grid for 140m then 282⁰ Grid to Red Burn
49	Hadrian's Wall Direct	Summit Shelter	231⁰ Grid for 140m then 282⁰ Grid to Red Burn
50	Smith's Route	Gardyloo Buttress	214⁰ Grid for 80m then 282⁰ Grid to Red Burn

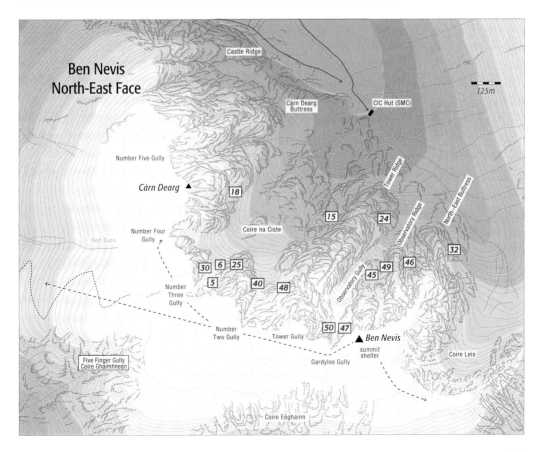

Ben Nevis North-East Face

CHAPTER 1 ▶ EARLY BIRD

Winter arrives quickly to high north facing
corries at the start of the season

Coire an Dubh Lochain, Beinn a' Bhuird; photo Simon Richardson

The spectacular Deep Throat in Coire an Lochain on Cairn Gorm, rimes rapidly with the first snows of winter and makes an excellent companion route to Savage Slit

Joris Volmer

The first snows of winter come surprisingly rapidly to the Scottish Highlands. In many places this wintry covering may appear cosmetic, but on well chosen cliffs these early season conditions can provide excellent climbing. Three decades ago, the convention was that the winter climbing season only began when the gully-lines started icing up in December or January. But modern mixed climbing has pulled the start back to late October or early November to create an early season, which typically runs from the first snows to the end of December. By then, at least one freeze-thaw cycle will have taken place and icier conditions are starting to develop.

The immediate thought with the first snows is to seek the coldest temperatures by going as high as possible. This is a good initial strategy, but cliff aspect and location with respect to the wind are equally important. Paradoxically, a heavy fall of snow on unfrozen ground is not necessarily a good start to the season as the snow can insulate the underlying vegetation, slowing down the freezing process and delaying conditions. Crags facing the prevailing winds are likely to have had more of their lying snow blown away, allowing more time for the exposed turf to freeze.

The Northern Corries of Cairn Gorm are popular early season venues. Not only are the cliff bases above 1000m, they also face north-west and bear the full brunt of the first winter storms sweeping across the Cairngorms. This cools the rock, an important factor as the mountains still retain significant summer and autumn heat, and allows rime ice to cover the cliffs in a beautiful layer of white.

Savage Slit and **The Hoarmaster** in Coire an Lochain, the most westerly of the two Northern Corries, are often the first routes of the season to be climbed. The high cliff base and the bowl-shaped nature of the corrie, together with its angular cliffs, means that it has a strong tendency to form rime ice. These climbs are Snowed-Up Rock routes which do not rely on frozen turf or ice for progress, but are more dependent on hooking and torquing techniques.

Climbs in the easterly and more accessible Coire an t-Sneachda are situated slightly lower and are less exposed to the wind. They take a few more days to come into condition following the winter's first icy blasts, however **The Message** and **Fingers Ridge** are well travelled early season favourites.

Over on the West, Ben Nevis is another excellent early season venue. The climbs on Number Three Gully Buttress are especially popular, and in a similar way to Coire an Lochain, it is fully exposed to north-westerlies and rimes rapidly. **Gargoyle Wall** is one of the established early season favourites on the mountain, but **Number Three Gully Buttress** itself, which is more commonly climbed as a Mixed route later in the season, is also a good Snowed-Up Rock route early in the winter.

For many climbers, early season is the optimum time to attempt technical Snowed-Up Rock routes as both early season enthusiasm and summer rock fitness come into play, and crucially, November days still have adequate daylight.

The very highest Cairngorm corries on Braeriach and Beinn a' Bhuird typically face east (away from the prevailing wind), and early in the winter the turf may be insulated by wind-blown snow and not fully frozen. A thaw and re-freeze will address this problem, and two or three weeks into the season Mixed routes that depend on frozen vegetation, as well as underlying rock features, come into play.

The east facing Coire an Lochain on Aonach Mòr is one of the highest cliffs in the West, and its plentiful granite cracks and copious turf makes it one of the more amenable mixed climbing venues in the country. Many climbers wait until the Gondola starts running at the beginning of the ski season (usually the end of December) to start climbing here, but for those prepared to walk, the Mixed routes can be excellent in November. **Grooved Arete**, one of the first routes climbed in the corrie, is a good early season choice.

Situated on the eastern side of the Highlands, Lochnagar is sheltered from the north-westerlies that often deposit much of their snow over the main Cairngorm massif. While the long routes in its great North-East Coire are not particularly good early in the season, being long with a relatively low cliff base, this is not the case elsewhere on the mountain. **Magic Pillar** in the Southern Sector has a higher cliff base, and comes into condition quickly if there is an easterly component to the wind. The west side of the mountain also rimes up quickly during early winter storms, and climbs on The Stuic such as **First Light** make good early season objectives.

The easily accessible Creagan Cha-no on the east side of Cairn Gorm is best visited early in the season before it is swamped by snow blown across the plateau. Routes like **Jenga Buttress** are climbable in a variety of conditions, and their quick access makes them suitable for half a day.

The Southern Highlands are not a traditional early season venue as the mountains tend to be lower than those further north. However, the north facing cliffs in Coire Chat on Ben Cruachan come into condition quickly and the climbing is similar in style to the Northern Corries (albeit with a longer approach). **Tainted Elixir** makes an excellent introduction to this recently developed crag that is rapidly gaining popularity.

Early winter used to be considered downtime from mainstream winter climbing because the ice and gully climbs had not yet formed. The emergence of mixed climbing changed this perception and created an early season which is now firmly established as one of the most popular and favourable times to enjoy Scottish winter climbing.

Roger Everett enjoying early season Grade III ground in Coire Ruadh on Braeriach

Simon Richardson

Helen Rennard enjoying superb early season conditions on the first pitch of Savage Slit. The route is perfectly rimed after the first storm of the winter

Joris Volmer

SAVAGE SLIT

Grade: 90m, V,6
Location: No.4 Buttress, Coire an Lochain, Cairn Gorm
Route Base, Aspect & Rock Type: 1100m, North-East facing, Granite
First Winter Ascent: George Adams, Jim White & Fraser Henderson, 21 April 1957

Cubby Images

Looking across the cliffs of Coire an Lochain towards No.4 Buttress

The first winter ascent of Savage Slit was a landmark in Scottish climbing history. The 1957 winter was a lean one, and by the end of March spring was well on its way in the high Cairngorms with many cliffs already snow and ice-free. However, a late cold snap towards the end of April left a covering of fresh snow on the tops, which prompted Cairngorms pioneers Adams, White and Henderson to visit Coire an Lochain and have a look at Savage Slit. This route had first been climbed as a summer Severe 12 years before, and their ascent in winter conditions was a tour de force. "The slit itself between the chockstones was blocked out partially with old ice, partially with packed powder," states their account in the 1961 Cairngorms guidebook. "The upper chockstone provided the hardest moves. These were heavily iced and the walls of the slit sheathed in verglas."

Although the route was originally graded IV, it was almost certainly the most difficult Cairngorms mixed climb achieved by that date, and nowadays it fully deserves its V,6 rating. The first ascent highlights the 'conditions conundrum' for this route. Later in the season the lower section can fill with ice and become a little easier, however this will inevitably lead to harder climbing above with icy cracks making protection difficult. As a result, Savage Slit is best climbed as a pure Snowed-Up Rock route – no frozen turf or ice is required – making it the perfect early season climb.

Savage Slit is justifiably popular and many climbers think of it as a rite of passage to harder Cairngorms mixed. It is a sustained route and an intimidating lead, and some prefer to climb inside the chimney rather than take the more elegant approach bridging up the outside. Either way, Savage Slit will provide a memorable experience, and should be high on the tick list of every Scottish winter climber. And as you wrestle your way up the corner, just remember, as one recent ascensionist noted; it's "wicked, squirmy, chimney, torquey, fun!"

Battling up the second pitch of *Savage Slit* in stormy weather. Climber Rob Marson

Jeremy Windsor

Approach

From the Coire Cas car park at the top of the Cairn Gorm ski road, follow the path that leads south-west. After 400m (NH987057) the path splits. Take the right-hand branch (the left-hand leads to Coire an t-Sneachda) and cross the burn of the Allt Coire an t-Sneachda. After 100m the path divides again. Either of the two branches ultimately leads to the two lochans at the foot of the corrie. The choice will depend on the depth of snow and whether an

Alternative Routes

If Savage Slit is busy, **Deep Throat** (V,6) and **The Third Man** (V,6) are good nearby alternatives on No.4 Buttress, and if the weather is poor, **Sidewinder** (III,4) is a good fall-back option. All these routes are possible at the beginning of the season. If you are there later in the year and Savage Slit is unhelpfully icy, then **Gaffer's Groove** (V,5) may be a more suitable option. Alternatively, **Oesophagus** (III) is likely to provide an easier icy alternative.

Guidebooks

The Cairngorms (SMC), *Scottish Winter Climbs* (SMC), *Winter Climbs in The Cairngorms* (Cicerone).

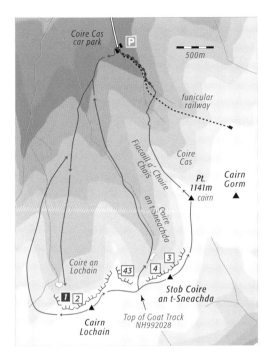

existing trail is in place. The left branch leads directly to the first of the two lochans, whilst the right branch continues to a burn crossing at NH980044, from where it is possible to strike up into the corrie. From the inner lochan go right (to avoid the Great Slab – avalanche risk) and then back left to reach the foot of No.4 Buttress (**1hr 30mins**).

Descent

It is not straightforward to return to the base of the route. The quickest descent is to the west. Follow the corrie rim to the south-west and descend the north-easterly slope back into the corrie. (Continuing down the ridge will avoid any potential avalanche risk). Alternatively, follow the corrie rim to the east and climb down the Goat Track (as for The Message p48) or continue to Pt.1141m (NH999040) and descend easily to the ski area from there.

Conditions

The high altitude of No.4 Buttress and its exposed location on the northerly edge of the Cairngorms plateau means that the cliff rimes quickly with north-westerly winds. As a result, Savage Slit comes into condition very rapidly, and is often the first route to be climbed at the beginning of the season (which can be as early as October). Savage Slit is the archetypal Snowed-Up Rock route, and just needs a coating of snow and/or rime to bring it into condition. No ice, consolidated snow or frozen turf is required.

Top Tips

It's best not to lead Savage Slit wearing a rucksack, but descending back to the foot of the route is awkward, so consider combining rucksacks and giving it to the second to carry. Alternatively, make a full 50m abseil from the top of the third pitch (anchor quite low down) above the right wall of the corner, back to your gear. Take care to avoid abseiling down the chimney as it can be difficult to retrieve the ropes.

Route Description

An outstanding line up the prominent right-angled chimney-corner in the centre of No.4 Buttress.

1. 15m A short initial pitch (harder than it looks) leads to a belay below the corner.

2. 25m Climb the chimney-corner to belay on the large chockstone at half-height.

3. 20m Continue following the chimney to a good ledge at its top.

4. 30m Ascend a left-trending gully and finish up a short wall at the top.

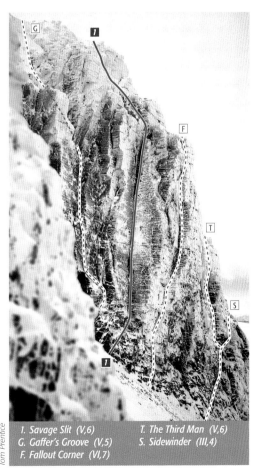

Tom Prentice

1. Savage Slit (V,6)	T. The Third Man (V,6)
G. Gaffer's Groove (V,5)	S. Sidewinder (III,4)
F. Fallout Corner (VI,7)	

Halvor Hagen contemplating the square-cut chimney of The Hoarmaster. Long feathers of rime ice, a characteristic feature of the second pitch, can be seen on the upper tower

Simon Richardson

THE HOARMASTER

Grade: 60m, VI,6
Location: No.3 Buttress, Coire an Lochain, Cairn Gorm
Route Base, Aspect & Rock Type: 1150m, North facing, Granite
First Ascent: Rab Anderson, Grahame Nicoll & Rob Milne, 19 November 1988

Rab Anderson

Grahame Nicoll back and footing up the bulging chimney of The Hoarmaster during the first ascent

Climbing in the Northern Corries went through a remarkable transformation in the late 1980s. Prior to that the 'Norries' were seen as something of a backwater and away from the cutting edge of Cairngorms winter climbing that was focused on the big cliffs of The Shelter Stone, Creag an Dubh Loch and Lochnagar. Hard mixed climbing in the early 1980s was a different game to now, and technical powder-covered rock was often climbed wearing thin gloves. In 1981, Andy Nisbet made some experimental mixed ascents on Càrn Etchachan. It was a poor winter with little snow and ice, but the deep cracks of the Northern Cairngorm granite proved ideal for torquing ice axe picks.

Later in 1985, Nisbet started working at Glenmore Lodge where he met Andy Cunningham. Although Cunningham was new to mixed climbing, the two Andys formed one of the most effective partnerships in the history of Scottish mountaineering. Over the next three winters they added over 25 challenging new routes across the Cairngorms and Northern Highlands. It was their routes in the Northern Corries however, such as Fallout Corner (VI,7) and The Migrant (VI,7), which were to have a profound influence on the shape of modern mixed climbing.

Rab Anderson was quick to recognise the area's potential. Together with his Edinburgh-based team of Rob Milne, Grahame Nicoll, Chris Greaves and Tom Prentice, he took up the charge with a string of excellent mixed routes in Coire an Lochain. As correspondent for the highly respected Mountain magazine and an excellent photographer (he always carried an SLR), Anderson had a major influence on the direction of winter climbing at the time. Within a couple of seasons the emphasis had changed and a 'cragging' atmosphere existed in the Northern Corries most week-ends. Routes such as The Hoarmaster immediately proved popular, and have introduced many climbers to the delights of mixed climbing in the Cairngorms.

2

The first pitch of Fallout Corner on No.4 Buttress. Climber Brian Duthie

Henning Wackerhage

Approach

From the Coire Cas car park at the top of the Cairn Gorm ski road, walk into Coire an Lochain as for Savage Slit (p40). From the inner lochan, go right (to avoid the Great Slab – avalanche risk) and then back left to reach the foot of No.3 Buttress (**1hr 30mins**).

Descent

In good conditions it is possible to descend back into the corrie by climbing down The Couloir (I), the broad slanting gully defining the left edge of No.3 Buttress. To return to the Coire Cas car park, follow the routes described for Savage Slit (p41).

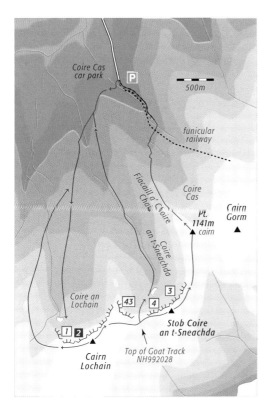

Conditions

The Hoarmaster is near the lower end of its grade and an excellent introduction to Cairngorms Grade VI winter climbing. Entering the square-cut chimney is

Alternative Routes

Hooker's Corner (VI,6) is the next line to the right and slightly more difficult than The Hoarmaster. It is often icy and can be harder to protect. **The Overseer Direct** (V,6) takes the line of corners to the left of The Hoarmaster and provides good technical climbing at a similar standard. Further left lies **The Migrant** (VI,7), the hard winter classic on the buttress. Left again is **Ewen Buttress** (III,4), a good back up route that takes the easier-angled left crest of the buttress overlooking the prominent gully of The Couloir. Another good alternative is **Fallout Corner** (VI,7) on No.4 Buttress.

Guidebooks

The Cairngorms (SMC), *Scottish Winter Climbs* (SMC), *Winter Climbs in The Cairngorms* (Cicerone).

difficult, and placing gear can be awkward if the cracks are iced and cannot take cams. The route is best climbed as an early season Snowed-Up Rock route, as its position on the exposed edge of No.3 Buttress ensures that it rimes up quickly in a northerly wind.

Top Tips

Too much frosting can be a bad thing, and the top pitch of The Hoarmaster is susceptible to significant accumulation of rime ice. The route is still possible in these conditions, but it will require tiring and time-consuming digging to find and place protection.

Route Description

An excellent steep Snowed-Up Rock route taking the square-cut chimney near the right edge of No.3 Buttress.

1. 30m Start at the bottom right corner of the buttress, ascend to a ledge, and climb the square-cut chimney on the right.

2. 30m Continue up the bulging chimney above to the top.

2. The Hoarmaster (VI,6)   O. The Overseer Direct (V,6)
E. Ewen Buttress (III,4)   H. Hooker's Corner (VI,6)

Henning Wackerhage

Graeme Gatherer placing a cam on the third pitch of The Message. Ice-free cracks mean Snowed-Up Rock routes are often easier to protect at the beginning of the season

Steve Elliott

THE MESSAGE

Grade: 90m, IV,6
Location: Mess of Pottage, Coire an t-Sneachda, Cairn Gorm
Route Base, Aspect & Rock Type: 1050m, North-West facing, Granite
First Ascent: Andy Cunningham & Willie Todd, 23 January 1986

Steve Elliott

Traversing the initial diagonal break of The Message with the main corner-groove cutting through the upper cliff

*C*oire an t-Sneachda, the most frequented of the two Northern Corries, has four main cliffs – Mess of Pottage, Aladdin's Buttress, Fluted Buttress and Fiacaill Buttress. They were all developed in the 1960s except for Mess of Pottage, which surprisingly waited until the 1980s before it was properly explored. Tom Patey and John Deacon, and later Dougal Haston, probed the crag with three routes in the early 1960s, but Patey naming the cliff 'The Mess of Pottage' suggests they were not too impressed and they didn't come back for more.

Today, The Mess of Pottage is home to some of the finest climbing in Coire an t-Sneachda, but it took a change of attitude for its true value to be appreciated. In the mid-1980s, Cairngorms mixed climbing was gaining pace and cliffs previously rejected for their lack of height were re-appraised. In January 1986 Andy Cunningham and Willie Todd revisited Patey's cliff and climbed the prominent groove up the centre of the buttress, which they called The Message. The three-pitch route provided absorbing and sustained mixed climbing (although nowadays many prefer to climb it as four pitches). The route name was deliberately provocative, and soon other climbers were exploring the cliff. Over the next few seasons more than a dozen winter routes of similar quality were found.

The Message remains the classic line. It is an excellent route, sustained all the way, with technical sections on all four pitches. There is good gear with 'bomber' hooks where you need them, and frequent places to rest. The climb builds to a crescendo on the last two corner pitches. Opinion is divided as to which of these is the hardest and there is a choice of finishes, but whichever way you climb it, The Message is a superb stepping-stone to the more difficult Mixed and Snowed-Up Rock routes in the Cairngorms.

3

Starting up the corner-groove on pitch 3 of The Message. Climber Roger Everett

Simon Richardson

Approach

From the Coire Cas car park at the top of the Cairn Gorm ski road, follow the path that leads south-west. After 400m (NH987057) the path splits. Take the left-hand branch (the right-hand leads to Coire an Lochain) and contour above the left bank of the Allt Coire an t-Sneachda to gain two small lochans just beyond the corrie lip. These will often be buried under snow. From here, head south-east picking the optimum way through the boulders, and climb a short snow slope to gain the foot of the cliff (**1hr**).

Descent

The simplest descent is to follow the corrie edge to Pt.1141m with its prominent cairn (NH999040) at the top of Fiacaill a' Choire Chais and descend the broad ridge (beware of a possible cornice on the right) into the ski area. Alternatively, descend the Goat Track, the steep strip of snow that rises up to the col between Fluted Buttress and Fiacaill Buttress at the south-west corner of the corrie at NH992028. Take care in conditions of heavy snow, or in strong westerly winds, as it can be avalanche-prone (there are accidents here most years).

Conditions

The Mess of Pottage faces north-west and bears the full force of early winter storms. This coupled with its relatively high elevation means that it freezes quickly, and a good coating of snow is all that is required to bring the route into condition. Much of the turf has

disappeared over the years, but fortunately there are plentiful hooks and torques to use instead. Requiring just an hour for the approach, the Mess of Pottage is one of the most easily accessible high mountain cliffs in the country.

Top Tips

The Message is best climbed early in the season before it becomes too icy. The route is towards the top end of its grade at IV,6 and this rating assumes that good protection is available. When icy, protection may be harder to find and the route can be V,6.

Route Description

The route follows the deepest groove in the centre of the face to the right of a prominent diagonal break. Start on the right side of a snow bay below the main dome-shaped section of cliff.

1. 40m Start by following the diagonal break up and left. Climb a short chimney followed by two short corner-steps to gain the base of the deep groove.

2. 10m Continue up a fault on the right, step left, and then go right into the steepest section of the groove.

3. 20m Climb the superb corner-groove to its top,

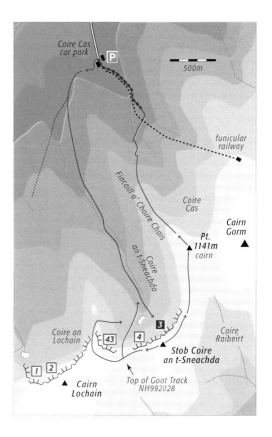

Andy Nisbet

3. The Message (IV,6)   P. Pot Of Gold (V,6)   D. Hidden Chimney, Direct Start (IV,5)
H. Honeypot (IV,6)   HC. Hidden Chimney (III)

step up and left and belay on a ledge below a right facing corner.

4. **20m** Climb the corner to a bulge. Avoid this by moving left and follow cracked slabs to the top. Alternatively, from the stance climb the parallel crack-line 2m right of the corner.

Alternative Routes

All the routes on The Mess of Pottage are worthwhile, but pride of place goes to **Pot Of Gold** (V,6) which takes an unlikely line of well protected cracks just right of The Message. If you find The Message straightforward, put this one on your list! **Honeypot** (IV,6) is another good route similar in standard to The Message. **Hidden Chimney** (III) makes an excellent introduction to the cliff and has a **Direct Start** (IV,5) that adds a little spice.

Guidebooks

The Cairngorms (SMC), *Scottish Winter Climbs* (SMC), *Winter Climbs in The Cairngorms* (Cicerone).

Simon Richardson

Kasper Berkowitz climbing Honeypot on the left side of the Mess of Pottage

Passing through the fingers in ideal Snowed-Up Rock conditions of light riming and powder snow

Henning Wackerhage

FINGERS RIDGE

Grade: 140m, IV,5
Location: Fluted Buttress, Coire an t-Sneachda, Cairn Gorm
Route Base, Aspect & Rock Type: 1000m, North facing, Granite
First Winter Ascent: John Dempster & Ian Wallace, 19 January 1969

Jim Higgins

Entering Coire an t-Sneachda. Fingers Ridge is near the right skyline

I first climbed Fingers Ridge during the 1997 International Winter Meet held at Glenmore Lodge. This was the first winter meet hosted by the BMC, and understandably nervous, the organisers requested that everyone climb in Coire an t-Sneachda on the first day. The weather was poor and it had been gently thawing for several days, but the Northern Corries still held a little snow and ice. Graeme Ettle and I were teamed up with two of the visiting stars – Andrej Stremfelj and Janez Jeglic from Slovenia. (I found out later that Andrej had won the inaugural Piolet d'Or for his alpine-style first ascent of the South Pillar of Kanchenjunga and Janez had climbed three new routes on Cerro Torre). As the local guru, Graeme suggested that Fingers Ridge would be possible whatever the conditions.

As we stepped out of the minibus at the Coire Cas car park, Janez and Andrej shot off up the mountain. Graeme managed to match their pace, but I was left to bring up the rear, jogging to keep up. By the time I had caught Andrej up at the base of Fingers Ridge and uncoiled the rope, Graeme had already led the first pitch. We sprinted up the route in tandem as two ropes of two, and whilst Graeme and Janez were waiting for us to climb the top pitch, they quickly nipped up Goat Track Gully. The whole route could not have taken more than 30 minutes, and as we descended the Goat Track, the rest of the meet was just arriving in the corrie.

I tell this story, not to recommend a rapid ascent of Fingers Ridge, but to demonstrate that it's possible in almost all conditions. The route improves the higher you go. The lower section after the diagonal entry pitch can give pause for thought; there is a tricky move past the eponymous fingers and an absorbing direct move up the headwall to finish. This looks blank from below, but once you commit to the moves, everything comes together to provide a very satisfying finale to an excellent and classic route.

4

Looking down Fingers Ridge in snowy conditions. Climber Jo George

Cubby Images

Approach

From the Coire Cas car park at the top of the Cairn Gorm ski road, follow the approach as for The Message (p48) into Coire an t-Sneachda. From the inner lochan, head south towards the broad Fluted Buttress, picking the optimum way through the boulders, to gain the foot of the ridge (**1hr**).

Descent

As for The Message (p48).

Conditions

Fingers Ridge is a genuine Snowed-Up Rock route, as it does not rely on frozen turf, consolidated snow or ice. It can be climbed with the first snows of winter, but it is best avoided when not frozen or in thaw conditions, as there are some large loose blocks in the groove leading towards the fingers. The ridge can be climbed at any time in the season, and it is a reliable route in a wide variety of conditions. The cornice is nearly always passable and later in the season the lower part of the route can provide good climbing up easy-angled ice and névé.

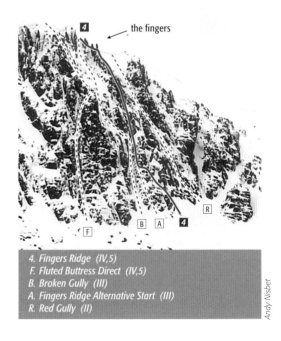

the fingers

4. *Fingers Ridge (IV,5)*
F. *Fluted Buttress Direct (IV,5)*
B. *Broken Gully (III)*
A. *Fingers Ridge Alternative Start (III)*
R. *Red Gully (II)*

Andy Nisbet

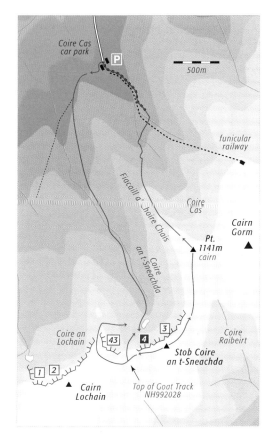

Alternative Routes

The gullies to the left and right of Fingers Ridge are **Broken Gully** (III) and **Red Gully** (II). Both provide worthwhile climbs and the lower part of Broken Gully is particularly good when lean. This section can be climbed to join Fingers Ridge just below the groove leading to the fingers; **Broken Fingers** (III,5). The other classic in the Fluted Buttress area is **Fluted Buttress Direct** (IV,5) which follows the narrow chimney system on the left side of the buttress. Unlike Fingers Ridge, it requires a little consolidated snow and ice to be at its best, so is not a good choice early in the season.

Guidebooks

The Cairngorms (SMC), *Scottish Winter Climbs* (SMC), *Winter Climbs in The Cairngorms* (Cicerone).

finger and climb a short technical wall to finish. Taken direct, this final wall is the technical crux (Tech 5), but it can be avoided on the left or right.

Top Tips

If the slabby ground at the start of the first pitch is bare (which can occur early in the season), it is possible to climb directly up to the right of Broken Gully to the first stance below the short steep wall. Higher up, if time is running short, there is an easy escape left from the col below the fingers into the straightforward upper section of Broken Gully. From here, finish either left or right of the final funnel.

Route Description

Fingers Ridge lies on the right side of Fluted Buttress and takes the slabby buttress between Broken and Red gullies that narrows into two prominent fingers near the top. The route is well marked by crampon scratches. Start at the foot of Red Gully and climb diagonally left for a ropelength over ledges and short slabs, to belay on a good ledge under a short wall on the left side of the buttress.

Bypass the wall on the left overlooking Broken Gully, then move up and right and climb a flake-crack to gain the prominent right facing groove that leads up to the narrow ridge crest and the fingers. Pass through the fingers, step around the right side of the second

Henning Wackerhage

Forrest Templeton leading the technical crux up the short wall at the top of Fingers Ridge

Konrad Rawlick and Sam Loveday tackling the superbly positioned Gargoyle Cracks pitch high on Gargoyle Wall. Climbing conditions are ideal with the cliff white from hoar frost and the cracks free of ice

Viv Scott

GARGOYLE WALL

Grade: 120m, VI,6
Location: Number Three Gully Buttress, Coire na Ciste, Ben Nevis
Route Base, Aspect & Rock Type: 1100m, North facing, Andesite
First Winter Ascent: Rab Carrington & Ian Nicolson, December 1977. Complete ascent
(as described), Simon Richardson & Chris Cartwright, 22 February 1998

Henning Wackerhage

Following the shattered corner on pitch 2 of Gargoyle Wall. Climber James Richardson

*I*t can take decades before the quality of some winter climbs is fully recognised and Gargoyle
Wall on Number Three Gully Buttress is a good example. Rab Carrington and Ian Nicolson made
the first winter ascent in December 1977 by starting up Thompson's Route, then traversing across
to the Gargoyle, a prominent head-shaped feature on the front of the face, and continuing up the
summer line on the vertical right edge of the buttress. Their description simply stated, "Follow the
summer route with difficulty on the upper cracks," and they graded the route IV.

Chris Cartwright and I started up the climb one poor day in February 1998. We felt rather
pleased with ourselves when we climbed the first two pitches of the summer line to join the existing
winter route at the Gargoyle. The two lower pitches had provided good mixed climbing up steep
cracks and thinly turfed corners, but when we traversed around the right edge of the buttress we
were in for a shock. The pitch above looked very steep, with few positive axe placements or
footholds, and was clearly going to be very awkward to protect. I then remembered Mal Duff had
made an early repeat of Carrington and Nicolson's line, finding it a lot tougher than he'd expected.
I should have taken more notice; Mal was a strong winter climber, at the vanguard of modern
mixed climbing on the Ben in the late 1980s.

Fortunately, the Gargoyle Cracks were not my lead, so I made myself secure and watched
Chris on the pitch, masterfully placing gear whilst tensioning his body to avoid barn-dooring. No
way was this a Grade IV. It was solid Tech 6, and in hindsight it was almost certainly the most
difficult mixed pitch on Ben Nevis until Mal Duff climbed Point Blank on Observatory Buttress in
1988. Today, Gargoyle Wall is considered to be one of the finest mixed routes on the mountain,
and sees many ascents, especially early in the season.

5

The infamous Gargoyle Cracks pitch on Gargoyle Wall. Climber James Richardson

Henning Wackerhage

Approach

Coire na Ciste is approached by heading over the domed rock west of the CIC Hut, then scrambling up a short vegetated wall at the foot of the main corrie. Number Three Gully Buttress lies at the head of the corrie, extends rightwards from Green Gully to Number Three Gully and consists of a broad slabby wall, then a very steep buttress of excellent rock (about **1hr** from the Hut, see p30-31).

Descent

See Ben Nevis Approaches & Descents (p30-33).

Conditions

The exposed position of Gargoyle Wall on the north-westerly edge of Number Three Gully Buttress, helps it to rime up very quickly and it is often the first route to come into condition on the mountain. Later in the season, icing can ease the difficulty of the first two pitches, but the route is best climbed as a Snowed-Up Rock route.

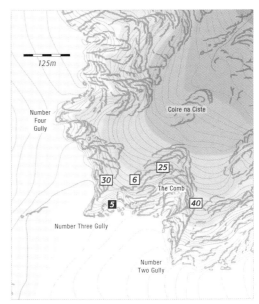

125m

Number Four Gully

Coire na Ciste

Number Three Gully

| 25 |
| 30 | | 6 |
The Comb
| 5 | | 40 |

Number Two Gully

5. Gargoyle Wall (VI,6)   B. Babylon (VII,7)

Iain Small

to reach the top of the Gargoyle. Climb the ridge above, passing a perched block, to gain a ledge. Traverse right into a shattered corner, and climb this to a stance and block belay below a steep cracked wall.

3. 15m Climb the Gargoyle Wall Cracks (crux) on the left side of the wall to a platform.

4. 35m Traverse 6m left to a chimney-crack, and climb this to where it steepens. Move left along a ledge to reach a right-trending ramp and finish easily along this to the top of the buttress.

Alternative Routes
Ben Nevis has become nearly as popular as the Northern Corries of Cairn Gorm as an early season mixed venue. There are many Snowed-Up Rock routes on the Ben, and routes on South Trident Buttress such as **The Slab Climb** (VI,7) and **Sidewinder** (VII,7) are particularly good at the start of the winter. On Number Three Gully Buttress, **Hobgoblin** (VI,7), (*see topo p61*), a direct version of Gargoyle Wall, is another excellent early season route.

Guidebooks
Ben Nevis (SMC), *Scottish Winter Climbs* (SMC), *Winter Climbs Ben Nevis and Glen Coe* (Cicerone).

Top Tips
Gargoyle Wall is an ideal introduction to Nevis mixed climbing. The situations are exciting and the moves well protected. The Gargoyle Wall Cracks normally have two or three pieces of in-situ gear that take the sting out of the pitch and allow the leader to focus on the technical moves.

Route Description
Start by climbing a short way up Number Three Gully to reach a right facing chimney-flake on the left wall, situated about 20m up and right of the prominent chimney of Thompson's Route.

1. 40m Climb the flake to a well defined ledge. From the left end of the ledge, descend slightly and enter the chimney on the left. Climb this, surmount a chockstone and gain a snow bay with the Gargoyle now visible on the right. In icy conditions it is possible to gain the chimney directly from below.

2. 30m Cross a groove and follow a short gangway

Simon Richardson stepping off the Gargoyle Flake during the first ascent of Hobgoblin

Chris Cartwright

Alex Runciman tip-toeing across the exposed final pitch of Number Three Gully Buttress. A short thaw and re-freeze has helpfully consolidated the snow

NUMBER THREE GULLY BUTTRESS

Grade: 150m, III,4
Location: Coire na Ciste, Ben Nevis
Route Base, Aspect & Rock Type: 1100m, North facing, Andesite
First Winter Ascent: Len Lovat & Donald Bennet, 18 February 1957

Simon Richardson

The spectacular final belay on Number Three Gully Buttress. Climber Robin Clothier

*A*way from its great ridges, there are only a handful of easier mixed routes on Ben Nevis. The majority of the well known mixed routes on the mountain weigh in at Grade VI or higher, which is a shame, because the Ben is fully exposed to the might of the first winter storms roaring in from the North Atlantic, and an excellent early season venue. Fortunately, there is one notable exception in the form of Number Three Gully Buttress. Lying high on the mountain and facing north, the route rapidly comes into condition, and its high altitude ensures that it is more likely to be in condition at the start of the season than any of the classic ridges.

Len Lovat and Donald Bennet made the first winter ascent on 18 February 1957, a landmark day for Scottish climbing, as next door in Observatory Gully, Tom Patey, Hamish MacInnes and Graham Nicol were making the first ascent of Zero Gully, the most sought-after winter route of its era. Perfect snow-ice conditions were ideal for step-cutting that day, and Lovat and Bennet enjoyed a classic climb on Number Three Gully Buttress, revelling in the ever-increasing exposure as the route reached its culmination, winding around the right side of the buttress overlooking an 80m vertical drop into Number Three Gully below.

Number Three Gully Buttress soon became a popular route, known for its sustained interest, heel-tugging situations, and good belays and protection. It can be climbed at almost any point in the winter, but is particularly good early in the season as a Snowed-Up Rock route. In those conditions it is probably worth III,4 and the steep step at the start of the fourth pitch, before the long traverse, can feel particularly hard. Many teams opt for the Direct Finish at this point. Climbing this steep 35m-long chimney is technically no easier, but possibly a little less exposed!

6

The awkward step up on Number Three Gully Buttress

Andy Brown

Approach
As for Gargoyle Wall (p56).

Descent
See Ben Nevis Approaches & Descents (p30-33).

Conditions
Number Three Gully Buttress is at its best either early in the winter, or later in the season when it can form good snow-ice. It is probably worth avoiding in conditions of heavy snow as the climbing can feel insecure and significant digging will be required to find protection.

Top Tips
Early in the season before the first major snowfalls, the approach up scree above Lochan na Ciste can be a slow process. On a day of good visibility, it may be simplest to approach from the plateau via the 'tourist' path and descend Number Three Gully.

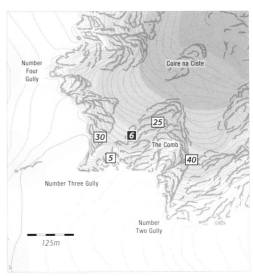

Alternative Routes

In recent years, a number of easier mixed routes have been climbed high in Coire na Ciste which come into condition with the first snows of winter. **Pinncer** (IV,4) is a fine expedition that takes the left crest of Pinnacle Buttress of the Tower and is started by climbing Broad Gully for 100m to below the foot of the ridge. The route continues up mixed ground for four pitches just right of the crest to reach the top of the Pinnacle. From here, continue along the easy-angled ridge to the foot of the Great Tower and continue up Tower Ridge. On the Upper Tier of South Trident Buttress (approached by traversing right out of Number Four Gully) there are two good Grade IVs. **Poseidon Groove** (IV,5) takes the steep groove-line splitting the central part of the wall, and **Triton Corners** (IV,5) starts 25m to the right and ascends a short bulging offwidth to gain a stepped corner system that leads up and right.

Guidebooks

Ben Nevis (SMC), *Scottish Winter Climbs* (SMC), *Winter Climbs Ben Nevis and Glen Coe* (Cicerone), *SMC Journal 2003, SMC Journal 2004, SMC Journal 2006. For SMC Journal new routes see* <www.smc.org.uk/new-routes>.

Route Description

The route is typically climbed in four or five pitches. Start at the top of a snowy depression just right of the centre of the front face of the buttress, gain a snow ramp, and follow it up and right to a large platform. Before it banks out, the last section before the large platform may involve an interesting little wall. Continue to a smaller platform, make an awkward step up, traverse right along an exposed snow terrace and finish up icy slabs. Alternatively, from the small platform move left to a steep icy chimney (Direct Finish) and climb this for 35m to the top.

Simon Richardson

6. *Number Three Gully Buttress (III,4)*
D. *Number Three Gully Buttress Direct Finish (III,4)*

5. *Gargoyle Wall (VI,6)*
T. *Thompson's Route (IV,4)*

H. *Hobgoblin (VI,7)*

The start of Grooved Arete in early season powder conditions. The crux upper section is looming above in the mist. Climber Henning Wackerhage

Henning Wackerhage

GROOVED ARETE

Grade: 130m, V,6
Location: North Buttress, Coire an Lochain, Aonach Mòr
Route Base, Aspect & Rock Type: 1100m, East facing, Granite
First Ascent: Simon Richardson & Roger Everett, 26 November 1988

Henning Wackerhage

Walking north along the Aonach Mòr plateau towards the summit ski tow at the end of the day

*T*he publication of The Munros by the Scottish Mountaineering Club in 1985 had a significant impact on Scottish climbing. It was the first fully illustrated book to describe the best ways of ascending Scotland's 3000ft peaks, and was a runaway success. The profits were ploughed back into Scottish mountaineering leading to the comprehensive series of SMC climbing guidebooks that we know today.

The pictures in The Munros revealed several potential new winter crags, and a shot of Coire an Lochain's icy cliffs on the east face of Aonach Mòr looked particularly interesting. In January 1988 Roger Everett and I decided to investigate the corrie by approaching from Torlundy. This was before the development of the Nevis Range ski area, and the north side of the mountain was trackless and rarely visited. Unfortunately visibility was very poor, so we started at the lowest point of the cliff and climbed three long and varied pitches to the top. The result was Morwind and the name reflected the bad weather we found that day.

Suitably encouraged we were back the following November. Again the weather was not on our side, so working from memory in the mist, we climbed the Grade III Icicle Gully near the right-hand side of the crag. This went quickly, so after an easy descent at the north end of the cliff, we set off up the attractive looking buttress to the left. An increasingly technical first pitch was followed by a superb second ropelength climbing steep grooves on turf and torques, before an exciting overhanging exit led to the final easier slopes. Such a climb deserved a traditional name, so we called it Grooved Arete.

Roger and I continued exploring the cliff throughout the rest of the season. As the route names suggest (Typhoon, Jet Stream, Force Ten Buttress, Hurricane Arete), the weather remained wild and windy but we knew that we had stumbled on a worthwhile new climbing ground that would be especially useful early in the season or when conditions were lean. Of all the routes we climbed that winter our favourite was Grooved Arete.

7

Robbie Miller starting the second pitch of Grooved Arete

Henning Wackerhage

Approach

The easiest way to reach the cliffs of Aonach Mòr is to take the Nevis Range Gondola to the top station at 650m. There is an early climber's lift at 8am and the Gondola runs continuously from 9am. The Quad chair to 870m also provides winter climbers with an uplift only service. Current arrangements can be checked at <*www.nevisrange.co.uk*>. On foot, the quickest way from the top station is to follow the line of the ski tows directly up the side of the main ski run, then continue alongside the summit ski tow to its end (**1hr 30mins**). This point is marked by a small shack and a large cairn (NN192740).

From here it is 150m to the rim of Easy Gully at NN191738 (bearing 185° Grid). In poor visibility it may be difficult to locate the top of the gully, and extreme caution should be exercised as the cornices can be very large. Early in the season, it is normally possible to enter the gully by its northern edge, which appears to escape much of the cornicing. Once in the corrie, all the approaches to all of the routes involve traversing steep avalanche-prone slopes, so climbing here should be avoided immediately after a heavy snowfall.

Descent

Easy Gully is the most commonly used descent back into the corrie. It is also possible to descend just to the north of the north-bounding ridge of the corrie.

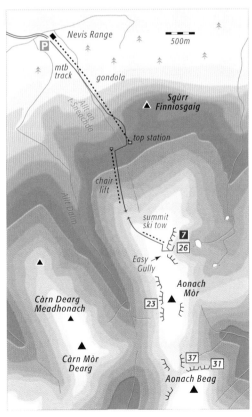

Alternative Routes

Other good early season mixed routes in Coire an Lochain are **Morwind** (IV,4), the classic line up the centre of Central Buttress, **Force Ten Buttress** (IV,4) to the right of Icicle Gully and **Lickety Split** (V,6), (see topo p149), in the Twins Area. In a similar way to Grooved Arete, originally graded IV, these routes have all been uprated from their first ascent grades. **Turf Walk** (III,4), which takes a vegetated line to the right of Morwind, is another excellent early season climb that has increased in popularity in recent years.

Guidebooks

Ben Nevis (SMC), *Scottish Winter Climbs* (SMC), *Winter Climbs Ben Nevis and Glen Coe* (Cicerone).

This is a useful alternative approach for Grooved Arete and other climbs on North Buttress. The best way off the mountain is to walk north along the summit plateau and descend the ski slopes and MTB Downhill course back to the start.

Conditions

Coire an Lochain is an excellent early season venue. The long line of granite cliffs up to 150m high have a cliff base of over 1100m, and the rock is generally well vegetated which means the Mixed climbs come into condition rapidly. A good freeze is required however, and unlike the Snowed-Up Rock routes in the Northern Corries, it is not possible to climb these routes unless the turf is properly frozen. In early winter however, after the first falls of snow and when the freezing level is hovering around the 1000m mark, Aonach Mòr is an ideal venue.

Top Tips

The Gondola is often shut for maintenance early in the winter before the skiing season starts. Since this is an excellent time to be enjoying the mixed climbing on Aonach Mòr, why not walk up from the valley? You will be guaranteed no queues on the routes, but make sure you take a headtorch! From the Nevis Range car park follow the line of the MTB Downhill course to the top station (**1hr 30mins**). From there it is another **1hr 30mins** to the top of Easy Gully.

Route Description

Grooved Arete lies on North Buttress, the last continuous section of crag at the northern end of the corrie. From the foot of Easy Gully, traverse snow slopes northwards for about 400m passing the deep gully of Molar Canal to reach two narrow buttresses at the left end of North Buttress. Grooved Arete takes the right-hand buttress immediately left of Icicle Gully.

   1. 45m Start at the foot of the gully and gain the arete to the left. Follow this, easily at first, then with increasing difficulty up grooves on its left side. Move back right to belay below a steep tower.

   2. 35m Climb a series of grooves on the crest of the tower, step left to a ledge and continue up a vertical corner. An excellent pitch.

   3. 50m Easy climbing on the crest leads to the plateau.

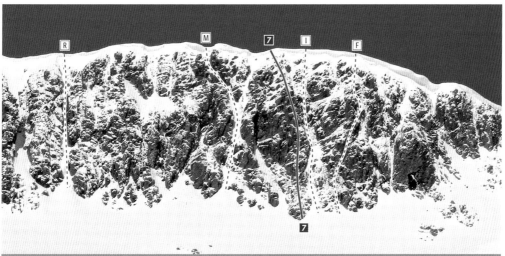

7. Grooved Arete (V,6)   *M. Molar Canal (III)*   *F. Force Ten Buttress (IV,4)*
R. Right Twin (II)   *I. Icicle Gully (III)*

Andy Nisbet

Good conditions of frozen turf, rime ice and hoar frost on Magic Pillar. Karolina Hain and Andrew Nivlem start up the superb second pitch

David Barratt

8

66

MAGIC PILLAR

Grade: 80m, IV,5
Location: The Cathedral, Southern Sector, Lochnagar
Route Base, Aspect & Rock Type: 950m, North-East facing, Granite
First Ascent: Chris Cartwright & Simon Richardson, 15 November 1998

Simon Richardson

Easy ground below the first pitch of Magic Pillar. Climber Chris Cartwright

Over the last two decades, the Southern Sector of Lochnagar has come into its own as a winter climbing playground. For many years it was overlooked as climbers rushed past on their way to the main North-East Coire, but the steep and easily accessible mixed climbing makes the Southern Sector a worthy venue. There are numerous isolated crags on the north-west side of the corrie, but the three buttresses on the north-east facing back wall contain the finest climbing. All three buttresses have their own distinctive character. Perseverance Wall has become popular for its mid-grade routes that follow vegetated grooves, whilst Sinister Buttress by contrast, is rarely climbed and has few natural lines. In between lies The Cathedral – the finest of the trio.

The buttress is well named as its configuration of grooves and pillars have an uncanny resemblance to the steeple and nave of a cathedral. The early routes focused on the groove-lines, which are superb, although they are a little steeper and smoother than they look. Climbers were a little slow to investigate the possibilities to either side, and the most surprising discovery in this second wave of development was Magic Pillar, which takes a prominent rib to the right of Cathedral Chimney.

From below, Magic Pillar appears ominously steep. Lochnagar can be a deceptive cliff, and the rounded nature of the rock often makes the mixed climbing more difficult than on the square-cut granite of the Northern Cairngorms. But Magic Pillar is an exception – the route really is magic and the climbing considerably easier than it looks. By a fortuitous geological coincidence, the crack-line splitting the pillar has offset parallel ledges creating a giant ladder of holds. There is turf on every ledge and the crack provides good protection. The main pitch up the front of the pillar will please even the most jaded climber, and Magic Pillar has now become the most popular of Lochnagar's Southern Sector routes.

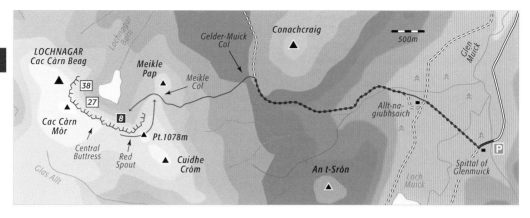

Approach

From the Spittal of Glenmuick car park (Pay and Display), turn right past the Visitor Centre and follow the vehicle track across the wide open Glen Muick to a junction with another vehicle track running up the other side of the glen (NO300858). Pass to the left of a barn and follow a narrow path for a short way to enter a forest, which leads to an estate track coming up from Allt-na-giubhsaich Lodge (NO296859). Follow this to a small cairn just before the Glen Muick-Glen Gelder Col (NO274861) and take a small path on the left that leads down to and across moorland in the direction of the col between Lochnagar and Meikle Pap. This path is often obscured by snow, and in heavy conditions the final pull up to the col (NO259858) can be hard work. From the Meikle Col, drop down and left across a band of boulders to enter the floor of the wide corrie bowl of the Southern Sector. The Cathedral is the central of the three buttresses on the north wall and is approached via steep snow slopes. These can be avalanche-prone and are best avoided after a heavy snowfall (**2hrs**).

Descent

From the top of the route, head south-east to the slight col above Red Spout at NO254852 (often wind scoured with exposed rust-coloured rocks), then bear north-east over Pt.1078m, before descending to the

James Edwards on the first ascent of Ghost Dance

Simon Richardson

Meikle Col. Even in the wildest of weather, you can breathe a sigh of relief here as you have done the hardest part of the descent. From the col, retrace your steps to the estate track and the Glen Muick car park.

Conditions

The relatively high cliff base of the Southern Sector routes means they come into condition faster than the longer climbs in the main North-East Coire, which start lower down the mountain. With a north-easterly wind, the Cathedral rimes up quickly and the turf freezes. Magic Pillar can come into condition from November onwards.

Top Tips

Lochnagar's easterly location means that approaching weather systems are often slowed by the bulk of the Cairngorms massif, and the Southern Sector can some-times provide a quick route just ahead of an approaching front. The relatively short walk-in means that with an early start a route can be completed before midday. It may be lashing with rain when you reach the plateau, but a strong south-west wind on your back will hurry you down to Glen Muick, happy in the thought that you have snatched a winter climb on a day that few would have considered going into the mountains.

Route Description

Start by climbing easy mixed ground to the base of the well defined pillar between Cathedral Chimney and No Worries Groove on the right side of the buttress.

1. 20m Follow the crack in the crest to a niche.

2. 40m Step round the roof to the right and continue up the crack-chimney to its top.

3. 20m Finish easily up the final gully of Cathedral Chimney.

Alternative Routes

In increasing difficulty, a logical progression of routes in the Southern Sector is **Quick Dash Crack** (IV,3) on Sunset Buttress, followed by Magic Crack and finally **Ghost Dance** (V,6) on The Cathedral. Also on The Cathedral, **Transept Groove** (IV,5) is a good early season route, as is **Cathedral Chimney** (IV,4), which is a little harder than its original rating of Grade III implied!

Guidebooks

The Cairngorms (SMC), Scottish Winter Climbs (SMC), Winter Climbs in The Cairngorms (Cicerone).

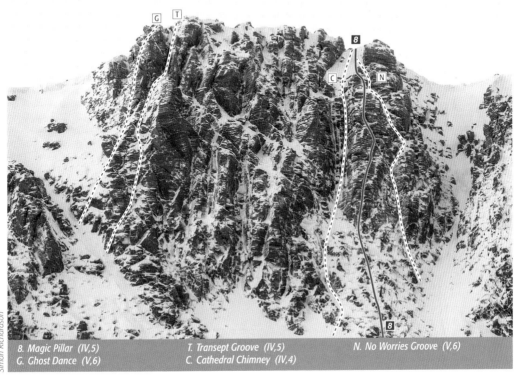

8. Magic Pillar (IV,5)   T. Transept Groove (IV,5)   N. No Worries Groove (V,6)
G. Ghost Dance (V,6)   C. Cathedral Chimney (IV,4)

Simon Richardson

Chris Cartwright climbing the first pitch of First Light during the first ascent. High and north-west facing, The Stuic rimes up quickly, and is one of the most accessible high altitude cliffs in the Southern Cairngorms

Simon Richardson

FIRST LIGHT

Grade: 70m, IV,5
Location: The Stuic, Lochnagar
Route Base, Aspect & Rock Type: 1000m, North-West facing, Granite
First Ascent: Simon Richardson & Chris Cartwright, 21 November 1999

Simon Richardson

Heading west along the Lochnagar plateau from the summit of The Stuic

Climbers flock to the North Cairngorms in November and December for good reason. High and north-west facing, the crags in the Northern Corries catch the full brunt of the early winter storms and rime up readily. Further east, the well known cliffs on Lochnagar lie in the shadow of the Cairngorms, and take longer to cool down and freeze. On the west side of Lochnagar however, there is a high altitude cliff flanking the north-west side of a prominent rock prow called The Stuic (pronounced Stooee). This cliff is at its best after the turf has frozen following the first snows of winter, and is the most accessible high altitude winter venue on the eastern side of the Cairngorms.

The Stuic offers a very different climbing experience to the main North-East Coire of Lochnagar. The approach through Ballochbuie Forest (one of the few remaining parts of the original Caledonian Forest) is varied and picturesque and once at the crag, the wide open views to the Central Cairngorms stretching from Cairn Toul to Ben Avon are unparallelled.

The superb blocky granite on The Stuic makes for relaxed climbing. There are plentiful cracks, the turf is good, and the belay ledges are wide and spacious. The climbs are not long and it is possible to climb two routes on a visit. First Light makes an excellent introduction to the cliff. It takes a line of turfy steps on the steep wall left of the deep cleft of The Stooee Chimney, the most prominent feature in the centre of the face. The steep wall itself is taken direct by A Wall Too Far, which at VII,8 is the test-piece of the crag, but the climbing on First Light can be extended by continuing up the third pitch of A Wall Too Far to give an excellent and sustained Grade IV outing.

The Stuic still sees relatively few visitors, but those that make the effort have reported back enthusiastically on the beautiful setting and enjoyable climbing. I suspect The Stuic will become more popular as time goes by!

Heavily rimed upper cracks on the second pitch of First Light. Climber Iain Small

Simon Richardson

Approach

From the Pay and Display car park (NO188912) at Keiloch, 3km east of Braemar and just north of the A93, go back to the A93 and follow this west for 200m until opposite Invercauld Gates. Cross the Old Bridge of Dee, then go south-east along the forest track towards Ballochbuie Forest. After 500m take a right fork, then go straight over the next cross-roads to reach a gate in the deer fence at NO197898. Go through this and follow the forest track to a left turn at NO195896. Follow the track out of the forest along the west bank of the Feindallachar Burn to a small barn at NO204873. Cut east from the track across rough ground to join the south bank of the Allt Loch nan Eun that leads to Sandy Loch. From here, bear south for a kilometre to reach the west bank of Loch nan Eun directly below the prominent prow of The Stuic (**2hrs 30mins**).

Descent

The simplest descent from the plateau to the foot of the cliff is to climb down the Grade I gully bounding the west side of the narrow Stegosaurus Rib (NO225851). To return to the parking, leave the small summit of The Stuic and follow the corrie edge west to a tor at NO221853, then cut down the line of Allt a' Choire Dhuibh, and head across open moorland to reach the small barn.

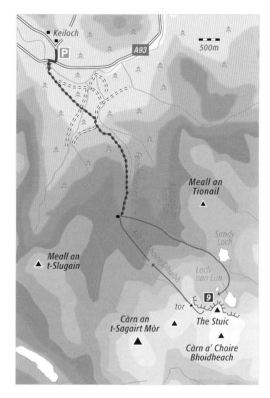

Alternative Routes

The longest route on the North-West Face is the 90m-long **Twilight Groove** (III,4), which makes a fine introduction to the cliff. **Daybreak Corners** (III) and **New Boot Groove** (III,4) are also worthwhile climbs. The attractive deep slit of **The Stooee Chimney** (IV,7) is considerably harder than it looks with an awkward exit from the top of the chimney. As far as I know it has only been climbed under powder but it may be easier if iced. **Morning Has Broken** (V,6) and **The Slot** (IV,6) are fine companion routes to First Light. There are several easier gullies on the right side of the cliff before the short spiky ridge of **Stegosaurus Rib** (II). The rocky promontory of The Stuic itself makes a good Grade I scramble possible in almost any conditions. The natural winter line on the North-East Face, which lies to the left of the crest of The Stuic, is **Plug Groove** (III). It often holds ice mid-season and is a useful back up if routes on the North-West Face have been stripped by a thaw.

Guidebook

The Cairngorms (SMC), *SMC Journal 2009*. For SMC Journal new routes see <*www.smc.org.uk/new-routes*>.

Conditions

Facing north-west with a cliff base of 1000m the routes on The Stuic come into condition quickly, however the turf needs to be frozen. The cliff is susceptible to thaw and strips quickly in a warm south-westerly wind, but the more sheltered north-east face is a useful back up if the main crag is bare. Heavy snow can make the approach laborious, so the crag is best visited early in the season, or following a freeze and snowfall after a major thaw.

Top Tips

Cycling along the forestry tracks as far as the small barn will save about 30mins on the approach, and more on the return. In conditions of good visibility and frozen snow, approaching via the tor at NO221853 (as described for descent) and descending the short gully west of Stegosaurus Rib provides a faster approach than following the Allt Loch nan Eun.

Route Description

A super little climb up the left side of the steep wall to the left of The Stooee Chimney. From Loch nan Eun ascend the lower slopes of the prow of The Stuic to where it steepens at NO227854, then traverse right for 100m along a broad grassy terrace to belay directly below the steep wall.

  1. **30m** Climb a steep groove to a ledge below the wall. Continue up the fault above, passing through a niche to reach a good stance.

  2. **40m** Move right and continue up the crest of the buttress to the top (as for A Wall Too Far).

Simon Richardson

9. First Light (IV,5)	**T. Twilight Groove** (III,4)	**N. New Boot Groove** (III,4)
S. The Stuic (I)	**W. A Wall Too Far** (VII,8)	**M. Morning Has Broken** (V,6)
D. Daybreak Corners (III)	**SC. The Stooee Chimney** (IV,7)	**SR. Stegosaurus Rib** (II)

Climbing the stepped corners at the beginning of the second pitch of Jenga Buttress. The cliff is in typical early season condition covered in a light layer of snow blown across the Cairngorm plateau

JENGA BUTTRESS

Grade: 70m, III,4
Location: Creagan Cha-no, Cairn Gorm
Route Base, Aspect & Rock Type: 950m, East facing, Granite
First Ascent: Sandy Simpson & Simon Richardson, 14 November 2010

Simon Richardson

Roger Webb pulling through the final barrier wall on Jenga Buttress

*H*igh on the eastern side of Cairn Gorm lies Creagan Cha-no, a steep and compact crag tucked under the east flank of the Cha-no spur. It provides a welcome alternative to the busy Northern Corries with a beautiful view and a 'remote' feel away from the hustle and bustle of the ski area. The routes are a little shorter than the Northern Corries, but the climbing is good and the walk-in is nearly as quick as Coire an t-Sneachda.

I came across Creagan Cha-no almost by accident. In September 2010, I was walking down Strath Nethy with a Duke of Edinburgh expedition, and noticed a frieze of granite crags high on the eastern flank of Cairn Gorm. It was difficult to estimate their height from afar, but they clearly merited further investigation as a possible winter crag.

A few weeks later it was mid-November and the new winter season was underway. With the promise of an unclimbed cliff to explore, it didn't take long to persuade Sandy Simpson to take a look, and after a quick approach from the plateau we made a beeline for the well defined central buttress. This provided enjoyable Cairngorm mixed climbing – steep moves on excellent blocky granite with good hooks and torques with plenty of gear and good ledges between. Two pitches later we were on the plateau and Jenga Buttress, a potential Cairngorm mini-classic, had been born.

The cliff is steeper than it looks, and is 70m high at its highest point. Easy access and good climbing means the venue has rapidly become popular and there are now 30 two-pitch routes, ranging from Grade II to VII. Creagan Cha-no may be a small cliff, but it is one of the few winter crags in Scotland where you can comfortably complete a good winter route in less than half a day.

Sylvain Baboud from France bridging up the first pitch of Arch Rival during the first ascent

Simon Richardson

Approach

From the Coire na Ciste ski car park cross the foot-bridge (NH999074) over the Allt na Ciste and follow the recently constructed path up the heathery spur of Creagan Dubh until a ski fence is reached. Follow this southward to an altitude of approximately 1000m, then traverse flatter ground north-eastward to reach the top of the crag. Be careful not to walk over the cliff edge as the plateau is very featureless at this point. A GPS will be useful to find the top of Recovery Gully (NJ017063), which lies approximately 300m north of Pt.1028m. The gully provides a straightforward descent, but under heavy snow it is safer to abseil down Anvil Gully from a thread (often in place) on the right of the distinctive Anvil Block which lies about 40m north of Recovery Gully. (**1hr** to **1hr 30mins** depending on snow conditions).

Descent

Reverse the approach, but take care not to descend directly to the Coire na Ciste car park via Coire Laogh Mòr which contains steep ground (**45mins**).

Conditions

Creagan Cha-no has a cliff base of 950m and comes into condition early. Later in the season some routes may bank out and have cornice difficulties, and the

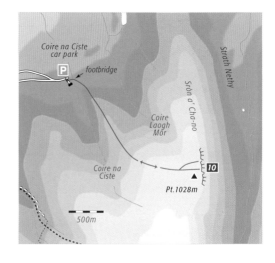

Alternative Routes

The front face of the prominent pinnacled rib guarding the left flank of Recovery Gully is split by the deep-cut **Chimney Rib** (III,4). Just right of Recovery Gully, the attractive stepped flake on the front face of the buttress is taken by **Flaked Out** (VI,7), and the prominent clean-cut corner on the left wall of the sharp arete of Anvil Buttress (defined by the prominent anvil-shaped block at its top) is **Anvil Corner** (VI,6). Between these two features lies **Anvil Gully**, which is situated at the foot of the abseil descent, and provides a very popular IV,4. The steep Arch Wall to the right of Jenga Buttress is home to the most difficult routes on the cliff such as **Smooth As Silk** (VII,7) and the eponymous **Arch Wall** (VII,7), together with the well defined groove-lines of **Arch Enemy** (V,5) and **Arch Rival** (V,5). Arch Wall is bounded on the right by the prominent gully of **Fingers And Thumbs** (IV,5). This is a popular route, but as the name suggests, it is a little more awkward than it looks.

Guidebooks

<www.scottishwinter.com>, SMC Journal 2011, Climber February 2013. For SMC Journal new routes see <www.smc.org.uk/newroutes>

---

crag strips quickly when the sun rises high in the sky in March and April. Beware of windslab when descending Recovery Gully and on the slopes beneath the cliff. If a strong westerly wind is blowing, especially after recent snowfall, spindrift conditions may be bad and the cliff is best avoided.

Top Tips

Take a long sling in case an abseil is required down Anvil Gully. A reasonably early start will allow at least two routes to be climbed. A good direct start to Jenga Buttress is **Daylight Robbery** (V,6), which climbs a steep turfy groove, and the impending corner above, to join the upper section of the original route.

Route Description

Excellent well protected climbing up the longest feature on the cliff. From the foot of Recovery Gully traverse right (north) for 50m and pass below the sharp-cut Anvil Buttress. Jenga Buttress is the next major feature that is situated beyond a little col, about 50m further right.

1. **40m** Start left of the steep lower wall and climb a short gully to gain the rib. Continue up this over a steep step to a good platform.

2. **30m** Surmount two stepped corners just right of the crest and continue up the prominent groove in the crest to a ledge. Easier climbing in the short gully above leads to a final barrier wall (awkward) and the top.

Sandy Simpson

10. Jenga Buttress (III,4)   F. Flaked Out (VI,7)   AC. Anvil Corner (VI,6)
C. Chimney Rib (III,4)   AG. Anvil Gully (IV,4)   D. Daylight Robbery (V,6)
R. Recovery Gully (I)

Chris Cartwright climbing the first pitch of Tainted Elixir during the first ascent. The north facing cliffs on Ben Cruachan's Noe Buttress are the most reliable early season venue in the Southern Highlands

Simon Richardson

TAINTED ELIXIR

Grade: 70m, V,6
Location: Coire Chat, Ben Cruachan
Route Base, Aspect & Rock Type: 950m, North facing, Granite
First Ascent: Chris Cartwright & Simon Richardson, 14 December 2003

Looking north from Ben Cruachan's summit ridge

*B*en Cruachan's distinctive outline to the south of the Glen Coe massif makes it an alluring peak. A traverse of its main summits along a sharp ridge of blocky granite is one of the finest expeditions in the area, but its winter climbs are little known and have only recently been developed.

The finest climbing lies on Noe Buttress that nestles into the north side of Coire Chat, just west of the main summit. The cliff remained untouched until 2002 when Southern Highlands pioneers Dave Ritchie and Mark Shaw climbed the prominent Noe Buttress (IV,4). Chris Cartwright and Iain Small visited the cliff during the winter of 2003 and left their mark with In the Knoe, a fine VI,6 fault-line cleaving the steepest section of the cliff.

Chris persuaded me to visit the following season and immediately it was clear that this was a gem of a winter cliff. It reminded me of Coire an Lochain in the Northern Corries, but with no people and a stunning view. All the climbs are good, but my favourite is the right facing corner of Tainted Elixir (V,6). The corner leads up to a cracked headwall cut by an overhanging tapered slot. As you lean back and pull through on hidden hooks and torques, the exposure suddenly bites and the ground opens out beneath you. Behind, the magnificent panorama stretches down Glen Etive to the mountains of Glen Coe with Ben Nevis standing proudly behind.

Of course, there is a small price to pay for the superlative position and little travelled terrain – a three-hour approach from Loch Awe over the summit. But somehow it all fits into a reasonable winter day. Leave your gear at the top of the cliff, whip down the descent gully, do a route (or two if you're quick), and then it's downhill all the way to the car (take walking poles). Cruachan is the crown jewel of Southern Highlands winter climbing – make sure you give it a go before it becomes too popular!

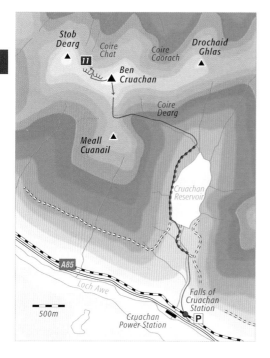

Approach

The cliff is best approached from the A85 Tyndrum to Oban road, via the summit of Ben Cruachan. Park in a pull-off just east of Falls of Cruachan station. Follow steps upto the station, go through an underpass and ascend steps to a path on the left, which rises steeply

up the right (east) side of the burn leading to a track at NN081277. Follow this to the base of the Cruachan Reservoir dam and ascend a ladder onto the dam to reach another track at NN078282. Follow this track to the north end of the reservoir then take an initially boggy track up Coire Dearg to the col (NN069298) between Meall Cuanail and Ben Cruachan. Continue up the south ridge of Ben Cruachan to the summit. From here, descend west for 250m, over one small rise, to the short East Gully, which lies at the eastern end of the crag (**3hrs**).

Descent

East Gully provides a straightforward descent to the cliff base and enables more than one route to be climbed in a day. To return to the valley, reverse the route of ascent. In good visibility the slope can be contoured from the top of East Gully to the south ridge to avoid re-ascent over Cruachan's summit.

Conditions

Facing north with a base above 950m, the cliff comes into condition rapidly with a cold northerly wind and fresh snow above 900m. Be wary that strong winds accompanying fresh snowfall may make the descent down East Gully avalanche-prone.

Top Tips

The routes in Coire Chat may be short (typically 70 to 80m), but they are continuously sustained from the first move to the very top. The granite is fractured into

11. Tainted Elixir (V,6)
E. East Gully (I)
C. Chatter Rib (III)
Q. Quickfire (III)

T. Toxic Brew (IV,4)
DC. Double Chaser (V,6)
I. In the Knoe (VI,6)
G. Goldfinger (VII,7)

DN. Dr Noe (VI,6)
N. Noe Gully (II)
T. Thunderbolt Chimney (IV,5)

Chris Cartwright

Dafydd Morris

Following the bulging corner on Tainted Elixir. The leader has belayed halfway up the second pitch. Climbers Ferdia Earle and Andy Moles

clean vertical crack-lines, and the blocky rock provides good nicks for frontpoints. This results in sustained and well protected mixed climbing, so take a good rack of nuts and cams. A selection of routes are described in *Scottish Winter Climbs* (SMC), but the cliff does not appear in a comprehensive guidebook, so consult SMC Journals for a full set of route descriptions. *Climb* magazine issue#2 (April 2005) has a detailed history of the development of the crag and a topo.

Route Description

Coire Chat lies on the north side of the ridge running west from Cruachan's summit. The climbing is divided between two main buttresses. The steep Chatter Buttress runs westwards from **East Gully** (I) to the prominent **Noe Gully** (II), and the easier-angled Noe Buttress lies to the right. Just right of East Gully is **Chatter Rib** (III), then the prominent recessed gully of **Quickfire** (III), followed by **Toxic Brew** (IV,4), a line of shallow chimneys. The wall right of Toxic Brew is cut by three parallel, left-leaning crack systems. Tainted Elixir is the leftmost and most prominent, and starts with a right facing corner. It is a must-do route with continu-ously sustained climbing and a puzzling crux.

  1. 25m Climb up between the corner and a large perched block. Continue up the bulging corner to a

belay on the left.

  2. 25m Surmount the cracked wall above and continue with interest to an overhanging barrier wall split by a tapered slot. Pull up and into the slot, then go left to belay overlooking Toxic Brew. An excellent pitch.

  3. 20m Step left into the final groove of Toxic Brew, and follow this to the top.

Alternative Routes

If you've got time rush back down and sample the icy grooves of **Toxic Brew** (IV,4) or explore the deep recess of **Thunderbolt Chimney** (IV,5) further right. **Double Chaser** (V,6) is a slightly more difficult companion to Tainted Elixir, taking the parallel crack-line to its right. The harder routes on Noe Buttress, such as **In the Knoe** (VI,6), **Dr Noe** (VI,6) or **Goldfinger** (VII,7), are more meatier affairs requiring separate visits, but will not fail to disappoint.

Guidebooks

Scottish Winter Climbs (SMC), *SMC Journal 2004, Climb April 2005*. For *SMC Journal* new routes see <*www.smc.org.uk/new-routes*>.

CHAPTER 2 ▷ COLD SNAPS

Cold and snowy conditions close down
options but also open up rare opportunities

Coire nan Clach, Braeriach; photo Simon Richardson

Mountain Icefalls such as Blue Riband in Glen Coe are a good choice when temperatures are low and the snow is unconsolidated

Winter grips hard across the Scottish mountains during the darkest months of December and January. Blizzards and low temperatures transform the hills into a Christmas cake of uniform white that appears to offer infinite promise to the winter climber. But for all their beauty, the mountains provide significant challenges. Approaches can be arduous from deep snow, route exits can be thwarted by wind-slab, cornices can be soft and descents can be avalanche-prone. Coupled with this, the days are barely eight hours long, which punishes any route finding errors or miscalculations on approach times. There are probably more failures in these conditions than at any other time in the season. This is doubly frustrating as these difficult conditions sometimes coincide with the popular Christmas and New Year holiday period.

This is the time to refer to the Strategy Guidelines and climb Mixed routes just above the snow line. Consider climbs on lower crags that may be closer to the road, or have a low-level approach that is largely below the line of the deep snow. There is little point flogging through chest-deep drifts to a route high on Ben Nevis, when lower lying crags such as those at Bridge of Orchy are in condition.

As always, the prevailing wind direction is important. After a heavy snowfall, a route facing into the wind is often preferable as it will not be swamped with snow caught in the lee. A northerly aspect is not critical at this time of year because the mid-winter sun is not high enough in the sky to strip routes of fresh snow, so this is a good time to consider those rarely visited south facing routes.

In general, accessible and lower lying mixed routes

Mike Gardner

routes, but unlike the routes in the Early Bird chapter, choose more accessible climbs such as the **South-West Ridge** of the Douglas Boulder on Ben Nevis.

Travelling to your chosen location can be a significant challenge when snowstorms sweep the country and high level roads are blocked. An advantage of Arrochar and many other cliffs in the Southern Highlands is that they are closer to the Central Belt and can be approached along roads that are not far above sea level.

Worth considering for these conditions is **Right-Angled Gully Direct** on The Cobbler, one of the few Mixed routes in the Southern Highlands that does not rely on frozen turf. When there is too much snow in the Cairngorms, Glen Clova is another accessible option worth considering. There are a number of recently developed climbs such as **Silver Threads Among The Gold** that provide good alternatives to better known Mixed routes deeper in the massif.

Low lying Icefalls such as Oui Oui on Creag Dubh, just off the A9 at Newtonmore, or Steall Falls in Glen Nevis, are good options if valley temperatures stay below minus 10°C for a week or more. Routes such as this are outwith the scope of this book which is focused on mountain routes, but if snow levels allow access to higher venues, then mountain Icefalls such as **Mega Route X** on Ben Nevis are worth considering.

When temperatures are cold, but there is little snow on the ground, then a different tactic is needed. The turf may be frozen, but the crags will appear black and be unappealing to climb. A good option in these circumstances is to seek out high-level watercourses which can provide excellent water ice climbing. **Rapunzel** on the south face of Beinn Fhionnlaidh south of Glen Coe is a good example. It follows an outstanding feature set deep into the hillside and is a permanent watercourse for most of the year.

Occasionally conditions are so challenging that they perplex even the most experienced winter climbers, but with an open mind and an inventive approach, good winter climbing is often there for the taking. Sometimes the solution can be found by thinking carefully about the wind direction, and routes on the south side of Cairn Gorm such as **Wobble Block Chimney** are good options when cold dry northerlies have blasted the Northern Corries bare.

There is huge satisfaction in pulling off a good route during the Cold Snaps that occur in the depth of winter. Inevitably you will be setting off and returning in the dark, and the rigours of the approach and descent are often as demanding as the climb itself. But the rewards are immense. The pink glow of dawn on a pristine white Scottish mountain is a moment to be savoured and the short daylight adds to the seriousness of the day.

such as **The Sting** on Beinn Dorain's Creag an Socach above Bridge of Orchy in the Southern Highlands, are the order of the day. The relatively short approach, moderate altitude and turfy nature of the crag, makes this an ideal choice in cold and snowy conditions.

In the far north-west, **Cul Of The Wild** on Cùl Beag in the Coigach hills illustrates the huge opportunities available in the Northern Highlands at this time of year. This route is low lying and close the sea, so cold and snowy conditions are essential. Some of Scotland's greatest winter routes are possible during this period, such as the **Fhidhleir's Nose Direct** on Sgùrr an Fhidhleir of Ben More Coigach. Keep big objectives like this at the forefront of your mind and seize the rare opportunity to climb them.

When heavy snow arrives soon after a thaw it is best to stick with ridge-lines or pure Snowed-Up Rock

Matt Buchanan starting up the corner pitch of *The Sting* in good conditions of frozen turf and powder snow

Dafydd Morris

THE STING

Grade: 130m, VI,6
Location: Creag an Socach, Beinn Dorain
Route Base, Aspect & Rock Type: 750m, North-West facing, Mica Schist
First Ascent: Graham Little & Kevin Howett, 19 January 1991

Tom Prentice

Ascending Coire an Dothaidh towards Creag an Socach. Climber Gerrie Fellows

*A*t the end of the cold and snowy November of 2010, Stuart MacFarlane and Gary Houston just missed out on an early repeat of The Sting on Creag an Socach, the steepest of the Bridge of Orchy cliffs. The pair abseiled off in the dark from below the top pitch of this sustained mixed route after climbing the crux (the 4c corner of the summer route Scorpion). Despite their failure, MacFarlane raved about the climb saying that it had "one of the finest pitches in the Southern Highlands". This was some accolade from a climber who has made winter routes in Arrochar and the surrounding mountains his speciality.

The following weekend, MacFarlane and Houston returned with Sam Burns to complete the route, only to find their retreat gear was no longer in place. As it turned out, Iain Small and Susan Jensen had made an ascent the day before. These repeats, together with MacFarlane's enthusiastic endorsement, led to a steady stream of further ascents, and swiftly made The Sting one of the most popular routes on the cliff.

Graham Little and Kevin Howett, who did the first ascent in January 1991, are masters at naming routes and proximity to the summer climb Scorpion wasn't the only reason for calling it 'The Sting'. The magnificent corner pitch also has an 'interesting move left' at its top... but is this really the 'sting' in the tail? The corner leads to a large ledge but the way above isn't obvious. The original route goes left and climbs a tenuous shallow left facing corner. It is also possible to climb a wide groove on the right, but this also leads to a difficult exit.

Whichever finish you take, The Sting has it all, from superb delicate moves up the initial ramp, to excellent well protected climbing in the corner and a delicate finish that is sure to add bite to the experience.

Excellent climbing in the sustained but well protected corner on pitch 4 of The Sting. Climber Susan Jensen

Iain Small

Approach

From the public car park at the Bridge of Orchy Hotel, follow the road leading up to the station and pass under the railway. Head north-east past an aerial to gain the right side of the Allt Coire an Dothaidh and ascend towards the col between Beinn an Dothaidh and Beinn Dorain. Where the path crosses the burn at NN320399 climb up southwards to the foot of the cliff (1hr).

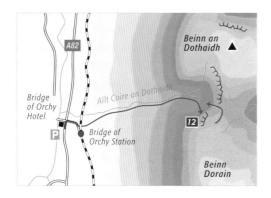

Descent

Follow steep slopes north-north-east to regain the path a little below the Dothaidh-Dorain col.

Conditions

Creag an Socach is a steep and vegetated medium altitude crag that faces north-west. Frozen turf is essential for progress so several days of sub-zero temperatures, followed by a substantial snowfall, will bring the cliff into good mixed climbing condition. But if it snows before it freezes, the turf will be insulated and will not be properly frozen. Creag an Socach has the shortest approach of all the Bridge of Orchy cliffs, which makes it a useful venue when other locations are too difficult to reach due to deep snow.

Top Tips

Take large hexes for the corner pitch together with a selection of pegs. All routes on Creag an Socach will benefit from turf-based protection. In the past this meant warthogs, but nowadays ice hooks provide a more mechanically robust solution.

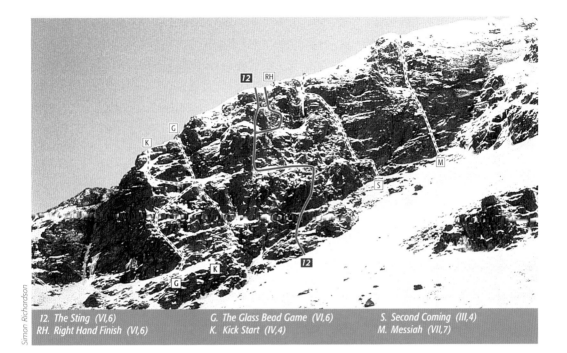

Simon Richardson

12. The Sting (VI,6)
RH. Right Hand Finish (VI,6)

G. The Glass Bead Game (VI,6)
K. Kick Start (IV,4)

S. Second Coming (III,4)
M. Messiah (VII,7)

Route Description

To the left of the prominent slanting weakness of Second Coming is a band of slabs situated below an area of dark impending rock, cut by a narrow right-slanting ramp.

1. 30m Climb the slabs to a block with a horizontal crack. (If the slabs have insufficient build up, it is possible to avoid them by coming in from the right). Go right up a snowy ramp before moving up to a niche at the foot of the narrow right-slanting ramp.

2. 25m Climb the ramp then continue steeply to the right end of the central break that girdles the left half of the cliff.

3. 20m Move left to below a prominent corner.

4. 15m Climb the excellent corner-crack (sustained and well protected) to its top and make an interesting move left to a ledge.

5. 40m Move up and slightly left to the foot of an imposing blunt rocky rib. Climb a short steep wall on its left side, then continue up and right on steep mixed ground to the top. Alternatively, from the top of the corner-crack move right along the ledge and climb the well defined corner until a traverse left can be made to gain ledges (possible belay). Boldly finish up the narrow groove cutting through the steep headwall above.

Alternative Routes

The classic medium grade route of the crag is **Second Coming** (III,4), which takes the left-slanting ramp-line in the centre of the cliff and holds conditions longer than any other route on Creag an Socach. **The Glass Bead Game** (VI,6) skirts just right of the steep left side of the cliff and relies heavily on turf for both pick placements and protection. **Kick Start** (IV,4) is a good counter-diagonal line that starts up a curving chimney. **The Prophet** (VI,7) takes a direct line between Kick Start and The Sting and follows a prominent open corner on the second pitch. The route is high in the grade and some teams think it merits VII,7. To the right of Second Coming the cliff considerably steepens and is broken by a prominent line of weakness taken by **Messiah** (VII,7). This is one of the most desired routes in the Southern Highlands, but requires the vertical ice-filled groove on the third pitch to be well iced.

Guidebooks

Arran, Arrochar and the Southern Highlands (SMC), *Scottish Winter Climbs* (SMC), *SMC Journal 2013*. For *SMC Journal* new routes see <*www.smc.org.uk/new-routes*>.

Chris Cartwright moving up to the notch during the first ascent of Cul Of The Wild. Routes on the low-lying mountains of Coigach make good objectives when higher peaks in the Northern Highlands are swamped by snow

Simon Richardson

CUL OF THE WILD

Grade: 250m, V,6
Location: Cùl Beag
Route Base, Aspect & Rock Type: 550m, West facing, Sandstone
First Ascent: Simon Richardson & Chris Cartwright, 30 December 2001

Simon Richardson

Approaching the flake-crack on pitch 6 of Cul Of The Wild

During Hogmanay 2001 Chris Cartwright and I were staying at the SMC's Naismith Hut at Elphin with our sights set on a route in the Assynt hills. There was about 15cm of snow at the hut, but as we drove north there were drifts two metres thick on either side of the road. Our small altitude gain made a huge difference to the snow depth and approaching the surrounding mountains was clearly going to be close to impossible. We make a quick change of plan and switched our attention south to Coigach and Cùl Beag. Our thinking was that being closer to sea level, the approach along the Achiltibuie road was likely to be clear, and the prevailing wind would have blown some of the fresh snow from the west side of the mountain.

This was all complete supposition, because it was still pitch black when we left the car and started breaking trail through thigh-deep drifts on the short approach to Cùl Beag. As far as we knew nobody had ever climbed here in winter, so we followed a prominent gully-line for three pitches to where the cliff steepened into a corner leading up to a distinctive sandstone tower. Two sustained pitches in the corner led to a deep notch in a ridge on the left. There was only one way out; a steep undercut crack exiting onto overlapping slabs arranged like tiles on a roof. Chris made a superb lead, but by the time we reached the summit ridge it was dark. Somehow we fumbled our way over the summit, descended the north-west slopes and ploughed through deep snow back to the car.

It was several years later that Northern Highlands pioneer John Mackenzie worked out exactly where we had gone. It turned out our line had joined the top of Lurgainn Edge, a Jim Bell summer route dating from 1958. And of course, we were not the first to climb the face in winter. Tom Longstaff (the first man to ascend a 7000m peak) had made an ascent of Y-Gully many decades before!

13

Looking down the prominent right facing corner on Cul Of The Wild

Simon Richardson

Approach
Park on the single track road between the A835 and Achiltibuie, beside Loch Lurgainn and directly below the West Face. Ascend the hillside directly to the cliff (**1hr**).

Descent
Cul Of The Wild finishes south of the summit just before a small col (the top of the right-hand exit to Y-Gully). From the summit it is easiest to descend the steep north-west facing slopes towards Lochan Fhionnlaidh, then follow the stalker's path back to Linneraineach and a short walk back along the road to the car.

Conditions
Cold and snowy conditions are a pre-requisite for winter climbing in Coigach. The sandstone mountains are typically very vegetated, low in altitude and lie close the sea. The most likely window is from late December through to the end of January.

Top Tips
When the snow levels are low be flexible and consider other Coigach venues. Other easily accessible cliffs include Stac Pollaidh, Bucket Buttress on Spidean Coinich and the Western Cliffs of Quinag.

Route Description
The West Face of Cùl Beag is split in its upper reaches by Y-Gully, which is defined on the right by the prominent line of Lurgainn Edge. Cul Of The Wild takes a natural

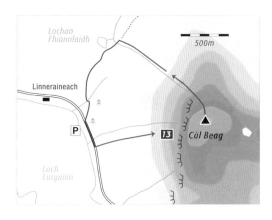

Alternative Routes

Y-Gully (I) is the most obvious winter line on the West Face and is best climbed via its right branch. In lean conditions it is Grade II. The bounding left edge of the face is the 200m-long **Kveldro Ridge** (III,5). The right side of Y-Gully is **Lurgainn Edge** (III,4), an interesting seven-pitch long mountaineering route that follows the original summer line fairly closely. Despite the ease of access, the West Face of Cùl Beag has been rarely visited in winter and its routes have seen few ascents.

Guidebooks

Northern Highlands North (SMC), *SMC Journal 2005*, *SMC Journal 2010*. For *SMC Journal* new routes see <*www.smc.org.uk/new-routes*>.

Simon Richardson

13. Cul Of The Wild (V,6)   Y. **Y-Gully Right Branch** (I)
K. Kveldro Ridge (III,5)   L. **Lurgainn Edge** (III,4)

winter line starting up a deep narrow gully 50m right of Lurgainn Edge.

1 to 3. 150m Climb the gully over several steep steps to a terrace and move up to a conspicuous right facing corner.

4 and 5. 70m Follow the corner to a prominent

notch at its top. Junction with Lurgainn Edge.

6. 30m Climb the flake-crack on the right (crux), step left and pull over a steep wall to easier ground and the top.

John Mackenzie

Neil Wilson climbing pitch 5 of Lurgainn Edge during the first winter ascent

The spectacular 400m-high Fhidhleir's Nose on Sgùrr an Fhidhleir of Ben More Coigach. The cliff is in perfect mixed climbing condition with frozen turf and some helpful ice draped in powder snow

Simon Richardson

FHIDHLEIR'S NOSE DIRECT

Grade: 300m, VII,7
Location: Sgùrr an Fhidhleir
Route Base, Aspect & Rock Type: 350m, North-East facing, Sandstone
First Ascent: Wilson Moir & Chris Forrest, 17 January 1987

Simon Richardson

Roger Everett setting off up the Second Pale Slab on Fhidhleir's Nose Direct

With the Atlantic Ocean as a backdrop, the mountains of Coigach rise straight out of an undulating landscape of rock, heather and water. None of the summits are high enough to reach Munro status, but their huge sandstone crags are impressively steep and provide some of the most adventurous climbs in the British Isles.

The queen of these routes is the Fhidhleir's Nose Direct. It takes a superb feature, which soars like a huge ship's prow for more than 400m to the 703m summit of Sgùrr an Fhidhleir, and is one of the finest pieces of mountain architecture in the Scottish Highlands. Despite a series of determined attempts stretching back to Ling and Sang in 1907, the Nose Direct was not climbed until the summer of 1962 by Neville Drasdo and Mike Dixon. The first winter ascent took place in February 1979 when Bob Smith and Norman Keir climbed a line approximating to the summer HVS Fidelio, by linking a series of grooves and icy corners high on the cliff left of the Nose. Their route has not been repeated and was one of the first Grade VIIs to be climbed in Scotland.

In January 1987, Wilson Moir and Chris Forrest climbed the summer line of the Nose Direct. Thinking they were on the 1979 route, they made a matter-of-fact ascent in just over six hours, although they used a point of aid in the crux groove at two-thirds height. A few weeks later Moir came across Keir's route description in the SMC journal and realised that they hadn't followed the original winter route, but had bagged the plum line up the very crest of the Fhidhleir's Nose.

Roger Everett freed the crux groove of its aid point in 1991, and since then the Fhidhleir's Nose Direct has become one of the most sought-after high standard winter outings in Scotland. The route is well protected and despite its low altitude, it is normally in condition at least once every season and has now seen more than 25 winter ascents.

14

Looking up the great sweep of the Fhidhleir's Nose Direct from the initial groove. Climber Gareth Hughes

Tony Stone

Approach

Park at the south-east end of Loch Lurgainn on the single track road between the A835 and Achiltibuie. Go through a gate in the deer fence (NC139067), cross the burn (stepping stones) and follow a faint path (boggy) that leads to the south bank of the Allt Claonaidh. Follow this to Lochan Tuath and continue to the base of the cliff (**2hrs 30mins**).

Descent

From the summit of Sgùrr an Fhidhleir, head south to the Ben More Coigach-Sgùrr an Fhidhleir col and descend the broad open couloir that leads down below the huge south-east face towards Lochan Tuath.

Conditions

The winter potential of Sgùrr an Fhidhleir's wet and vegetated north facing cliffs is clear, but lying so close to the sea they require specific conditions. The weather pattern was ideal during New Year 2000 when Arctic air swept south across the country over the Christmas period. Initially a series of strong northerlies froze the turf solid, before the wind veered to the north-east covering the cliffs with snow. The result was the best climbing conditions in the far north-west for more than five years, but access was impossible until the roads were cleared. The first climbing team made it in by following right behind the first snow plough after the Christmas break. The message is clear – when routes like the Fhidhleir's Nose are in condition, drop everything and go!

Top Tips

Recent forestry operations mean that the approach can be difficult to find in the dark. Reconnaissance the day before or on a prior trip, will save precious time when the rare conditions arrive.

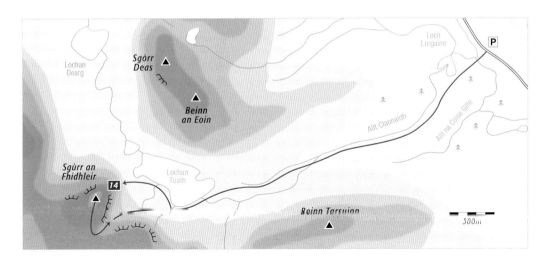

Route Description

The route starts with a pronounced turfy groove which twists up the lower buttress to gain the Pale Slabs (something of a misnomer because they are deceptively steep), before finishing up the crest of the spur in a magnificent position.

1 to 2. 100m Climb the turfy groove for two pitches to belay in a cave below a large roof.

3. 20m Step right and follow another groove to below the First Pale Slab.

4. 20m Bypass this by climbing turf rightwards to a further groove on the right and continue up this to a small bay.

5. 15m Traverse the turf ledge left to the 'Hansom Cab' stance.

6. 15m Climb a turfy groove on the left (the Second Pale Slab) to a ledge.

7. 15m Step left around the edge and climb an impending corner just left of the arete.

8. 25m Step right, pull over an overlap and trend left up the slab above, using well spaced turf to gain a good ledge.

9. 30m Climb the steep corner above to a thin crack

14. Fhidhleir's Nose Direct (VII,7)   C. Castro (VII,7)

Jim Teesdale

(old peg) that leads up the crux wall to the Upper Shoulder, where the angle eases. Easy climbing (**50m**) now leads to the sharp summit of Sgùrr an Fhidhleir.

Alternative Routes

Castro (VII,7) takes an obvious line of vegetated grooves on the impregnable-looking south-east face and is similar in standard to the Fhidhleir's Nose Direct. Unfortunately, its more southerly aspect means it is less often in condition. The aptly named **Consolation Gully** (III) is the well defined right-slanting feature at the right end of the north face of the mountain, and is a useful back up if there is insufficient time to complete the main route. The start lies at NC098051, about 300m east of the Ben More Coigach-Sgùrr an Fhidhleir col.

Guidebooks

Northern Highlands North (SMC), *SMC Journal 2009*. For *SMC Journal* new routes see <www.smc.org.uk/new-routes>.

The South-West Ridge of the Douglas Boulder is an excellent choice when large amounts of snow limit options higher on the mountain. Climbers Andreas Wild and Simon Edwards

Mike Pescod

SOUTH-WEST RIDGE

Grade: 120m, IV,5
Location: Douglas Boulder, Ben Nevis
Route Base, Aspect & Rock Type: 800m, South-West facing, Andesite
First Winter Ascent: James Macdonald & Herbert Turnbull, March 1934

Alex Messenger

Deep snow on the approach to the South-West Ridge of The Douglas Boulder. Climber John Roberts

*T*he 200m-high Douglas Boulder is the first summit on the kilometre-long Tower Ridge.
Elsewhere in the country it would be a significant cliff in its own right, but here it is dwarfed
by the scale of the North-East Face of Ben Nevis. The Victorians were quick to realise the size of
the feature and in April 1896 they jokingly called it a 'boulder' and named it after Willie Douglas,
the first editor of the SMC Journal. Douglas had just joined Raeburn, Hinxman and Brown for the
first ascent of the Direct Route up the front face. This was probably the second time the small
exposed summit had been reached – the first was by the Hopkinson brothers a couple of days
after they had (down)climbed Tower Ridge in 1892, the earliest recognised route on the mountain.

The diminutive status of the Douglas Boulder continued for over a century and it is only
recently that its true value as a winter venue has been realised. A steady stream of routes have
been added to the Boulder in recent years and although many are deceptively difficult, they point
to the value of the cliff when the snow level is low, precluding climbing higher on the mountain.

The South-West Ridge was first climbed in winter 80 years ago. Dismissed in earlier guidebooks as simply the easiest route on the Douglas Boulder, it is now recognised as an excellent
winter climb taking the prominent crest overlooking West Gully. Successive SMC guidebooks
(including mine!) rather euphemistically describe it as 'good value for money' and grade it III, but
today it is thought to be a full grade harder than that at IV,5 and provides a brilliant way of reaching
this satisfying summit.

15

Rose Pearson making the first recorded winter ascent of the East Ridge of the Douglas Boulder

Simon Richardson

Approach

From the CIC Hut, head over the domed rock west of the Hut, then negotiate a short, vegetated wall at the foot of Coire na Ciste, before heading south to the foot of West Gully which separates the Douglas Boulder from the rest of Tower Ridge (about **30mins** from the Hut, see p30-31).

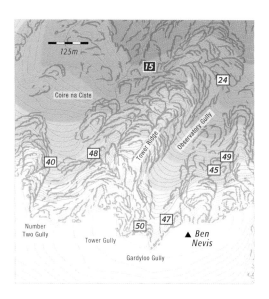

Andreas Wild high on the South-West Ridge

Mike Pescod

Alternative Routes

An ascent of **West Gully** to the Douglas Gap, followed by a descent of **East Gully** is a classic Grade I expedition and possible in wild weather, but watch out for avalanche conditions in the gullies. Another good route to the summit of the Boulder is the **East Ridge** (IV,5) which climbs the south-east edge right of East Gully, via a prominent square corner. The steep grooved wall left of the South-West Ridge contains several routes including the clean-cut corner of **Cutlass** (VI,7) and **Jacknife** (IV,6). Both routes finish up the upper section of the South-West Ridge.

Guidebooks

Ben Nevis (SMC), *Scottish Winter Climbs* (SMC), *Winter Climbs Ben Nevis and Glen Coe* (Cicerone), *SMC Journal 2004, SMC Journal 2014*. For *SMC Journal* new routes see <www.smc.org.uk/new-routes>.

Descent

From the summit of the Boulder abseil into the Douglas Gap and descend East Gully (I). There is an in-situ abseil tape around a large block next to the summit, but this can be obscured by snow. There is another anchor about 3m down on the Gap side that may be more visible in winter. In heavy snow conditions, a long abseil into East Gully should take you clear of any potential avalanche danger in the gully, but if in doubt, make a second abseil to gain the easy slopes at the foot of East Gully.

Conditions

A freeze and snowfall quickly bring the South-West Ridge into condition and it's a popular choice when large amounts of snow preclude climbing on the Ben's higher cliffs. The blocky nature of the rock means that it can be climbed in a variety of snow conditions, and when banked out (particularly at the start), the standard drops to Grade III. The Douglas Boulder is an excellent venue to shelter from strong westerlies blowing over the summit of the Ben, however easterly winds can deposit windslab on the approach slopes, so be careful in these conditions.

Top Tips

You may want to consider taking some spare cord or tape to save leaving behind your best sling if you decide to back-up the abseil from the top of the Boulder.

Route Description

The route follows the prominent rib left of West Gully and is usually climbed in four pitches. The start, which lies 10m up from the entrance to West Gully, ascends a short cracked wall that is easily the most difficult section of the route. This bit is often avoided by continuing another 20m up the gully and cutting back left along a turfy ramp to gain the crest of the ridge and a good belay. Continue up a series of steep steps on well protected and blocky terrain. The exit from the chimney on the last pitch can feel awkward, and the route ends abruptly on the small summit of the Boulder.

Simon Richardson

15. South-West Ridge (IV,5)   **J. Jacknife (IV,6)**
C. Cutlass (VI,7)   **W. West Gully (I)**

Ian Dempster wrestling up the final V-groove of Right-Angled Gully Direct. Due to its south facing aspect, this route is best climbed when the weather is cloudy or overcast

Andy Bain

RIGHT-ANGLED GULLY DIRECT

Grade: 80m, V,6
Location: North Peak, The Cobbler
Route Base, Aspect & Rock Type: 800m, South facing, Mica Schist
First Ascent: Harold Raeburn & William Tough, 31 October 1896;
Simon Richardson & Chris Cartwright, 30 December 1990

Rab Anderson

The North Peak of The Cobbler in good mixed climbing condition – except for the sunshine!

*I*n the rush up the A82 to Glen Coe and Ben Nevis, the Arrochar hills are often overlooked as a winter climbing venue. Lying further south and lacking the altitude and mass of the larger mountain ranges, they are not very resistant to thaw and need a hard freeze to come into condition. However, they offer a worthwhile and easily accessible venue when large levels of snow and avalanche conditions preclude climbing on the higher peaks.

There is good winter climbing on all the Arrochar mountains, but the shapely peak of The Cobbler at the head of Loch Long offers the widest variety on north and south facing cliffs. The Cobbler is a famous and iconic mountain, but it is relatively low-lying at 884m and the majority of its winter routes rely on frozen turf, so low temperatures followed by snowfall are essential ingredients for success.

One notable exception is Right-Angled Gully Direct on the North Peak. There is no vegetation on the climb, so it can be climbed as a pure Snowed-Up Rock route when the turf is not fully frozen elsewhere. It is very well protected too. Considerable care should be taken when climbing in these conditions however, as The Cobbler has many classic rock climbs and the soft mica schist is easily damaged by over-enthusiastic pick placements and imprecise crampon work.

Right-Angled Gully Direct is a short route, but it packs a punch with a deceptively technical initial pitch and a daunting back and foot V-groove at its top. Although it can be climbed as a route in its own right, it is often combined (when the turf is frozen) with an ascent of Ramshead Ridge (IV,5) resulting in a fulfilling three-pitch outing.

16. Right-Angled Gully Direct (V,6)
RG. Ramshead Gully (IV,5)
RR. Recess Route (V,6)

Rab Anderson

Approach

From the Pay and Display car park (NN294049) by Loch Long, just beyond Arrochar village, follow the new forestry track to the south-west, then continue straight up at a telecommunications aerial to reach a dam on the Allt a' Bhalachain. Follow a path on the east side of the burn, then cross over it beyond the Narnain Boulders. From here, climb up the corrie below the North Peak. If intending only to climb Right-Angled Gully Direct (without the Ramshead Ridge start), continue up to the col between the Centre and North Peaks, otherwise traverse right to reach the left side of the South Face of North Peak (**2hrs**).

In deep snow this approach can be hard going, so in winter an approach from Glen Croe is often used. From a small bridge on the A93 (NN243060), follow the north side of the burn descending from Bealach a' Mhaim (the col between Beinn Ime and Beinn Narnain) for about a kilometre to reach a small dam at NN253067. From here, cross the burn and strike up a spur on The Cobbler to reach the col between the Centre and North Peaks (**1hr 30mins**).

Descent

From the summit of The North Peak, descend south-westwards with one short scrambling section to the col between the Centre and North peaks. From here, descend easily to join either approach route.

Conditions

Cold temperatures followed by significant snowfall will bring The Cobbler's North Peak into condition. However, the south facing aspect of this cliff, compared with the north-east faces of the South and Central Peaks, means its routes strip rapidly with any sun, so a cold, overcast, or even a stormy day is required. This is a cliff to visit when the weather is not perfect!

Top Tips

Watch out for the pothole-type entrance to the Cobbler Cave (it burrows for 45m under the North Peak), situated near the foot of Ramshead Ridge. If you do not fancy the final V-groove of Right-Angled Gully Direct it is possible to keep the standard at IV,5 by following a terrace out right and finishing up the short, steep corner above. This is the line of Raeburn and Tough's first winter ascent of Right-Angled Gully way back in 1896.

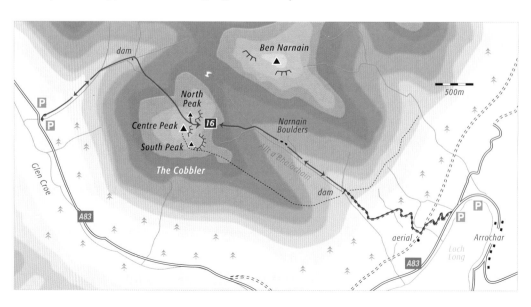

Alastair MacLean

The lower gully-corner of Right-Angled Gully Direct. Climber Graeme Barr

Route Description

The routes on the North Peak fall into two sections with Right-Angled Gully Direct lying on the upper section, above a terrace that can be reached from the col between the Centre and North peaks. The gully spectacularly divides the two overhanging prows that define the peak. If the turf is fully frozen, Ramshead Ridge, which lies on the lower tier to the left of the prominent Ramshead Gully, provides a good introductory pitch.

1. **45m** Ramshead Ridge: Start up a rocky recess on the right side of the ridge to gain the crest and follow a wide crack to a terrace.

2. **20m** Right-Angled Gully Direct: Ascend to the top of the terrace, belay at the foot of the gully-corner, and climb it on slabby holds to where it steepens. This pitch is steeper than it looks!

3. **15m** Right-Angled Gully Direct: Continue straight up the V-groove above.

Alternative Routes

The great winter classics on The Cobbler include **South-East Ridge And The Arete** (III) – a traverse of the South and Centre Peaks, **North Wall Groove** (VI,6) on the north-east face of the South Peak and **Recess Route** (V,6) on the North Peak. All these routes require good conditions and frozen turf. There are few pure Snowed-Up Rock routes on The Cobbler aside from Right-Angled Gully Direct, however **S-Crack** (VI,7) on the South Peak is comparable. It is sustained and well protected, but needs a good covering of rime ice or hoar frost, as it is too steep to catch much falling snow.

Guidebooks

Arran, Arrochar and the Southern Highlands (SMC), *Scottish Winter Climbs* (SMC).

Cold and snowy conditions on Silver Threads Among The Gold. Henning Wackerhage moving left across the headwall on the third pitch

Henning Wackerhage

SILVER THREADS AMONG THE GOLD

Grade: 140m, IV,5
Location: Corrie Farchal, Glen Clova
Route Base, Aspect & Rock Type: 700m, East facing, Mica Schist
First Ascent: Henning Wackerhage, Simon Richardson & Tim Chappell, 10 March 2013

Henning Wackerhage

Approaching Corrie Farchal. Climber Simon Richardson

*W*inter climbing in Glen Clova has a reputation for being rather fickle and not often in condition. This view is largely based on Look C Gully, probably the area's best known winter route. When fully formed, this broad icy gully-line is undoubtedly superb, but it follows a vigorous watercourse in the relatively low-lying Corrie Fee, and takes a mini-ice age to freeze.

Glen Clova is undergoing something of a winter renaissance at the moment with a steady stream of quality mixed climbs added over the past few seasons. Henning Wackerhage, Robbie Miller, Brian Duthie and Forrest Templeton have been at the forefront of these developments with dozens of new routes, but the one that has attracted the most repeats is Silver Threads Among The Gold in Corrie Farchal. Henning Wackerhage has climbed the route three times and considers it, "arguably the best winter buttress climb in the Angus glens," but the quick approach and Tim Chappell's evocative route name also add to the appeal.

Silver Threads lies on the back wall of the recently developed Corrie Farchal. "There are plenty of chimneys, technical walls, a cave and some variation," Henning enthuses. "After that a tunnel pitch, a troglodyte's dream, leads to the bottom of the final wall. This is steeper than it looks and balancy but it has, like the rest of the climb, good gear. Overall it's a great climb which is not at all obvious from the road, but reveals its qualities to those who climb it."

The big attraction of Clova is that it is not a high altitude area; a real advantage in a snowy season. Easily accessible from most of the Central Belt, Glen Clova is worth keeping in mind when deep snow swamps the rest of the Cairngorms and the mountains further west, and road conditions are too poor to make the long trek up to the North-West.

17

Approach

From the Glen Doll car park (Pay and Display) at the head of Glen Clova, walk back along the road for 500m to Braedownie Farm. Go through a gate just west of the farm and follow a track on the east side of the River South Esk to a small bridge at NO289751. Go over the bridge, continue along a track south-east through an open area of forest, cross a small burn followed by a deer fence, and climb directly to enter the corrie (**1hr 15mins**).

Descent

Head east to the broad col between Driesh and Hill of Strone and descend the open snow gully to the corrie floor.

Conditions

The route can be climbed in a wide variety of conditions. The key requirement is that the turf is well frozen.

Top Tips

Unlike the rest of the Cairngorms, the Glen Clova hills are comprised of mica schist which can be difficult to protect. Take pegs and a couple of ice hooks for turf and vegetated cracks. The Clova rock often fractures into wide cracks, so medium to large cams can be useful too.

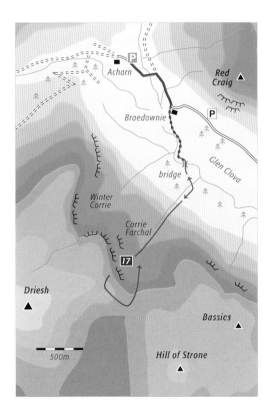

Jenny Hill climbing the icicle-festooned chimney of Age Is Only A Number on the first ascent

Alex Thomson

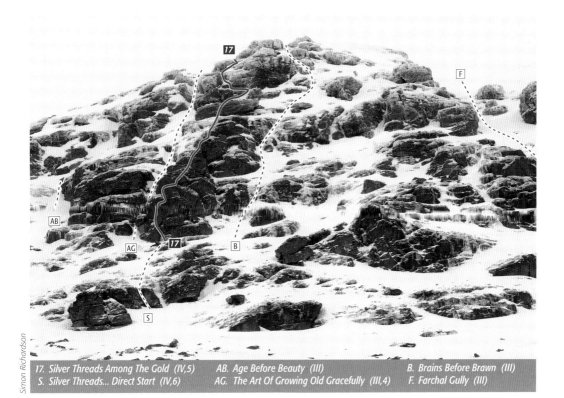

17. Silver Threads Among The Gold (IV,5)   AB. Age Before Beauty (III)   B. Brains Before Brawn (III)
S. Silver Threads... Direct Start (IV,6)   AG. The Art Of Growing Old Gracefully (III,4)   F. Farchal Gully (III)

Route Description

The prominent Farchal Gully roughly splits the crag into two. The broad cliff to its left is cut by the deep gully of The Art of Growing Old Gracefully, and Silver Threads Among The Gold follows the well defined buttress just to the right of this. The pitches are easily split if rope drag is a problem.

1. 50m Start on the terrace above the short lower tier just right of the gully and climb the corner-ramp cutting through the left side of the initial wall. Above, continue right via a steep chimney and climb two steep walls to a terrace.

2. 40m Climb the centre of the short impending wall above and continue through the chimney-tunnel splitting the giant boulder above. Belay on the prominent terrace.

3. 50m Ascend the headwall by climbing first right, then left up a steep turfy wall to reach an easier gully leading to the top.

Alternative Routes

Corrie Farchal lies just to the east of the well travelled Winter Corrie, but following the first ascent of the prominent Farchal Gully in 1980, it was neglected for more than 30 years. It is now home to over a dozen medium grade mixed and gully climbs. **Farchal Gully** (III) itself is a good line, but it takes a cold and snowy season for the lower ice pitch to form. The prominent gully of **The Art Of Growing Old Gracefully** (III,4) quickly comes into condition and can be ascended as a mixed climb, so it makes a good early season alternative. Other worthwhile gullies include **Age Before Beauty** (III) and **Brains Before Brawn** (III). High up on the steep buttress right of Farchal Gully,, **Age Is Only A Number** (III,4) finds a cunning way through steep and impressive terrain. **Silver Threads Among The Gold** has a **Direct Start** (IV,6) that takes the undercut right facing corner in the lower tier.

Guidebooks

SMC Journal 2013, SMC Journal 2015. For SMC Journal new routes see <www.smc.org.uk/new-routes>.

March 2016 and Mega Route X in full Grade VI condition. In fatter years the ice can be thicker and the route a little less intimidating

Steve Holmes

MEGA ROUTE X

Grade: 70m, VI,6
Location: Central Trident Buttress, Ben Nevis
Route Base, Aspect & Rock Type: 950m, East facing, Andesite
First Ascent: John Murphy & Alasdair Cain, 18 December 1982

Ben Cooling

Alistair Todd climbing the spectacular second pitch of Mega Route X

*I*n the early 1980s the last great problem on Ben Nevis was a thin hanging icefall on Central Trident Buttress. To anyone walking up Coire na Ciste it was a striking line and an obvious challenge, but the ice rarely formed more than an inch or two thick and never reached the base of the buttress. Like all last great problems it was named before it was climbed and spoken about in hushed tones. In December 1982, John Murphy the strongest of the regular Nevis ice climbers at the time, took on the challenge with Alasdair Cain. Murphy spent a long time bouldering-out the lower mixed wall and it was only after he was fully committed five metres off the ground, that the ice was thick enough for solid placements. It was dark by the time they reached the first belay, so they abseiled off. The following day they traversed in to climb the second pitch, and Mega Route X was in the bag. The aura of the route was broken a few days later when Martin Lawrence and Roger Webb repeated it in a single push.

Mega Route X was probably near the limit of what was possible on steep ice before banana picks became commonplace in Scotland, and such was the climb's reputation that it was not until 1987 that it saw any further ascents, an unusual length of time for such a prominent and accessible line on Ben Nevis. In those five years equipment had developed considerably, although it was still a far cry from today's leashless tools, monopoint crampons and super-efficient ice screws.

Fortunately, the steep icefall routes on the Ben such as Mega Route X now seem to form thicker and with greater regularity than they used to do. Various theories abound as to why this is so, but the likely causes are a more active water table due to wetter summers and milder winters that promote the crucial freeze-thaw sequence required for good ice formation.

Approach

From the CIC Hut, head over the domed rock east of the Hut and negotiate a short vegetated wall to enter Coire na Ciste. The Trident Buttresses are on the right side of the corrie and extend from Number Four Gully to Moonlight Gully. The steep rounded wall of Central Trident Buttress lies to the right of the prominent ramp of Jubilee Climb (about **45mins** from the Hut, see p30-31).

Descent

It is possible to downclimb the sloping shelf at the top of the route into Coire na Ciste, but many teams choose to make a long abseil from the snow terrace at the top of the route (take 60m ropes). The climb has also been descended using Abalakov threads. Alternatively, if conditions are not too snowy or avalanche-prone, continue up **Jubilee Climb** (II) to the plateau.

Conditions

Mega Route X sometimes forms during the first sustained low temperature period of the season, and in these conditions it will be worthy of a meaty VI,6

18. Mega Route X (VI,6)   F. Feeding Frenzy (VI,6)
J. Jubilee Climb (II)

Simon Richardson

grade. The first section can be very thin and requires a bold and forceful approach before the ice is thick enough to take an ice screw. Later in the season (until exposed to the sun in early March), the ice can form fatter and even lead to the formation of a cone at the foot of the route. With modern ice screws the route can be well protected and drop a grade to V,6. Although it takes cold temperatures for the climb to form, it will be easier if the temperature is hovering just below zero to avoid brittle ice. Like many mountain icefall routes, it is difficult to predict Mega Route X's conditions from afar and firsthand knowledge, or real time information from the Internet, will pay dividends.

Top Tips

Mega Route X is the steepest ice route in this book, and although it is never quite vertical, it is guaranteed to give a good pump. The trick to climbing steep ice is to keep a level head, break the route up into short sections, and make the most of available features such as grooves and the tops of bulges to rest the calves and shake out the forearms. Never miss the opportunity to place a good ice screw – it is worth taking eight screws on this route so you have enough for the belay.

Route Description

The icefall forms down the line of the summer route Steam (HVS).

   1. 40m Climb the icefall directly, then a left-slanting ramp, to a belay in the corner below an overhang.

   2. 30m Continue up right to easier ground and a block belay.

Cubby Images

Superb icefall climbing on the second pitch of Mega Route X

Alternative Routes

Left of Mega Route X is the attractive hanging-icicle frieze of **Feeding Frenzy** (VI,6); unfortunately this very steep continental-looking route is rarely in condition. To the left of the Grade II **Jubilee Climb**, on the right side of Jubilee Buttress, is the vertical icefall of **Mega Reve** (VI,6). Left of this is the ice-line of **Jubilation** (IV,4), which is reliably in condition, and makes a good back-up if the steeper ice lines are not sufficiently formed. Elsewhere on Ben Nevis, **The Curtain** (IV,5) on Càrn Dearg Buttress is an excellent climb and the most popular pure ice route on the mountain. Further right on the North Wall of Càrn Dearg is the spectacular free-hanging icicle of **The Shroud** (VI,6). Together with Mega Route X it is the most sought-after high standard ice route on the Ben, but it is not often in condition and should only be attempted when the hanging fang has connected with its base.

Guidebooks

Ben Nevis (SMC), *Scottish Winter Climbs* (SMC), *Winter Climbs Ben Nevis and Glen Coe* (Cicerone).

Matt Shaw leading the lower section of Rapunzel in well frozen conditions. The huge iced chimney hangs over the middle section of the watercourse above

Dave Ritchie

RAPUNZEL

Grade: 350m, IV,4
Location: Beinn Fhionnlaidh
Route Base, Aspect & Rock Type: 600m, South facing, Mica Schist
First Ascent: Simon Richardson & Robin Clothier, 11 January 1987

Ian Stennett

Looking west down the Allt Bealach na h-Innsig to Beinn Sgulaird, Loch Creran and the Mull hills beyond

The south side of Beinn Fhionnlaidh, a Munro to the south of Glen Coe, is split by a very deep chasm. One Sunday in January 1987, Robin Clothier and I were driving through the Coe wondering what to do in the cold and snowless conditions. The temperature was low but the gullies were bare. The buttresses were black and the icefall of Blue Riband was not fully formed. Spirits were low until I suggested Beinn Fhionnlaidh's chasm, so with nothing to lose, we decided to take a look.

Four hours later, we had driven south around Loch Linnhe to Glen Creran and made the long trackless approach to below the south face. We entered the mouth of the chasm and climbed an ice pitch to a steep corner. Thin ice on the right wall, followed by a series of short ice steps and some easy snow, led to below the crux. A huge iced chimney reared above for 50m, capped with two huge chockstones draped with long icicles. It was a daunting-looking feature and we could see why the local name for the chasm is Eas nan Clach Reamhar – 'waterfall of the large boulders'.

It looked a difficult pitch, but we were fully committed now. Fortunately, the icicles were more solid than they appeared and the placements were good. The gully split above, and we took the right fork before moving together up the final slopes.

On the summit ridge the wind was biting hard and we could see storm clouds moving in from the west, so we bundled the gear into our sacks, skipped the summit, and headed down the west ridge. It was dark by the time we reached the forest above Glenure and we arrived back at the car tired but satisfied. We hadn't seen anybody all day, and the remoteness had intensified the experience. It had been a real adventure!

Superb ice climbing in the upper gully of Rapunzel. Climber Matt Shaw

Dave Ritchie

Alternative Routes

To the left of Rapunzel is the hidden **Icicle Buttress Gully** (II). This appears as a slanting ramp from below and lies right of a broad buttress, about 75m left of Rapunzel. The gully is mainly easy-angled but includes several short icy steps before it splits. The easier right-hand branch leads to the summit slopes, but a more difficult finish takes the narrow gully on the left (III) with two short vertical sections. About 150m right of Rapunzel a shorter and less well defined gully system leads to a terrace at about one-half height on the face. This is the line of **The Witch** (III,4). In Glen Coe, the most sought-after mountain ice cascade is the 600m-long **Blue Riband** (V,5) on the South Face of the Aonach Eagach. Similar to Rapunzel, a sustained freeze is required to bring it into condition.

Guidebooks

Glen Coe (SMC), *Winter Climbs Ben Nevis and Glen Coe* (Cicerone), *SMC Journal 2010*. For *SMC Journal* new routes see <*www.smc.org.uk/new-routes*>.

huge iced chimney

19. Rapunzel (IV,4)   I. Icicle Buttress Gully (II)

Tom Prentice

Approach

From the car park at the end of the public road in Glen Creran (NN036489) just before Elleric, take the private road south-east to Glenure House. From here follow a track north to a forest (NN046484) and pick up a path heading east on the southern slopes towards the Allt Bealach na h-Innsig. After 3km this leads to a small building (NN072485) where the path fades and the going becomes slow. Continue up the Allt Bealach na h-Innsig for another 2km until the South Face of Beinn Fhionnlaidh comes into view, with its deep chasm extending almost to the floor of the glen at NN091491. The chasm isn't visible until almost directly underneath it (**2hrs 30mins**).

Descent

Descend the well defined west ridge followed by the more open slopes of the Leac Bharainn to rejoin the approach just north of Glenure.

Conditions

Rapunzel's relatively low altitude and south facing aspect means it takes a couple of weeks of sub zero temperatures to bring it into condition. Remember this is a permanent watercourse and it can take a long time for free-flowing water to freeze. It is worth the wait however, because it is an excellent climb with great character, a variety of interesting pitches, and a feeling of remoteness.

Top Tips

If the steep corner near the bottom of the route is not fully frozen and the water is still running, it is possible to climb thin ice on the right wall.

Route Description

Walk into the chasm and climb a short ice pitch followed by a steep corner. Short ice steps and easy snow lead to the huge iced chimney. Climb this using thin icicles to pass two huge chokestones at its top where the gully splits. Take the right-hand branch and climb two long ice pitches then a short ice step, leading to a general easing in the angle. Follow the gully up snow, with several short ice pitches, for 150m to reach the summit snow slopes.

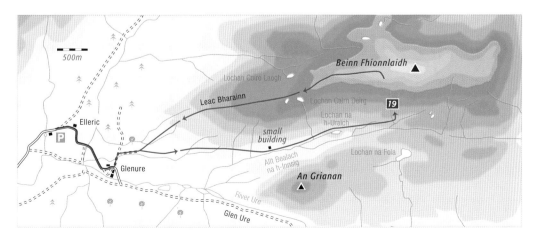

Roger Webb fighting through a gale during the first ascent of Wobble Block Chimney. The vegetation is well frozen and wind-blown snow from the plateau has collected deep in the chimney

Simon Richardson

20

WOBBLE BLOCK CHIMNEY

Grade: 80m, IV,5
Location: Stac an Fharaidh, Cairn Gorm
Route Base, Aspect & Rock Type: 1000m, South-East facing, Granite
First Ascent: Simon Richardson & Roger Webb, 2 January 2012

Henning Wackerhage

The wonderfully secluded Loch Avon Basin with the south flank of Cairn Gorm and Stac an Fharaidh on the left

*I*t has taken me nearly 30 years to realise it, but wind is the most important factor determining *Scottish winter conditions. Most people look to temperature as the key ingredient, but the direction and strength of the wind is paramount. Clearly the direction the wind comes has a direct influence on temperature, but how the wind moves and transfers snow is just as important. This will impact the ease of travel on wind-blown ridges, create windslab on lee slopes, and also define the angle the snow hits the crags and whether it stays in place after it has fallen.*

A good example of the importance of paying careful attention to wind direction was the winter of 2012, when the Cairngorms were battered by ferocious northerlies for several weeks. The underlying air temperature was cold, but the winds were so strong that north facing cliffs were blown bare. Very little was climbed in the Northern Corries during that period because the crags were black and wind-scoured.

Ironically there was good climbing to be had a short distance away on the south facing cliffs above Loch Avon. The snow driven across Cairn Gorm came to rest in the lee of the plateau on the upper tier of Stac an Fharaidh, a cliff best known in winter for its ice climbing. In the prevailing conditions, the previously neglected upper tier provided a handful of good two-pitch routes. Wobble Block Chimney takes the classic line of the bunch, and whilst it could never be considered a major route, it provided an excellent back up climb when other locations were poor.

The south facing cliffs overlooking Loch Avon were also a good choice during the 2014 winter which had the reverse problem, with continuously strong snow-bearing south-easterly winds. These deposited huge amounts of snow in the Northern Corries, burying the crags and creating significant avalanche and cornice danger. Southerly aspects escaped all these problems and due to the easterly component of the wind, they were not scoured completely clean either.

Cairn Gorm summit

descent from plateau

20

I

20

20. *Wobble Block Chimney (IV,5)*   I. *Ice Axe Elbow (V,7)*

Simon Richardson

Approach

From the Coire Cas car park at the top of the ski road, follow the broad ridge of Fiacaill a' Choire Chais to Pt.1141m (prominent cairn). Descend gently and contour across the upper reaches of Coire Raibeirt to reach the west end of Stac an Fharaidh at NJ010028. Descend a short gully to reach the terrace below the upper tier (**1hr 30mins**).

Descent

Reverse the approach to Pt.1141m and descend by the side of the ski area to the car park. This route requires an ascent of approximately 150m to gain Pt.1141m.

Conditions

Wobble Block Chimney makes a good back up when more established venues in the Cairngorms are not available due to too much, or too little, snow. The first two pitches are turfy so need to be well frozen. It is worth bearing in mind the wind direction and its strength for the uphill return to Pt.1141m, and it is best to avoid climbing here in strong south-westerly winds which can whip up punishing spindrift.

Top Tips

Gearing up on the plateau can be an ordeal in a strong wind, so it is preferable to put on crampons

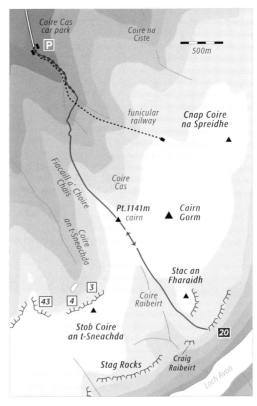

Coire Cas car park

Coire na Ciste

P

500m

funicular railway

Cnap Coire na Spreidhe

Fiacaill a' Choire Chais

Coire an t-Sneachda

Coire Cas

Pt.1141m
cairn

Cairn Gorm

Stac an Fharaidh

3

43   4

Coire Raibeirt

Stob Coire an t-Sneachda

20

Stag Rocks

Craig Raibeirt

Loch Avon

(which you will need for descending to the foot of the route) as soon as you find a sheltered spot on the approach.

Route Description

The upper tier of Stac an Fharaidh is comprised of three distinct buttresses separated by well defined gullies. Wobble Block Chimney takes the left side of the rightmost buttress that is cut by a long straight gully with an impending chimney at its top.

1. **45m** Deceptively steep moves up a vegetated offwidth lead into the gully. Climb this over a steep step to reach the easier angled gully above and follow this to a pronounced steepening.

2. **15m** Continue up the steep section to a good ledge below the impending chimney.

3. **20m** Climb the chimney (easier than it looks) to a good platform. The eponymous wobbling block was trundled and is no more!

James Edwards

The first pitch of Ice Axe Elbow on Stac an Fharaidh.

Simon Richardson

Roger Webb on the first ascent of Lightning Corner on Craig Raibeirt

Alternative Routes

Ice Axe Elbow (V,7) and **Wrist Flexor** (VI,7) climb the prominent central buttress to the left of Wobble Block Chimney starting from an undercut niche. Approximately 200m west-south-west of Stac an Fharaidh lies the compact Craig Raibeirt (see map) which has several mixed routes that can be climbed in similar conditions to Wobble Block Chimney. Approach by descending from the plateau at NJ008026. The right edge of the front face is cut by attractive twin corners taken by **Lightning Corner** (V,6) and **Thunderbolt Crack** (V,7). **Hurricane Rib** (III,6) climbs the well defined left edge of the cliff. It has a couple of steep sections, but is a pure Snowed-Up Rock route that does not rely on frozen turf, and is possible in almost all conditions.

Guidebooks

SMC Journal 2012, SMC Journal 2014. For *SMC Journal* new routes see <*www.smc.org.uk/new-routes*>.

CHAPTER 3 ▶ LEAN TIMES

After a major thaw winter retreats to the higher cliffs, but good climbing opportunities still remain

Creagan Cha-no, Cairn Gorm; photo Simon Richardson

Helen Rennard taking advantage of some rarely formed ice high on Lochnagar. Heavy snowfall followed by deep thaw and a re-freeze can sometimes form ice in unusual places

Simon Richardson

Major drainage lines such as Green Gully on Ben Nevis, rapidly fill with ice after a thaw followed by a re-freeze

John Trudgill

We've had the early season storms and the mid-winter cold snaps, and then disaster – a major thaw strips the mountains bare. This is extremely disappointing. Overnight, the mountain cliffs lose their sculptured icy glaze and rapidly slip back to dull shades of yellow and brown. But all is not lost – the freeze-thaw process is essential for Top Nick conditions to develop and even when the hills seem completely stripped, good winter climbing can reappear in a matter of hours.

The big difference between a major thaw at the beginning of the season and one in January, is that below the surface the ground and bedrock are now cold and the groundwater is only just above zero. It doesn't take much of a freeze for ice to start oozing from cracks and minor drainage lines. But best of all, the remaining snow beds are fully saturated and a re-freeze of only a few hours can transform them into perfect névé. This can bring snow filled gullies into the first decent condition of the season, and make approaches and descents a breeze.

Long approaches are a characteristic of Lean conditions. Climbs located in high Cairngorm corries such as **Cherokee Chimney** on Braeriach may be difficult to get to, but they are situated in the coldest places in the country. Many of the routes freeze up almost immediately after a thaw and just need a brief snowfall to turn them white. Lean conditions are ideal for remote routes as they make for easier and quicker approaches. Fast travel over snow free ground is a key criterion when accessing a route like **Alderwand**, which is a significant distance from the road.

Low-angled ridges such as **Western Rib** on Aonach Mòr are another good option after a major thaw as they retain snow and ice on slopes, ledges and platforms. Routes like **Tower Ridge**, which are climbable throughout the winter, are often at their best in Lean conditions as re-frozen snow can provide fast progress over moderate ground, transforming the route into a handful of short technical pitches between longer sections of easier mountaineering terrain.

A major thaw followed by a re-freeze turns deep gullylines into ice-making machines, especially when the gullies are high, north facing and natural drainage lines such as **Green Gully** on Ben Nevis. A touch of mid-winter sun can accelerate this ice formation and the gullies on Aonach Mòr are at their best mid-season after a deep thaw and re-freeze. **Left Twin** is the classic objective here and its east facing aspect encourages the daily freeze-thaw cycle, ensuring snow is rapidly converted to climbable ice. **Raeburn's Gully** on Lochnagar is undoubtedly at its best after a major thaw. When it's choked with snow the climbing can feel precarious, especially if the headwall is unconsolidated.

Sometimes it can be difficult to predict exactly what is happening high in the mountains, but fortunately some routes are resilient to a variety of conditions. **Deep Cut Chimney** on Hell's Lum Crag works just as well as an icy Mixed climb or a Snowed-Up Rock route and provides an excellent option when winter is returning to the crags after a sustained period of thaw.

After a long dry cold spell, Mixed routes benefit from a thaw because it allows the vegetation to re-saturate and prevents the turf dehydrating and becoming brittle. Vegetation re-freezes remarkably quickly, especially on climbs located at a high altitude, such as **Top Gun** on the West Face of Aonach Beag.

Finally, some predominantly Snowed-Up Rock routes can benefit from a little section of ice or hard névé. **Darth Vader** on Ben Nevis has a difficult crux sequence, but it is noticeably easier when good placements in re-frozen snow or ice are available in the niche just above the cave on the third pitch. However, beware of verglas on re-frozen Snowed-Up Rock routes; icy cracks can make protection very difficult to place.

Once the early season has passed and the mountains have cooled down, Lean conditions can occur at any time. These periods can make for very satisfying winter climbing and with a little extra effort and slightly longer approaches, many excellent routes are there for the taking.

Henning Wackerhage

Approaching Tower Gap on Tower Ridge. Long routes such as Tower Ridge are often at their best in Lean conditions as re-frozen snow allows rapid movement over lower-angled terrain (see also p14)

Chris Cartwright climbing the first pitch of Cherokee Chimney during the first ascent. Ideal mixed climbing conditions that day were largely due to an overnight storm

Simon Richardson

CHEROKEE CHIMNEY

Grade: 90m, V,6
Location: Garbh Choire Mòr, Braeriach
Route Base, Aspect & Rock Type: 1150m, North facing, Granite
First Winter Ascent: Chris Cartwright & Simon Richardson, 17 November 1996

Simon Richardson

Looking down the second pitch of Cherokee Chimney

arbh Choire Mòr is almost certainly the coldest place in the British Isles. Cutting deep into the Braeriach plateau, not only is it high, but the deeply enclosed corrie is shaped like a lipped bowl, and perfectly formed to hold the cold. The snow patch below Sphinx Ridge is almost permanent, and has remained intact for all but six summers in the last 100 years.

The corrie's suitability as a winter climbing ground is offset by its remoteness; this is a challenging place to get to, especially within the confines of a short winter's day. For several years I thought it was a cliff I would never visit. Constrained by a Sunday-only schedule, the classic approach from Glen Derry up the Làirig Ghrù and overnight at Garbh Choire bothy would have taken too much time. Ever thoughtful, Roger Everett came up with the idea of cycling in from Gleann Einich, following the stalkers' path up onto the plateau and approaching the corrie from above. Over the years this has proved a very workable formula for accessing Garbh Choire Mòr and its superb winter routes.

Cherokee Chimney lies high on the exposed north wall of Great Gully and is one of the fastest routes in the country to come into condition. The day before we made the first ascent, Chris Cartwright and I had to retreat from an unfrozen Aonach Mòr. However, Cherokee Chimney provided a superb mixed climb with rimed up rock and well frozen turf. We knew we were in for a good day because as we climbed higher onto the Braeriach plateau, the ground hardened and the wet grass began to glisten with hoar frost. Cherokee Chimney is a little gem with three pitches of varied and well protected mixed climbing. But best of all, if you climb it in lean conditions you will have the double satisfaction of snatching a good climb and getting a route done when other venues are either too warm or devoid of snow.

Moving up to the right-hand of the two corners on the third pitch of Cherokee Chimney

Simon Richardson

Approach

This is the most serious venue in this book and careful planning and forethought are required. Only descend Great Gully if conditions are stable – doing so in heavy snow could be extremely dangerous. Starting from Coylumbridge (NH915107), cycle 12km up Gleann Einich (now spelt Eanaich on new OS maps) to the start of the stalkers' path (NH920001) about 500m before the track ends at Loch Einich (Eanaich). Follow the path to where it ends on the edge of the Braeriach plateau, at the second of two burns at NN926980. (If frozen, crampons will be required to cross the first burn – be careful, it forms a frozen waterfall below and there have been accidents here).

Follow a bearing of 090º Grid to reach the top of Great Gully at NN939980 (incorrectly marked on some editions of the OS 1:25000 map). Pass the cornice on the right (south) or abseil from a small, buried boulder on the plateau (5m sling required). Descend Great Gully to below Cherokee Chimney, the right-hand of the two prominent chimney-slots on the north wall (**4hrs** to **5hrs**).

Alternative Routes

There are several good mixed routes in the vicinity of Great Gully that are quick to come into condition. **Little Big Chimney** (VI,7) is Cherokee Chimney's harder left-hand twin. It is steep and committing – a short route with a big feel. **Crown Buttress** (III) is one of the finest easier mixed climbs in the corrie. It is a Braeriach classic and climbed relatively often. **Coronet Arete** (IV,5) is a harder alternative just left of Crown Buttress with good positions. **She-Devil's Buttress, Original Route** (V,5) lies on the wall right of Great Gully and has an easier lower section leading to two interesting and contrasting mixed pitches above.

Guidebooks

The Cairngorms (SMC), *Winter Climbs in the Cairngorms* (Cicerone).

Mòr holds the cold and snow more readily than any other venue in the Cairngorms. High winds can make the cycle up Gleann Einich an arduous task and conditions on the plateau can be ferocious, so don't attempt the route in poor weather. The surface of the track up the glen softens after a hard freeze followed by a thaw, which makes cycling difficult and can add an hour to the approach.

Top Tips

In over 20 visits to Garbh Choire Mòr, I've only had one clear day, so use a GPS to mark the top of the stalkers' path and rope up when close to the cornice edge. If you are unable to locate the top of Great Gully, or if the cornice is too large, it is normally possible to go down the headland between Garbh Choire Mòr and Garbh Choire Dhaidh. It can be difficult to locate from above, but the cornice is normally small and passable on the Garbh Choire Mòr side. This way will add at least an hour to the approach.

21. Cherokee Chimney (V,6)   *L. Little Big Chimney (VI,7)*
CA. Coronet Arete (IV,5)   *G. Great Gully (I)*
CB. Crown Buttress (III)

Simon Richardson

Descent

This reverses the approach, but the crux is finding the start of the stalkers' path which is not evident from above. In early to mid-season aim to finish climbing by 3pm, so you can locate the start of the path in daylight. Allow three hours back to the road.

Conditions

This is a route to attempt when conditions across the Scottish mountains are very lean, either during the first few weeks of the season, or after a major thaw. Although the turf needs to be frozen, Garbh Choire

Route Description

An excellent technical climb up the overhanging chimney-slot to the right of Little Big Chimney, the prominent steep chimney on the right flank of Crown Buttress. Start 5m to the right of Little Big Chimney.

  1. 25m Climb the chimney over a bulge with a chockstone, to a niche.

  2. 25m Continue up the overhanging slot and short continuation corner to a ledge.

  3. 40m Move up the slabby wall above and climb the right-hand of two corners to reach easy ground and the top.

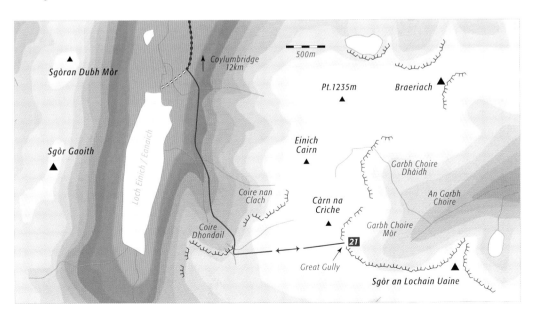

Roger Everett high on Alderwand during the first ascent. Following a major thaw, high altitude east facing corries such as Ben Alder's Garbh Choire Beag, hold snow well

Simon Richardson

ALDERWAND

Grade: 300m, III
Location: Garbh Choire Beag, Ben Alder
Route Base, Aspect & Rock Type: 850m, East facing, Mica Schist
First Ascent: Simon Richardson & Roger Everett, 31 January 1987

Looking west from the summit of Ben Alder towards the Mamores, Ben Nevis and the Grey Corries

*B*ack in the 1980s there was an air of mystery about climbing on Ben Alder, with rumours of impressive unexplored crags. But Ben Alder is an elusive mountain, situated in the centre of the vast tract of land between Rannoch Moor and Dalwhinnie, and rarely visited in winter. In January 1987 Roger Everett and I decided to take a look for ourselves. Early one Saturday morning we set off from Culra bothy, after a long walk in from Dalwhinnie the previous night. As dawn broke, our eyes were drawn to the great east facing cliffs of Garbh Choire Beag, glowing red in the rising sun.

After racing across the moorland, we immediately set to work on the prominent line of ice running up the centre of the face. The climbing was interesting, but never difficult, and later that morning as we pulled through the cornice and walked the short distance to the summit, we were pretty sure that we were the only winter climbers around.

We climbed two more routes that weekend and by the time we returned to the car late on Sunday night we had walked more than 56 kilometres. The other climbs were technically harder, but the route of the trip was undoubtedly that very first climb on Garbh Choire Beag. We knew that we had to give it a memorable name. The face reminded us of an Oberland north wall and 'Alderwand' seemed to perfectly capture the tiered nature of the mica schist, as well as the magical nature of the mountain.

Twenty-five years on there are now a couple of dozen winter routes on Ben Alder courtesy of Andy Nisbet and others, but it is the very first climb that attracts the bulk of the attention. Pick a settled winter spell, go and climb Alderwand and enjoy a unique mountaineering experience in a very special place.

22

The final snow slopes of Alderwand. Climber Roger Everett

Simon Richardson

Approach

You do not have to walk long distances to reach the climbing on Ben Alder nowadays, as the estate tracks are well maintained and ideal for cycling. Most parties plan on an overnight stop, although in good walking and cycling conditions it is possible to climb in Garbh Choire Beag in a day trip. From Dalwhinnie cycle the estate track on the north-west shore of Loch Ericht past Ben Alder Lodge to Loch Pattack. Continue round its southern shore, then south to Culra bothy (NN523762), situated just before Culra Lodge, (15km from Dalwhinnie, about **3hrs** by bike). The bothy made a good base in the past, but is currently closed due to asbestos issues – there are good camping spots nearby.

On foot from the bothy, go 300m downstream, cross the Allt a' Chaoil-rèidhe by a bridge and follow the good stalkers' path under the west side of Beinn Bheòil. Cross the burn near the outflow of the lochan in the vicinity of Bealach Beithe to reach easy slopes leading up to Garbh Choire Beag and the foot of the climb (**1hr 30mins** from Culra).

On foot in dry conditions, or if snow blocks the track, this approach can be shortened by following the stalkers' path that leaves the track by a stable building at NN548787 about 2km beyond Ben Alder Lodge, and follows the east side of the Allt a' Chaoil-rèidhe.

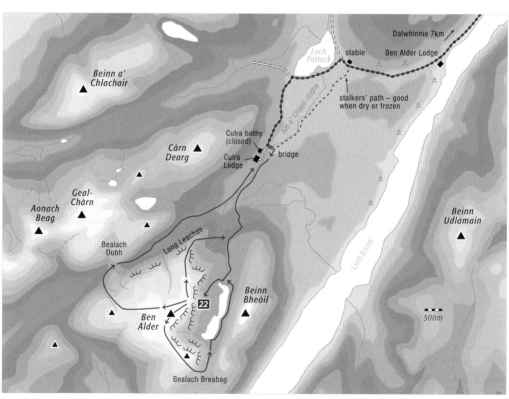

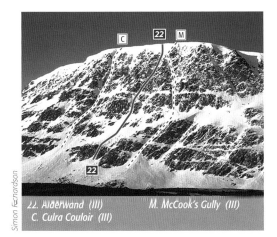

Simon Richardson

22. Alderwand (III)   M. McCook's Gully (III)
C. Culra Couloir (III)

Descent

With its deeply incised corries and huge cornices, the summit plateau of Ben Alder is a serious place in winter, and careful navigation is required. The safest (and longest) descent is to head west-north-west from the top of the climb and descend easy slopes to the Bealach Dubh. In good visibility it is simpler to follow the plateau rim southwards (visiting the summit en route) around Garbh Choire Mòr and descend steeply to the Bealach Breabag where the stalkers' path can be joined below the east side of the mountain. Alternatively, a confident party can descend the Long Leachas, which provides the most direct descent.

Conditions

The high east facing Garbh Choire Beag collects snow well and is at its best mid-season following a re-freeze after a deep thaw. Cold and dry conditions will also make the approach faster as it is possible to cycle much of the stalkers' path when frozen. Late in the season the corrie catches too much sun for Alderwand to be in condition, however some of the gully-lines may be possible with a very early start, but beware of possible cornice collapse.

Top Tips

Since you will be travelling large distances, keep your rucksack as light as possible. The climbing is not technically difficult, so a small rack of a few slings, a handful of nuts, two pegs and a couple of ice screws will suffice. If planning an overnight stop you will need to bring lightweight camping gear as Culra bothy is closed. Alternatively, an early start from Dalwhinnie with bikes and good walking conditions underfoot, will allow the route to be round-tripped in a day.

Route Description

An excellent mountaineering route taking the depression between the two left-hand gullies (Culra Couloir and McCook's Gully) directly up the centre of the face. Start with an (avoidable) ice pitch to reach a snow terrace and continue by four long pitches up the icy open groove-line above to exit on mixed ground. Snow slopes lead to the cornice.

Alternative Routes

There are more than a dozen routes in Garbh Choire Beag ranging from Grade II to IV. The most prominent line on the face is **Culra Couloir** (III), which takes the left-slanting wide gully-line to the left of Alderwand. Being more recessed (and low in the grade) this route is often in condition and contains just one short ice pitch. It makes a good back up option if Alderwand is not sufficiently iced.

If climbing conditions in Garbh Choire Beag are poor, the **Short Leachas** (I), which takes the eastern spur of the north ridge of the mountain makes a fine mountaineering route, especially if climbed direct. The **Long Leachas** (I) climbs the north-eastern spur, which narrows in its upper section and is slightly harder than its neighbour to the left.

Guidebooks

Ben Nevis (SMC).

Simon Richardson

Chris Cartwright on the crux section of Culra Couloir

Richard Hewison at half-height on Western Rib where the difficulties begin to ease. Many teams start moving together at this point

Scott Muir

WESTERN RIB

Grade: 500m, III
Location: West Face, Aonach Mòr
Route Base, Aspect & Rock Type: 900m, West facing, Granite
First Ascent: Simon Richardson, 17 December 1988

Scott Muir

The excellent third pitch of Western Rib. Climber Richard Hewison

*T*he 2km long West Face of Aonach Mòr is a wonderful mountaineering playground, defined by an attractive series of granite ridges separated by deep gullies. The steepest part of the cliff, the Summit Ribs, lie in a recessed bay directly below the summit. These climbs are open to considerable variation and good route finding will determine the most rewarding line for the conditions of the day. A reasonably short approach, followed by some 500 metres of good climbing leading directly to the summit cairn, have proved a popular formula for an enjoyable yet not too exacting winter expedition.

Alan Kimber recognised the potential here way back in 1979, when he soloed the second rib from the left to give Golden Oldy (II). He left the route unrecorded at the time, for without the spotlight of the Nevis Range Gondola and ski development, the Aonachs were considered very much off the beaten track and not a significant climbing venue.

Ten years later, during the initial development of Coire an Lochain on the east side of the mountain, Roger Everett, Nick Barrett and I decided to have a look at the West Face. We were unaware of Alan's previous exploratory visit, but as luck would have it, when we found the recessed bay we chose to climb the prominent Daim Buttress (III) further right. A later visit resulted in Western Rib (III), which in my view is a finer and more balanced climb. It looks part of Daim Buttress from below, but is in fact distinct, and provides a long and delightful mixed outing up a narrow ridge of clean, rough granite.

23

Claire Hutchinson enjoying good powder snow conditions on Western Rib

Alan Halewood

Approach

From the Nevis Range Gondola top station, contour round into the Allt Daim. The West Face Gullies are reached first, but the Summit Ribs area lies in a slightly recessed bay and the ribs are not visible until just past the prominent East Ridge of Càrn Dearg Meadhonach on the glen's west side. They can be awkward to find in poor visibility – the start of Western Rib lies at NN189730 (**1hr** to **1hr 30mins**).

Descent

From the summit walk north for 1km along the plateau to reach the summit ski tow and descend the ski slopes to the Gondola top station. For those who reach the summit with plenty of time to spare, the mountaineering flavour of the day can be extended by a traverse over Aonach Mòr's tops. This starts with a descent of the sharp **East Ridge** (Grade I) to Stob an Chul-Choire. Continue north-east over Stob Coire an Fhir Dhuibh and north over Tom na Sroine, then down to forest tracks that lead back to the Nevis Range car park.

Conditions

The Summit Ribs are a good option when strong westerlies have deposited unstable snow in the lee slopes of east facing corries on Ben Nevis and Coire an Lochain on Aonach Mòr. Western Rib comes into condition fast, but the freezing level should be 900m or below to ensure the turf is frozen. Beware of deep snow, which can make the approach up the Allt Daim long and laborious.

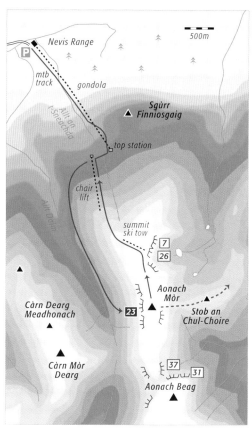

Top Tips

If the visibility is poor, the foot of the face can present a confusing picture, with uncertainty about the true starts to the climbs. A first visit here is best made on a day when the base of the Summit Ribs area is free of cloud and the routes can be identified.

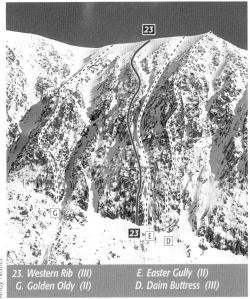

23. Western Rib (III)	**E. Easter Gully (II)**
G. Golden Oldy (II)	**D. Daim Buttress (III)**

Andy Nisbet

Euan Whitaker

Moving together up the final slopes to the summit plateau of Aonach Mòr

Route Description

Less sustained and committing than Tower Ridge on Ben Nevis, or the North-East Ridge of Aonach Beag, Western Rib provides an excellent adventure in a wild and remote setting, well away from busy Coire an Lochain and the ski development. There are six defined Summit Ribs in the recessed bay below the summit. The most distinctive is Daim Buttress, the fourth from the left, which contains a prominent slab at half-height. Western Rib is the third rib from the left and appears as a flying buttress to Daim Buttress on its right. The line is obvious and follows the crest of the rib until it merges into easier ground leading to the summit plateau. A popular alternative is to start on the left and climb a subsidiary rib to join the main line at a small col just below one third-height.

Alternative Routes

Gendarme Ridge (II) is a pleasant mixed climb up the leftmost rib and has a small rock finger near its top. **Golden Oldy** (II), the other established classic of the crag, follows a groove in the centre of the second rib from the left, to reach the better defined ridge-line higher up. **Daim Buttress** (III) is the fourth buttress from the left. It takes snow and rocky corners for 200m to the base of the prominent slab, which is climbed by cracks on the left edge. **Easter Gully** (II) climbs the gully between Western Rib and Daim Buttress for three pitches to reach easier ground. Either continue up the gully, or move right onto the upper part of Daim Buttress and follow this to the top. The West Face Gullies lie at the northern end of the face and are passed on the approach up the Allt Daim. They are not often climbed, however they can give pleasant outings in cold dry weather, when they form icy watercourses with little snow.

Guidebooks

Ben Nevis (SMC), *Scottish Winter Climbs* (SMC), *Winter Climbs Ben Nevis and Glen Coe* (Cicerone).

Climbing out of Tower Gap, with the upper ridge in favourable conditions of consolidated snow and ice-free rock

Henning Wackerhage

TOWER RIDGE

Grade: 1000m, IV,3
Location: North-East Face, Ben Nevis
Route Base, Aspect & Rock Type: 1000m, North-East facing, Andesite
First Winter Ascent: Norman Collie, Godfrey Solly & Joseph Collier, 30 March 1894

Tower Gap and the Great Tower from the east

John Trudgill

*T*he great north-east face of Ben Nevis falls abruptly from the summit plateau in a magnificent series of cliffs. More than 3km long and 500m high, this is the most impressive mountain face in the British Isles, and the scale is so vast that it can be difficult to appreciate, especially on a first visit. The dominant feature in the centre of the face is Tower Ridge, which separates Observatory Gully and Coire na Ciste, the two great corries on the north side of the mountain.

It is no surprise that this imposing feature caught the imagination of the climbers at the birth of Scottish mountaineering. Tower Ridge was the first route to be climbed on Ben Nevis, and its first winter ascent in 1894 by Collie, Solly and Collier was a tour de force. Years later, in his book *Mountaineering in Scotland*, Bill Murray enthused a new generation of post-War Scottish climbers with an inspiring account of an ascent with Jim Bell and Douglas Laidlaw in December 1938. Nowadays Tower Ridge sees many ascents, but its alpine scale should not be underestmated. This magnificent classic requires good mountaineering skills to climb it efficiently and has seen innumerable epics and benightments.

When I was putting the finishing touches to the 2002 edition of the SMC's Ben Nevis guide-book, Roger Wild from the Lochaber Mountain Rescue Team asked me to consider upgrading the route to Grade IV. This was to emphasise its seriousness and hopefully lead to a reduction in rescue call-outs. At first, this seemed a big wrench from its traditional Grade III, but a IV,3 rating makes absolute sense. Tower Ridge is a long expedition and the difficulties are high on the route.

A winter ascent of Tower Ridge is one of the finest mountaineering routes in the country. It is accessible to all climbers, and whatever your climbing grade, it is guaranteed to provide an enjoyable and memorable experience.

Looking down the central section of Tower Ridge towards the Little Tower. Climbers Chris Hutchison and Martin Ross

Mike Pescod

Approach
The normal winter ascent bypasses the Douglas Boulder by climbing East Gully to gain the Douglas Gap. From the CIC Hut, skirt under the front face of the Douglas Boulder to its east side and move up to the foot of the gully (about **20mins** from the Hut, see p30-31).

Descent
See Ben Nevis Approaches & Descents (p30-33).

Conditions
Tower Ridge is possible in a wide range of conditions and often provides a safe option when other routes on the mountain are avalanche-prone or swamped with deep snow. Although roped teams have climbed the route in less than 45 minutes, it should be considered a major undertaking and 6 to 10 hours allowed for the ascent.

Tower Ridge provides a fine climb in Lean conditions in the middle of the season, as firm snow lying on easier-angled sections of the Ridge make for fast progress. Early in the winter however, when coated in powder snow and verglas, Tower Ridge may be very time-consuming, and when covered in deep snow, belays and runners can be almost non-existent apart from on the Eastern Traverse and at Tower Gap.

The route is often climbed at the end of the season too, when it can feel very alpine with short exposed sections of dry rock.

Alternative Routes
Castle Ridge (III) is the easiest of the four great ridges on the north-east face of Ben Nevis. Whilst not in the same class as Tower Ridge, it does have a distinct quality of its own, and has superb views. It is possible in most conditions, but should be avoided after heavy snowfall as the approach slopes are prone to avalanche. **Ledge Route** (II), which starts from the lower reaches of Number Five Gully and winds up the left flank of Càrn Dearg Buttress, is the best route of its grade on the mountain with sustained interest and magnificent situations. It is a safe undertaking and possible in a wide variety of conditions.

Guidebooks
Ben Nevis (SMC), *Scottish Winter Climbs* (SMC), *Winter Climbs Ben Nevis and Glen Coe* (Cicerone).

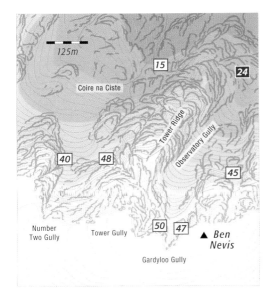

Simon Richardson

circumstances it is probably best and safest to push on up the Ridge to the top.

Route Description

Start by climbing **East Gully** (I) to the Douglas Gap. The chimney above the Gap can be tricky, but after this the Ridge is straightforward as far as the Little Tower. In dry or good icy conditions, the Little Tower is best climbed on the left, but under heavy powder it may be easier further right. Above, easy but spectacular ground leads to the foot of the Great Tower, which rises abruptly in a 30m-high vertical wall.

This is bypassed by the exposed Eastern Traverse, which takes a narrow ledge on the left side of the crest and is normally banked out to a steep level. This leads to a chimney formed by a fallen block (usually buried), followed by short tricky walls that lead to the top of the Great Tower. From here, follow the knife-edge ridge, descending slightly to reach Tower Gap.

The descent into the Gap is short but steep and awkward. Some of the blocks are loose, so it is best to set up a good belay in the Gap once you are down. Climb out the other side by a short wall, or avoid it by moving round to its left and climbing back to the crest. The Ridge now eases until the final steepening, which is best taken by a groove on the right-hand side.

Top Tips

If time is running out it is possible to escape from Tower Gap into Tower Gully by making a short abseil. From here, the slopes leading across to the top of Observatory Gully can be steep and icy and feel very exposed with the cliffs of Tower Scoop below. Whilst this exit may appear a tempting option, in almost all

24. Tower Ridge (IV,3)

Joe Smith leading the final pitch of Green Gully. A recent storm has left a thin covering of snow over re-frozen ice

Ali Rose

GREEN GULLY

Grade: 180m, IV,3
Location: Coire na Ciste, Ben Nevis
Route Base, Aspect & Rock Type: 1100m, North facing, Andesite
First Ascent: Harold Raeburn & Eberhard Phildius, April 1906

Henning Wackerhage

Descending from Ben Nevis as a break in the clouds reveals Loch Linnhe and the setting sun

*G*reen Gully is a much-loved Scottish winter classic. For more than three decades it was thought that Jim Bell, Dick Morsley, Percy Small and Jack Henson had made the first ascent in April 1937, but in 1972 Robin Campbell unearthed an account by Harold Raeburn in the SMC Journal. This revealed that Raeburn had climbed the gully 31 years previously with Eberhard Phildius, a visiting Swiss climber from Geneva. Raeburn was notoriously poor at recording his routes and his account of an icy ascent of The Comb needed careful unravelling by Campbell to determine exactly which line Raeburn and Phildius had taken. The cause of the confusion was that Raeburn had set out to climb The Comb, the prominent steep buttress at the head of Coire na Ciste, and was disappointed not to follow a route closer to the crest. Raeburn and Phildius started up a long right-trending ramp (now taken by Pigott's Route) and made a difficult traverse right into the lower reaches of Green Gully on the right flank of the buttress, before following that to the top.

The realisation that a Grade IV ice route was climbed in Scotland as early as 1906 was a remarkable discovery and Green Gully was one of the hardest technical ice routes in the world at the time. Cutting steps up steep ice with a long and heavy axe and no front points is difficult to imagine in today's world of leashless tools and monopoint crampons, and Raeburn's account of climbing through the cornice still sends tingles down the spine, "... I must confess to a feeling of helplessness for a moment as I stood on my ice-axe, driven horizontally into the vertical snow wall, some hundreds of feet of little less than vertical ice-plastered rocks stretching away down into the depths of the mist beneath, while my fingers slid helplessly from the glassy surface of the cornice névé...".

Moving fast up the central section of Green Gully. Climber Al Todd

Hamish Frost

Approach

From the CIC Hut, head over the domed rock west of the Hut, then negotiate a short vegetated wall at the foot of Coire na Ciste before heading up into the corrie bowl, passing to the right of a small lochan. Climb snow slopes to reach the right flank of The Comb, which is the most prominent feature dividing the back wall of the corrie (about **1hr** from the Hut, see p30-31).

Descent

See Ben Nevis Approaches & Descents (p30-33).

Conditions

With a north facing aspect and a cliff base of 1100m, Green Gully is reliably in condition from mid-season until early spring. It can be climbed in thin conditions as it has no particularly steep sections, but is at its best when the ice is well formed after a re-freeze following a significant thaw. The route has good in-situ peg belays, although they can be difficult to find on the central section of the route.

Top Tips

Green Gully is an excellent first Grade IV lead. In good conditions it is straightforward, but the route is sustained, the pitches are long and it can feel a little bold. The belays are likely to be in place, but even so it is worth carrying one or two pegs and a selection of ice screws.

Route Description

Climb a steep ice pitch (which can vary in length and difficulty depending on the snow build up) to a peg belay on the left wall at 45m. Continue up the gully for two or three ice pitches with peg belays on the right wall. Above this the gully fans out and various finishes are possible. The easiest options are to traverse left to the ridge at the top of The Comb, or bear right up easy snow. The finest finish is straight up via a direct ice pitch, but a large cornice often makes this difficult.

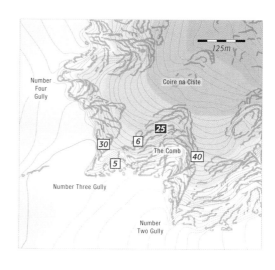

25. *Green Gully (IV,3)*
6. *Number Three Gully Buttress (III,4)*

S. *The Survivor (VII,7)*

Simon Richardson

Pete Trudgill starting the direct exit to Green Gully. A thaw and re-freeze has resulted in lean, icy conditions

John Trudgill

Alternative Routes

Comb Gully (IV,4) is the classic companion to Green Gully (*see topo p209*). It flanks the left side of The Comb and has a similar elevation and aspect, so it is climbable in similar conditions. It is slightly steeper than Green Gully and more confined, so it holds ice for a long time. (Robin Clothier and I once climbed it during an October freeze by using the remnants of snow and ice from the previous winter). There are many excellent Grade IV gully climbs in this area of the Ben. **Thompson's Route** (IV,4) is a favourite choice and lies high up on Number Three Gully Buttress (*see topo p145*). It ices well and is resistant to thaw. Further right on Creag Coire na Ciste, **South Gully** (IV,4) is another worthwhile route that is often overlooked and right again **Central Gully Right-Hand** (IV,4) fully deserves its reputation as one of the finest ice gullies on the mountain.

Guidebooks

Ben Nevis (SMC), *Scottish Winter Climbs* (SMC), *Winter Climbs Ben Nevis and Glen Coe* (Cicerone).

145

Thomas Davy enjoying perfect conditions in Left Twin. Heavy snowfall followed by multiple freeze-thaws and a healthy dose of sun have generously filled the gully with ice

Richard Hines

LEFT TWIN

Grade: 120m, III,4
Location: Coire an Lochain, Aonach Mòr
Route Base, Aspect & Rock Type: 1100m, East facing, Granite
First Ascent: Roger Everett & Simon Richardson, 22 January 1989

Simon Richardson

Looking towards the cliffs of Coire an Lochain from Aonach an Nid

*F*rom a winter climbing perspective, Aonach Mòr is the perfect complement to Ben Nevis. The mid-grade routes come into condition earlier in the season and need less time to form ice. The routes are shorter and the approach is quick from the Nevis Range Gondola, so overall, climbing on Aonach Mòr is a less committing affair. Many folk visit Aonach Mòr as a wind-down after a big Saturday climbing on the Ben.

The cliffs can be seen from the A86 when driving west towards Roybridge, but they are dwarfed by the scale of the east side of the mountain which plunges 800m into the extensive Leanachan Forest below. Before the Nevis Range ski development opened in December 1989, the only way of accessing Aonach Mòr's lonely Coire an Lochain was by a long approach through the forest up the trackless north face of the mountain. It's probably for this reason that the routes in Coire an Lochain remained undeveloped until the late 1980s, although it is possible that some of the easier gullies were climbed by RAF Mountain Rescue Team members in the 1960s.

The east facing aspect and high cliff base of 1100m, produce multiple freeze-thaw cycles and the gully-lines readily build ice. The classic gullies are Left Twin and Right Twin that run straight as a die up the centre of the crag. They are the most frequently climbed routes on the cliff and Left Twin in particular has become a modern classic with dozens of ascents each season. The route is no pushover at Grade III and in lean conditions it can be a continuous run of ice and feel a little tough for the grade.

White Shark on the Ribbed Walls forms ice readily and is an excellent companion route to Left Twin. Climber Rab Anderson

Cubby Images

Approach

The easiest approach is to take the Nevis Range Gondola and continue to the top of the summit ski tow, (see Grooved Arete p64), (**1hr 30mins**).

From here it is 150m to the rim of Easy Gully (bearing 185⁰ Grid). In poor visibility it may be difficult to locate the top of the gully, and extreme caution should be taken as the cornices overhanging Coire an Lochain can be very large. Early in the season, it is normally possible to enter Easy Gully by its northern edge, which appears to escape much of the cornicing. However, from mid-season onwards it may be necessary to abseil over the cornice using a snow bollard. This is often in place and once in Easy Gully, the downclimbing is straightforward.

From the foot of Easy Gully, all the approaches involve traversing steep, avalanche-prone slopes beneath the routes. In heavy snow conditions, or if a high category avalanche warning has been issued (particularly for east facing slopes), the corrie should be avoided. Some teams bypass the traverse under the cliffs by abseiling the line of Left Twin or the nearby Morwind. This is a good tactic often used by local guides, but it requires detailed knowledge of where the abseil points are, and is not a good plan at busy times when other climbers may be below.

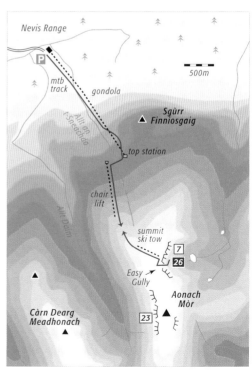

Descent

Walk north along the summit plateau and descend the ski slopes to the Gondola top station. The last gondola departs between 4 and 5pm depending on daylight (check before you set off), but if you miss it (or poor weather has caused it to close early), there is a good track following the MTB downhill course back to the car park. This takes an hour or so and is known locally as the 'walk of shame', however I think it is more a sign that you have had a long and fulfilling day!

Conditions

Left Twin is a traditional icy gully that forms readily and is resistant to thaw, but it is not a good option after a heavy snowfall, and a large cornice can sometimes threaten the route. For these reasons, Left Twin is ideal when a major thaw has been followed by a hard freeze. In these conditions, Left Twin will be icy and the approach down Easy Gully will be safe and the cornice stable. The traverse to the foot of the route will involve front pointing on hard snow, so take your time and be careful of the continuous 40⁰ slope that drops for 300m down to the lochan below. Left Twin faces east so it catches the sun and is rarely in condition from mid-March onwards.

Top Tips

The excellent fine-grained Aonach Mòr granite has fractured along a vertical plane, resulting in many

Alternative Routes

The narrow and well defined **Right Twin** (II) is the natural companion to Left Twin and another very popular route. **Tunnel Vision** (III) takes the wide gully between the Ribbed Walls and Central Buttress, but in full conditions, the final back wall may bank out to a frightening angle with an impassable cornice. The **Left Branch** provides a steep and technical alternative (III,4), and it should always be possible to climb the right branch to reach the upper section of **Morwind**. The classic Aonach Mòr Grade IV ice routes include **White Shark** (IV,5) on the Ribbed Walls, **Typhoon** (IV,4) on Central Buttress (IV,4) and **Jet Stream** (IV,4) on North Buttress. These are all excellent routes, but are a step up in difficulty from Left Twin. **The Split** (IV,4) lies just to the right of Left Twin and is more mixed in nature. The two routes can be combined by climbing Left Twin to the good spike at the top of the gully, abseiling down in two pitches and climbing The Split to finish. Right again lies **Lickerty Split** (IV,5).

Guidebooks

Ben Nevis (SMC), *Scottish Winter Climbs* (SMC), *Winter Climbs Ben Nevis and Glen Coe* (Cicerone).

26. Left Twin (III,4)
T. Typhoon (IV,4)
TS. The Split (IV,4)
L. Lickety Split (IV,5)
R. Right Twin (II)

Andy Nisbet

cracks, chimneys and gullies. The buttress routes are generally well protected, but the rock on the sidewalls of the major fault-lines is often quite compact, so belays in the gullies can be hard to find. This is especially so in Left Twin, but if 60m ropes are used, it is possible to climb the route in three pitches from in-situ belay to in-situ belay. Carry at least three ice screws for the long, crux second pitch.

Route Description

From the foot of Easy Gully traverse right (north) below the Ribbed Walls which are divided into a series of grooves and ribs, and separated from Central Buttress by the deep gully of Tunnel Vision. Further right are two narrow buttresses separated by three deep gullies. This is the Twins Area. The left-hand buttress is cut by the deep cleft of The Split, a useful landmark in poor visibility, and easily recognised by its large jammed blocks. Left Twin takes the deep gully immediately right of Central Buttress. It is normally climbed in four short pitches with in-situ belays at the end of pitch 1 (sling and nut) and pitch 3 (good spike over the top of the main gully). The final pitch is a snowfield leading to the cornice, which may require a traverse to find a way through.

Raeburn's Gully holds snow well after a deep thaw and is often at its best in lean conditions of hard snow and ice

Simon Richardson

RAEBURN'S GULLY

Grade: 200m, III
Location: North-East Coire, Lochnagar
Route Base, Aspect & Rock Type: 900m, North-East facing, Granite
First Ascent: Roy Symmers, Sandy Clark, Bill Ewen, 27 December 1932

Niall Ritchie

Approaching the North-East Corrie of Lochnagar at dawn

*T*here are over a dozen routes named after Harold Raeburn across the Scottish Highlands, which is not surprising, as Raeburn was the climbing superstar of his generation. His routes were at the cutting edge of what was possible at the time and many went unrepeated for 25 years.

The great slanting rift of Raeburn's Gully on Lochnagar, which slices through the cliff between the Tough-Brown Face and the Black Spout Pinnacle, was a natural target for the Victorian pioneers. There were several attempts until Raeburn finally succeeded in November 1898. Rather surprisingly, Raeburn, Rennie and Lawson are credited with the first summer ascent, even though they climbed it in early season conditions of soft snow and thin ice. After surmounting an overhanging chockstone and dropping their only axe, they passed the next bulging section via an intriguing through-route that led to the summit snow bowl.

The first full winter ascent fell to Roy Symmers, Sandy Clark and Bill Ewen in December 1932. The chockstone was almost completely banked out, but nevertheless their ascent was a landmark in winter climbing on Lochnagar. Climbing Raeburn's Gully in these conditions with a full armoury of modern axes and crampons removes much of the technical challenge, although the hazards of an avalanche-prone exit and difficult cornice still remain. For these reasons, I suggest an ascent in very lean conditions more akin to those found by Raeburn's party.

Following a deep thaw and re-freeze, the gully forms an attractive ribbon of ice, assisted by a natural spring near its top. Although the route is more sustained in these conditions, the chockstone will still provide the technical crux. Overall, expect a full-on Grade III, but don't count on finding Raeburn's cunning through-route to finish. Unfortunately, this has changed with subsequent rock-falls and has been lost in the mists of time!

Moving up to the crux bulge on Raeburn's Gully

Dave Riley

Approach

From the Spittal of Glenmuick car park (Pay and Display), follow the approach to the Meikle Col as for Magic Pillar (p68). From the col drop down and cross the broad corrie of the Southern Sector and ascend a little to gain rocks at the foot of Central Buttress, which divides the Southern Sector from the North-East Coire. The large metal first aid box at NO251857, situated on a platform approximately 100m from the foot of Central Buttress, is a popular gearing up spot. From here, Raeburn's Gully cannot be seen as it slants left behind the prominent Tough-Brown Ridge, but it lies approximately 100m left of the prominent couloir of The Black Spout on a bearing of 278° Grid (**2hrs**).

Descent

Follow the cliff edge back to the Meikle Col (beware of cornices). In stormy weather, a simpler but longer descent can be made via Glas Allt and Loch Muick. For this, head south from any point near the cliff top, and descend easy snow slopes that lead into the upper basin of Glas Allt, which is followed to Loch Muick.

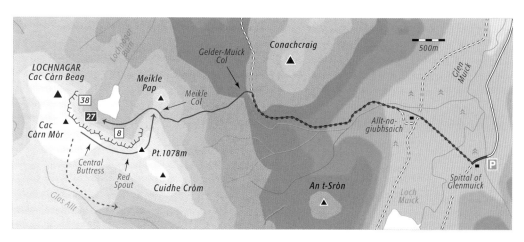

Conditions

The gully has a large catchment area that includes the corniced rim of the Amphitheatre. For this reason Raeburn's Gully is more prone to avalanches than any other gully in the corrie, and is best avoided in conditions of deep snow or warm temperatures. Raeburn's Gully is the deepest gully on the mountain and holds snow well after a major thaw. The optimum time to climb it is after it has re-frozen when the upper pitches often form a continuous run of ice.

Top Tips

There have been a number of accidents in Raeburn's due to avalanches and late in the season the route can be exposed to cornice collapse. Note that even after the cornice has apparently fallen, there is sometimes a section remaining on the right-hand side of the Amphitheatre that cannot be seen from below.

Route Description

This classic gully is often very good early in the season when it holds continuous ice and is Grade III, but it fills quickly to leave only one ice pitch at one-third height. In lean conditions the route is typically climbed in four long pitches comprising straightforward snow, an initial ice step, the crux bulge over jammed blocks by a cave, an ice-choked groove and a final snow bowl. The exit is often defended by an enormous cornice that can be outflanked by an exposed traverse left to the crest of Tough-Brown Ridge, which leads easily to the plateau.

Alternative Routes

Parallel Gully A (III) is the natural companion route to Raeburn's Gully, but it is more open and less resistant to thaw. The first pitch often forms an attractive 30m-high icefall, but if this is not complete, it is possible to gain the gully by climbing turfy mixed ground from the left (the start of Tough-Brown Traverse). **Pinnacle Gully 1** (III) leads up to the col behind the Black Spout Pinnacle and is another worthwhile route and a safe option under powder, although it only takes the form of a gully in its upper half. Similar to Raeburn's Gully it is not a good option late in the season as it is exposed to cornice collapse from the Amphitheatre. Its sister route **Pinnacle Gully 2** (II) starts from high up in the Left Branch of the Black Spout and leads to the col behind the Pinnacle from the other side. In peak conditions the gully is often straightforward snow, but if conditions are lean, two chockstones will provide difficulties and the route can be as hard as III,4. If all else fails, **Crumbling Cranny** on the right wall of Black Spout Left Branch provides a short Grade II.

Guidebooks

The Cairngorms (SMC), *Scottish Winter Climbs* (SMC), *Winter Climbs in the Cairngorms* (Cicerone).

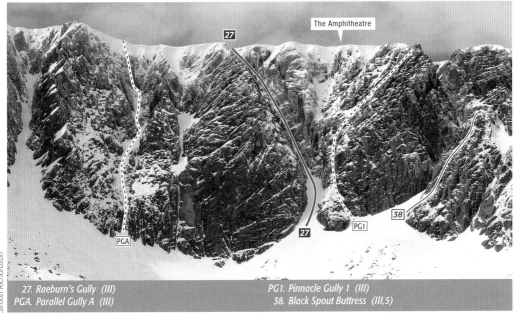

Simon Richardson

27. Raeburn's Gully (III)
PGA. Parallel Gully A (III)

PG1. Pinnacle Gully 1 (III)
38. Black Spout Buttress (III,5)

Deep Cut Chimney is possible in a variety of conditions. Here, Brian Duthie contemplates the powder-choked upper section, but the route also makes an excellent climb when conditions are lean

Henning Wackerhage

DEEP CUT CHIMNEY

Grade: 150m, IV,4
Location: Hell's Lum Crag, Loch Avon Basin
Route Base, Aspect & Rock Type: 900m, South-East facing, Granite
First Winter Ascent: Tom Patey & Derek Holroyd, 19 January 1958

Ian McIntosh

Back and footing up the spectacular crux section of Deep Cut Chimney. Climber Steve Langton

*H*ell's Lum Crag at the head of the Loch Avon Basin was one of the last great cliffs of the Cairngorms to be explored. The left side of the crag is characterised by the deep gully of Hell's Lum itself, and to the right of this is the prominent slit of Deep Cut Chimney. Ian Brooker and Marie Newbigging made the first ascent in September 1950, back and footing up the sidewalls to avoid the lush vegetation at the rear of the slit, to give a surprisingly good rock climb.

It was no surprise when the great Scottish climber Tom Patey made the first winter ascent of Deep Cut Chimney in January 1958. Patey had burst onto the winter scene seven years earlier with the first winter ascent of Douglas-Gibson Gully on Lochnagar, the first Grade V gully climbed in Scotland and pre-dating the famous Zero Gully on Ben Nevis (another Patey route) by six years. Patey was a mere 19 years old when he climbed Douglas-Gibson and over the next ten years he went on to make first ascents of dozens of the finest routes across the Highlands. In 1958 he was in his prime, and his matter-of-fact ascent of Deep Cut Chimney with Holroyd was summed up by the comment that he thought it similar in difficulty to Comb Gully on Ben Nevis.

This, of course, was a typical case of underselling and hundreds of subsequent ascents have confirmed Deep Cut Chimney as one of the great winter classics. The interest builds throughout the climb and reaches a peak below the outrageous-looking final pitch that looms above and looks a daunting prospect. Once you start back and footing there are some excellent hooks for your tools and somehow it all comes together. As my good friend Henning Wackerhage recounted, "It's a must-do climb, and the return from Inner Earth is good value for the grade!"

28

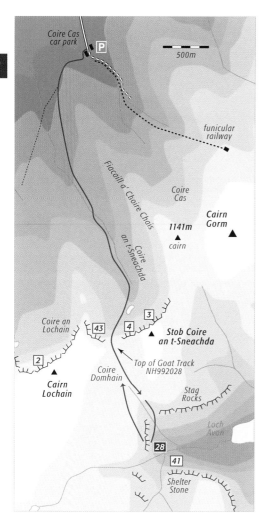

Conditions

Hell's Lum Crag takes significant drainage and faces south-east which makes it perfect for ice formation. However, this southerly aspect also makes it susceptible to thaw from mid-season onwards and although Deep Cut Chimney itself is well shaded, the cliff is not a good venue beyond early March. A variety of conditions may be encountered on the route, but it is a similar grade whether lean or iced. Under heavy snow, the chimney can become full of bottomless powder and is best avoided. Optimum conditions are likely to occur after a thaw and re-freeze, but the route is resilient to a variety of conditions.

Top Tips

It is best to avoid carrying rucksacks up the route, so gear up and leave them on the approach before descending to the crag. You may want to carry a GPS to mark the exact position of your kit.

Route Description

The narrow Deep Cut Chimney cuts into the buttress to the right of the prominent fault of Hell's Lum Crag. The normal approach uses a left-slanting diagonal fault, but the chimney can also be gained directly from below when the lower slabs are banked out. Climb the chimney and back and foot in a spectacular position around the capping chockstones.

Alternative Routes

The deep gully at the left end of the crag is **Hell's Lum**, which provides a classic climb that can vary from Grade II to IV,5 depending on When completely filled with snow it is a straight-forward route through remarkable scenery and highly recommended, but early in the season it can be a tougher mixed proposition. On the right side of the cliff, **Kiwi Gully** (III,4) follows a left-slanting line that readily forms ice. It is also more sheltered from the sun, so it is likely to remain climbable later in the season. **Escalator** (II), a well travelled route following a shallow fault on the very right side of the cliff, often forms shallow-angled ice, and makes a good back up if time is short or conditions are too poor to attempt any of the routes on the main face.

Guidebooks

The Cairngorms (SMC)*, Scottish Winter Climbs* (SMC), *Winter Climbs in the Cairngorms* (Cicerone).

Approach

From the Coire Cas car park at the top of the Cairn Gorm ski road, follow the approach into Coire an t-Sneachda as for The Message (p48). From the inner lochan, head south past the broad Fluted Buttress and ascend the Goat Track to its top at NH992028. From here walk down the easily-angled Coire Domhain for about 600m until the ground steepens, then cross the burn and descend diagonally under the cliff. The descent into Coire Domhain can be avalanche-prone in north-westerly winds, whereas the Goat Track often forms windslab if the wind has been from the opposite direction, so careful judgment of potential avalanche danger is required (**2hrs**).

Descent

From the top of the climb, head north-north-west into Coire Domhain to join the approach route.

Henning Wackerhage leaving the belay on the second pitch of Deep Cut Chimney

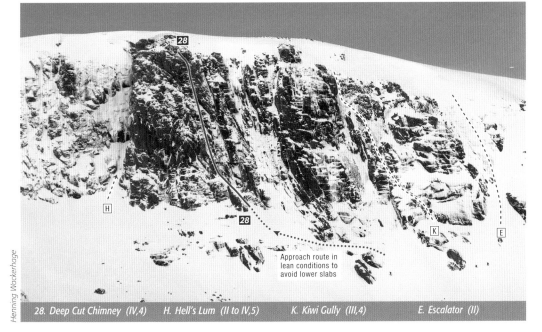

Approach route in
lean conditions to
avoid lower slabs

28. Deep Cut Chimney (IV,4)   **H. Hell's Lum (II to IV,5)**   **K. Kiwi Gully (III,4)**   **E. Escalator (II)**

Alan Mullin tackling the steep corner on the fourth pitch of Top Gun. Aonach Beag is the seventh highest mountain in Scotland and the west facing Raw Egg Buttress freezes hard and rimes up rapidly during a storm

Simon Richardson

TOP GUN

Grade: 160m, V,6
Location: Raw Egg Buttress, Aonach Beag
Route Base, Aspect & Rock Type:1000m, West facing, Mica Schist
First Ascent: Alan Mullin & Simon Richardson, 23 February 1999

Simon Richardson

Looking across to the West Face of Aonach Beag from Ben Nevis. The inverted triangle of Raw Egg Buttress lies right of centre, left of a prominent gully

*A*onach Beag is one of my favourite mountains. At 1234m it is one of the highest summits in Scotland, but it is a shy and retiring peak, dwarfed by the towering bulk of Ben Nevis next door. The same is true of its climbing, and it was only in the late 1980s that the winter potential on the mountain was seriously explored.

Early one morning in February 1999, Alan Mullin and I set off for Raw Egg Buttress, the finest feature on the West Face. Alan had swept into the limelight with a string of impressive repeats in the Northern Corries and the second winter ascent of The Needle on the Shelter Stone. Our plan was to climb the groove cutting through the centre of the buttress's impending headwall, so I set off up a long chimney-ramp that led to a short icefall. Alan attacked the icefall with impatient gusto, but three moves up I was dismayed to see his blunt crampons skate off the ice. His tools ripped and he landed in the soft snow at my feet in a tangle of ropes and slings. Alan dusted himself off, ignored my raised eyebrows and promptly dispatched the icefall with panache before disappearing into the chimney above.

Two pitches later we were below the headwall. It was very steep and cut by a corner with a prominent series of flakes on the left wall. Alan took the rack and without hesitation powered through the undercut start, and bridged elegantly up the corner above, slotting in protection first time. When my turn came I realised that this was a route full of surprises. Whenever the ground looked impossibly steep, there were hidden holds, perfect torques and slots for runners. We bubbled with excitement as I tackled the final puzzling overhang to stand on the flat top of the buttress. I called our route Top Gun, as much a tribute to Alan's raw talent, as it was to a brilliantly enjoyable climb.

29

Starting the steep corner on pitch four of Top Gun during the first ascent. Climber Alan Mullin

Simon Richardson

Approach

The Nevis Range Gondola provides easy access to Aonach Beag's icy North Face, but the mica schist buttresses on the West Face are best approached from Glen Nevis. From the car park at the head of the glen, follow the path through the gorge to the ruins at Old Steall. Leave the main glen here and head north up the hillside on the west bank of the Allt Guibh-sachan until under the West Face. A long pull from the glen floor up steep approach slopes leads to the foot of the crag (**2hrs 30mins**). About 30 minutes can be taken off this approach via a brutally steep shortcut over Bealach Cumhann (NN178700). This is best approached by taking the west side of the small burn which descends from the bealach, starting from where it cuts the upper minor path through the Glen Nevis gorge.

Descent

The wide snow gully to the right of Raw Egg Buttress provides a straightforward descent to Glen Giubh-sachan. Alternatively, and a safer option in poor snow conditions, go down the long south-west ridge and descend steep ground to the flats of the Allt Coire Giubhsachan opposite Meall Cumhann.

Conditions

High and exposed, the winter climbs on Raw Egg Buttress are climbable any time from November to April.

It is a good venue in a lean winter, as it rimes quickly in a north-westerly wind and comes into condition after a fresh snowfall. The main requirement is that the turf is frozen. Given the altitude and relatively remote situation this is not a good crag to visit under heavy snow, and beware approaching the cliff after strong easterly winds as the slopes may be avalanche-prone.

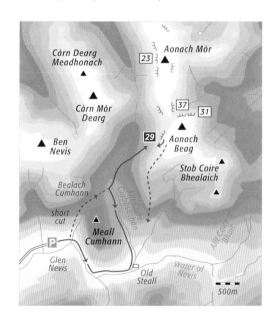

Top Tips

Mixed climbing on mica schist can be an unpredictable game; what looks straightforward from below, can often be very tricky. Bring a large and varied rack (including a selection of pegs and ice hooks) and take your time.

Description

High on the west face of Aonach Beag, a line of crags runs southwards for a kilometre from the Aonach Mòr-Aonach Beag col. Broken Axe Buttress lies at the northern end of the face, just left of a deep easy gully which slants up from the right. The slopes to its right include several rocky outcrops, and a number of icefalls form down the broken mixed ground between. Some 500m from the col, just to the left of a broad snow gully, is the prominent Raw Egg Buttress. Start 30m right of Raw Egg Buttress (the original line on the buttress) below a left-slanting chimney-ramp which begins a few metres up and right of the lowest rocks.

1. 40m Climb the chimney-ramp to its top, and move up to the barrier wall of Raw Egg Buttress.

2. 40m Climb the wall by a short icefall, and continue up, then right via chimneys to a good platform.

3. 50m The upper buttress is cut by three parallel right-slanting grooves. Climb the central one to a good

Alternative Routes

Raw Egg Buttress boasts several excellent summer and winter routes. The five winter routes on the front face all provide technical but well protected mixed climbing, while the south-west wall, one of the most impressive rock features in the area, has two excellent summer routes. **Raw Egg Buttress** (IV,5) is the easiest winter line on the buttress and takes the obvious right trending weakness across the front face. To the right of the south-west wall, **Ruadh Eigg Chimney** provides a short, but atmospheric IV,5 mixed climb.

Guidebooks

Ben Nevis (SMC), *Winter Climbs Ben Nevis and Glen Coe* (Cicerone).

ledge below the right side of the headwall. Step left and belay below a steep corner with a prominent series of vertical flakes on its left wall.

4. 20m Climb the steep corner to a good platform. An excellent pitch.

5. 10m Continue up the impending groove to the top.

Simon Richardson

29. Top Gun (V,6) — **RB. Raw Egg Buttress (IV,5)** — **RC. Ruadh Eigg Chimney (IV,5)**

Kevin Avery pulling through the crux section of Darth Vader. The difficulty of this pitch depends on the amount of build up deep in the chimney and the route is best climbed after a thaw and re-freeze

Bob Wightman

DARTH VADER

Grade: 100m, VII,7
Location: Creag Coire na Ciste, Ben Nevis
Route Base, Aspect & Rock Type: 1100m, North-East facing, Andesite
First Ascent: Simon Richardson & Chris Cartwright, 30 March 1997

Murdoch Jamieson

Descending Number Three Gully with the deep slit of Darth Vader hanging overhead on the right wall

*I*n the late 1990s Chris Cartwright and I started to investigate the untapped mixed climbing potential on Ben Nevis. The compelling chimney-crack (that we were later to name Darth Vader), which slices through the vertical wall at the left end of Creag Coire na Ciste, caught our imagination, and in the winter of 1997 we made a determined effort to climb it.

By the end of March most climbers had given up for the season and it was quiet in the CIC Hut over the Easter weekend. Although we didn't like to admit it, deep down we were both scared of Darth Vader because we knew we would have to stop somewhere in the chimney and had visions of a hanging belay in a monstrous offwidth crack. To counter this we had brought along my 'secret weapons' – homemade chocks constructed from scrap aluminum bar that I had found washed up on a beach on Skye.

Chris said it was his turn for a big lead so he set off up the vertical barrier wall leading into the chimney-crack. He calmly dealt with loose rattling holds, before disappearing into the chimney above. The rope ran out surprisingly quickly and soon I heard him whooping for joy. When I came up Chris was sitting in a hidden cave. It was the perfect belay and there was no need for the secret weapons. The downside was that the cave had a capping roof, which gave me a good struggle, because there was no build up on the ledge above to provide any placements. Another steep pitch and Darth Vader was finally in the bag.

Chris and I went on to climb another 30 new mixed routes on the Ben, but Darth Vader is our most popular route. It has seen dozens of ascents, and now that the pick placements have been cleaned out and it has become easier to protect, it makes an excellent target for a first Scottish Grade VII.

30

John Varco on the final chimney of Babylon. This popular mixed test-piece makes a fine companion to Darth Vader

Ian Parnell

Approach
From the CIC Hut, head over the domed rock west of the Hut, then negotiate a short vegetated wall at the foot of Coire na Ciste before heading up into the bowl of the corrie passing to the right of a small lochan. Climb snow slopes to reach the foot of Number Three Gully and bear right to the start of the route (about **1hr** from the Hut, see p30-31).

Descent
See Ben Nevis Approaches & Descents (p30-33).

Conditions
Although there is no vegetation on the route, Darth Vader is best approached as a Mixed climb rather than a pure Snowed-Up Rock route. This is because the exit from the cave on pitch 3 is considerably easier if there is ice or névé at the base of the bottomless groove. The optimum conditions for an ascent therefore, are a heavy snowfall followed by a deep thaw, then a freeze and second snowfall to bring the route back into acceptable winter condition.

Positioned at the left end of Creag Coire na Ciste the route rimes easily, however it receives the sun from the end of March onwards so is not a good late season route.

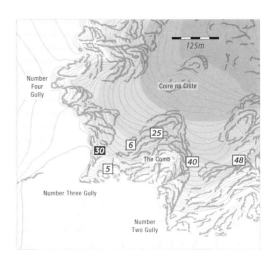

Top Tips

Despite its formidable offwidth appearance, a rack of large gear is not required. A set of wires (doubling up on small sizes) and cams up to size 3 plus a peg or two will suffice.

Route Description

Start directly below the chimney, just right of the foot of Number Three Gully.

1. 25m Climb an open icy groove to a ledge running beneath the vertical wall. Move right to belay on blocks just right of the chimney-crack.

2. 20m Entry to the chimney is barred by a 3m wall. Climb this (awkward) and continue up the chimney to a surprise cave stance.

3. 25m Pull over the roof of the cave and enter a bottomless groove (crux). Continue up the chimney above to belay on a large platform.

4. 30m Continue in the line of the main chimney-crack by moving slightly left, surmounting a short step and climbing the chimney at the back of the platform, before moving up and right to finish.

Starting the awkward 3m wall at the beginning of the second pitch of Darth Vader. Climber Kenny Grant

Viv Scott

Tim Neill

30. Darth Vader (VII,7)   C. Cornucopia (VII,8)

Alternative Routes

There are now many high standard mixed routes on Creag Coire na Ciste and the nearby Number Three Gully Buttress. **Babylon** (VII,7), which takes the right edge of Gargoyle Wall, (*see topo p57*), is the second most popular Grade VII in the vicinity. Similar to Darth Vader it requires a degree of freeze-thaw to come into condition, especially on the easier entry pitch. **Cornucopia** (VII,8), which lies opposite Babylon on the left wall of Creag Coire na Ciste overlooking Number Three Gully, is a well known test-piece but is at least a technical grade harder than Darth Vader. **The Survivor** (VII,7) on the left side of Number Three Gully Buttress (*see topo p145*) is another worthwhile mixed route that has yet to see the traffic of its better known neighbours.

Guidebooks

Ben Nevis (SMC), *Scottish Winter Climbs* (SMC), *Winter Climbs Ben Nevis and Glen Coe* (Cicerone), *Scottish Mountaineering Club Journal 2008.* For *SMC Journal* new routes see <*www.smc.org.uk/new-routes*>.

CHAPTER 4 ▶ TOP NICK

Winter climbing conditions at their best with hard névé, plastic ice and frozen turf

Stob Coire nan Lochan, Glen Coe; Cubby Images

Excellent ice conditions on Stand and Deliver, Aonach Beag

Guy Steven

*T*op Nick conditions are a winter climber's dream. The long wait through the early part of the season enduring thin conditions, gales, blizzards and thaws has all been worthwhile. Gullies are filled with ice, Mixed routes are rimed white, turf is frozen, and mountain Icefalls are thick and fat. Throw in the lengthening days of February and March, together with a high pressure system sucking in cold air from Scandinavia, and the great winter routes are ready and waiting.

More daylight means longer routes can be climbed and there is more time for approaches. This is a great opportunity to tackle long ridges like the **North-East Ridge** of Aonach Beag, which can be accessed from Glen Nevis to maximise the mountaineering nature of the day. Another established mountaineering must-do is **North-East Buttress** on Ben Nevis, where extra daylight and quick progress over consolidated snow and ice will allow more time for technical intricacies such as the Mantrap. Aptly named, this short steep wall lies near the top of the route, from where persevering on is a far better option than going down. It is no coincidence that the Victorian pioneers chose the longer days of early April to climb these routes.

Scottish winter climbing is famed throughout the world for its icy gullies and this is the time to climb them. Successive snowfalls followed by patterns of thaw and freeze, will fill gullies, chutes and clefts with soft plastic ice that is a delight to climb. By mid-February the great gullies on Creag Meagaidh such as **South Post Direct** should be well iced, and if the weather has been favourable with heavy snow carried on light winds, rarer routes such as **Smith's Gully** should be forming too. Gully climbing is a superb way of sampling steep ice. Narrow and enclosed, steep sections can often be overcome by bridging rather than vertical icefall techniques, and the climbing is more akin to rock climbing. Protection can be easier to arrange too, and there will often be a choice between ice protection in the gully or rock gear on the side walls. However, **Crowberry Gully** on Buachaille Etive Mòr requires an exceptional depth of snow to fill. As a consequence it does not come into condition every year, but when full and icy it is worth seeking out.

Lower lying ice routes such as **Hanging Garden Route** on Creag an Dubh Loch are less reliant on snow depth and are more reliably in condition when the weather is cold. Some routes are very difficult to predict. Ice conditions on the North Face of Aonach Beag can be fickle, so it is best to make a visit to **Royal Pardon** when reports of recent ascents have filtered through via the grapevine or been posted on the Internet.

With the fitness and confidence gained from climbing shorter routes earlier in the season, now is the time to push your limits. For a Grade III leader, **Black Spout Buttress** on Lochnagar is sure to provide a challenge and the experience will set you up for the next grade. Likewise, **Raeburn's Route** on Stob Coire nan Lochan is an excellent first Grade IV. Amongst the harder routes, **Tower Face Of The Comb** on Ben Nevis is the perfect follow-on from early season outings such as Gargoyle Wall, and the stature of **Postern** on the majestic Shelter Stone ensures its status as one of the prized Mixed routes in the Cairngorms.

Of course in reality, optimum conditions and blue sky weather rarely coincide, especially for the weekend climber with limited flexibility. In practice the number of perfect days may be limited to one or two a season, so it always makes sense to follow the Strategy Guidelines and plan for a back up route.

In addition, some climbs can be particularly difficult to find in condition. Emerald Gully on Beinn Dearg has frustrated many climbers looking for this elusive *Cold Climbs* tick, so should conditions prove disappointing, knowing that **Archway** offers a good alternative might well save the day.

When perfect conditions and good weather align, almost anything seems possible. This is a magical time in the winter season, so take every opportunity to savour it to the full.

Simon Richardson

Dave Hesleden enjoying Top Nick conditions of névé-encrusted slabs and steep plastic ice on Creag Coire na Ciste, Ben Nevis

Roger Webb high on the North-East Ridge. Hard snow and frozen turf combined with a snow-free approach are the ideal conditions for climbing this route the 'traditional' way from Glen Nevis

Simon Richardson

NORTH-EAST RIDGE

Grade: 500m, III
Location: North Face, Aonach Beag
Route Base, Aspect & Rock Type: 750m, North-East facing, Mica Schist
First Ascent: James Maclay, William Naismith & Gilbert Thomson, April 1895

Mike Watson

Looking south from the summit plateau of Aonach Beag. The prominent peak on the right is Sgùrr a' Mhaim

The Victorians were exceptional mountaineers. By the late 19th Century the Alps had been highly developed and technical standards were surprisingly high. The Highlands of Scotland by contrast had scarcely been touched. The main reason for this was lack of access, but the start of the West Highland Railway in 1894 unlocked the gates. All of a sudden Ben Nevis and its surrounding peaks were open to exploration.

In 1895, the SMC held its Easter meet in Fort William. On a tip-off from Norman Collie, James Maclay, William Naismith and Gilbert Thomson set off early from Spean Bridge bound for the North-East Ridge of Aonach Beag. During the long walk across peat bogs, the weather closed in and the party mistook the easy north-bounding spur of Stob an Chul-Choire for Aonach Beag's North-East Ridge. Whilst the party were questioning Collie's mountaineering judgment, the skies cleared to reveal their objective to the south. They made a swift descent to the foot of the ridge and climbed it in four hours, before returning over the summit of Aonach Mòr to Fort William. The first ascent of Aonach Beag's great North-East Ridge was a significant step forward in unravelling the mountaineering potential of the area.

The approach from Spean Bridge is long and emphasises the exceptional fitness and speed of the Victorians over rough ground. Three years earlier, Naismith and Thomson had made a remarkable 66 kilometre (41 mile) cross-country journey from Dalwhinnie to the Inveroran Hotel near Bridge of Orchy. They arrived at 8pm in time for dinner after a 16-hour march that included an ascent of Ben Alder, and were fresh enough to climb the Upper Couloir on Stob Ghabhar the following day.

Nowadays, Aonach Beag's North-East Ridge can be accessed via the Nevis Range Gondola, but the longer approach from Glen Nevis is probably more in tune with the spirit of the Victorian pioneers.

Alan Hardie moving up towards the pinnacles on the North-East Ridge

Karl Stewart

Approach

From the car park at the head of Glen Nevis, follow the path through the gorge to the ruins at Old Steall. Continue along the glen for 2km before heading north up the hillside near the Allt Coire a' Bhuic to the bealach at 731m (NN211705), which lies just east of Stob Coire Bhealaich (**2hrs**). Descend 100m, then head north-north-west for nearly 2km, crossing three burns (the second and third are deeply-cut), to enter An Cùl Choire at an elevation of approximately 700m. Climb a snow slope under the north side of the lower section of the North-East Ridge for 100m, to gain a short wide gully that slants up left to the start of the main ridge (**3hrs** from Glen Nevis).

Descent

The summit plateau of Aonach Beag is ringed by large cornices on its east and north faces and is a serious place in winter. The small summit cairn lies perilously close to the corniced edge and is normally buried by snow. The surest way off is to head north-west down snow slopes to gain the sharp north ridge of the mountain and zigzag down this to the safety of the Aonach Mòr-Aonach Beag col (NN194719). From here, descend the steep west slopes of the col and follow the Allt Coire Giubhsachan down to the ruins of Old Steall. If the weather is clear on the summit, it is quicker to go down the south-west ridge and descend steep ground to the flats of the Allt Coire Giubhsachan opposite Meall Cumhann.

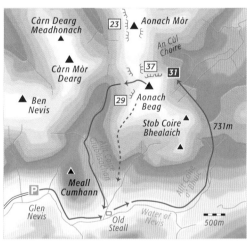

Conditions

Ascents of the North-East Ridge have been made in winter conditions as early as October, however it is probably best to wait until later in the season to ensure faster travel on consolidated snow. The route should be avoided in heavy snow conditions, as the approach will be laborious.

Top Tips

This is a long route and a big day out. Restrict the amount of equipment you carry to a minimal rack of a few slings, a handful of nuts and one or two pegs.

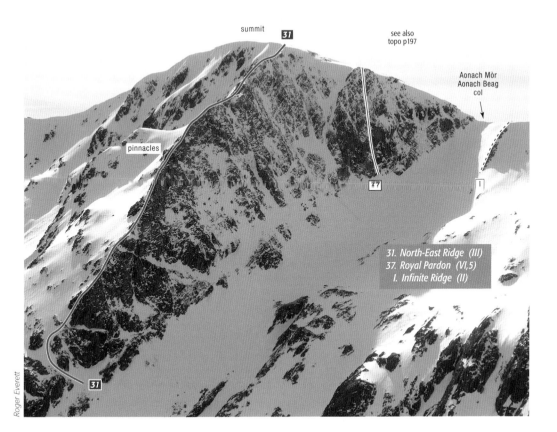

summit
31

see also
topo p197

Aonach Mòr
Aonach Beag
col

pinnacles

37

I

31. *North-East Ridge (III)*
37. *Royal Pardon (VI,5)*
I. *Infinite Ridge (II)*

31

Roger Everett

Route Description
Climb the wide gully to reach the lower section of the ridge, which is broad, broken, and open to much variation. After 100m the climbing becomes steeper and leads to a short level section before the blade-like pinnacles. The pinnacles can be climbed direct, but this section will be significantly harder than the rest of the route. Instead, turn them at half-height on their right side, regain the crest of the ridge, and pass an overhung nose on its left. A knife-edge snow ridge above leads to the easier and broader upper section that finishes approximately 50m from the summit.

Alternative Routes
West of An Cùl Choire, the upper corrie enclosed by the south and east ridges of Aonach Mòr, contains a prominent schist buttress, which is a conspicuous feature when viewed from the Aonach Mòr-Aonach Beag col. The crest of this is taken by the **Aonach Seang** (III). This has a high route base (1000m), so it provides a good back up if the lower section of the North-East Ridge is bare of snow. From a large ledge at the start of the main difficulties, climb the shallow chimney-groove that leads to a steep corner pitch on the left side of the buttress (crux). Above, climb more easily on the crest to a narrow neck, followed by easier ground to the plateau. The nearest buttresses to the Aonach Mòr-Anoach Beag col, lie to the left of the Aonach Seang and are **Infinite Ridge** (II) and **Inverted Ridge** (III,4). This second buttress resembles an inverted-V and the route follows its right leg.

Guidebooks
Ben Nevis (SMC), *Scottish Winter Climbs* (SMC), *Winter Climbs Ben Nevis and Glen Coe* (Cicerone), *Scottish Mountaineering Club Journal 2010 & 2011*. For *SMC Journal* new routes see <www.smc.org.uk/new-routes>.

Andy Harrison doing battle with the 40ft Corner, the last of the difficulties high on North-East Buttress

Rob Reglinski

NORTH-EAST BUTTRESS

Grade: 500m, IV,5
Location: Coire Leis, Ben Nevis
Route Base, Aspect & Rock Type: 1000m, North-East facing, Andesite
First Winter Ascent: William Naismith, Walter Brunskill, Alexander Kennedy, William King & Frances Squance, 3 April 1896

Henning Wackerhage

The imposing profile of North-East Buttress defines the Nevis skyline when approaching up the Allt a' Mhuilinn

"*B*en Nevis, the most malevolent, most elevated lump of rock on these islands, is itself an island, humping hideous flanks from endless bogs, hard to equal for hidden depths and character." The words of Jimmy Marshall often come to mind when I see Ben Nevis on the horizon from mountains to the south. The Ben is instantly recognised, not just by its height, but by its huge bulk and rounded shape; truncated on its right by the steep shoulder of North-East Buttress, which along with Tower Ridge is one of the two dominant structural features of the mountain.

The steep crest of North-East Buttress forms an imposing skyline when ascending the Allt a' Mhuilinn and it is no surprise that it was climbed in summer as far back as 1892 by the Hopkinson Brothers. The first winter ascent by Willie Naismith's team took place four years later, but details of their climb were forgotten until the 1970s. Over time North-East Buttress has become an established winter classic, regarded as one of the finest mountaineering expeditions in the country. The major difficulties are at the top and the infamous Mantrap, an insignificant looking three-metre high rock-step, has confounded many parties. After this, the difficulties are still not over as the second crux, the 40ft Corner, lies just above.

Even today, many teams find North-East Buttress a long and time-consuming adventure. It is not to be underestimated, but somehow over the years guidebook writers have toned down its difficulty. The climb was originally graded III, which later crept up to III/IV and it is now given IV,4. But with the technical difficulty of the Mantrap at least Tech 5, perhaps an even higher grade is justified? I have suggested a grade of IV,5 for this book, but somehow even this does not fully capture the commitment required for success on this magnificent route.

High on North-East Buttress looking over Tower Ridge towards Càrn Dearg Buttress and the Allt a' Mhuilinn

Peter Duggan

Approach
From the CIC Hut, continue up the glen and under the toe of the First Platform into Coire Leis. North-East Buttress starts well within Coire Leis and follows a right-trending ramp leading to the top of the First Platform, the first level section on the buttress (about **1hr** from the Hut, see p30-31).

Descent
See Ben Nevis Approaches & Descents (p30-33).

Conditions
North-East Buttress is climbable in a variety of conditions and being a ridge, it can save the day when it is too warm elsewhere on the mountain. The

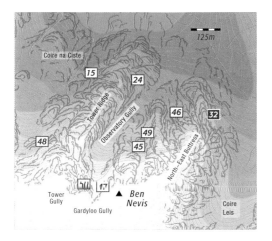

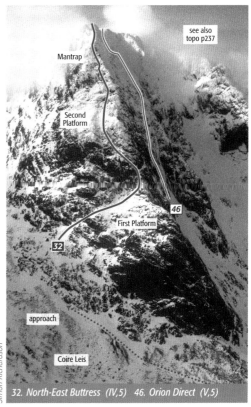

Simon Richardson

32. North-East Buttress (IV,5)   46. Orion Direct (V,5)

best opportunities are likely during the second half of the season when there will be consolidated snow and more daylight. The route should be avoided under heavy snow as the best line can be difficult to follow, and significant clearing will be required to find gear. The ideal scenario is being able to move together except for the short step above the Second Platform, the Mantrap, and the 40ft Corner. The Mantrap will normally be the crux and in times of old it was normal for a leader to remove any crampons and stand on the second's shoulder. The Mantrap is often bare of snow and typically has several pegs in place. The 40ft Corner can be straightforward under ice or névé, but in those conditions protection may be hard to get.

Top Tips
Using Slingsby's Chimney as an alternative start to gain the First Platform is suggested in some guidebooks. This is a direct and elegant route to take, but Slingsby's Chimney is often full of unconsolidated

Alternative Routes
The only ridge on Ben Nevis comparable in stature is **Observatory Ridge** (IV,4). Similar to North-East Buttress, this is a major undertaking that has had its difficulty underestimated over the years and some believe it merits a grade of V,4. Unlike North-East Buttress, the most difficult climbing is near the start, but the upper section can be very time-consuming under heavy snow.

Guidebooks
Ben Nevis (SMC), *Scottish Winter Climbs* (SMC), *Winter Climbs Ben Nevis and Glen Coe* (Cicerone).

powder, so unless you know it to be in good condition, it is advisable to start North-East Buttress from Coire Leis. The Mantrap can be avoided via the Tough-Brown Variant on the right flank of the buttress, by stepping down and moving into a groove which leads up to the foot of the 40ft Corner. Both the Mantrap and the 40ft Corner are relatively short sections, so having climbed that far, it is probably better to battle upwards rather than face a long retreat.

Route Description
Climb the right-trending ramp on snow to the crest of the buttress and the First Platform, then continue easily up the ridge to where the buttress steepens. Follow a shallow gully slanting up and left, before heading right up a series of grooves and short corners to gain the Second Platform, a snowfield on the left side of the crest. Climb the snowfield to its top and avoid the impending wall above by climbing a corner and a large step. Regain the ridge crest and follow it to the Mantrap. This is exposed and the technical crux, but it is short and well protected. Continue up the 40ft Corner above, or avoid it on the left by a short gully, to reach the summit slopes.

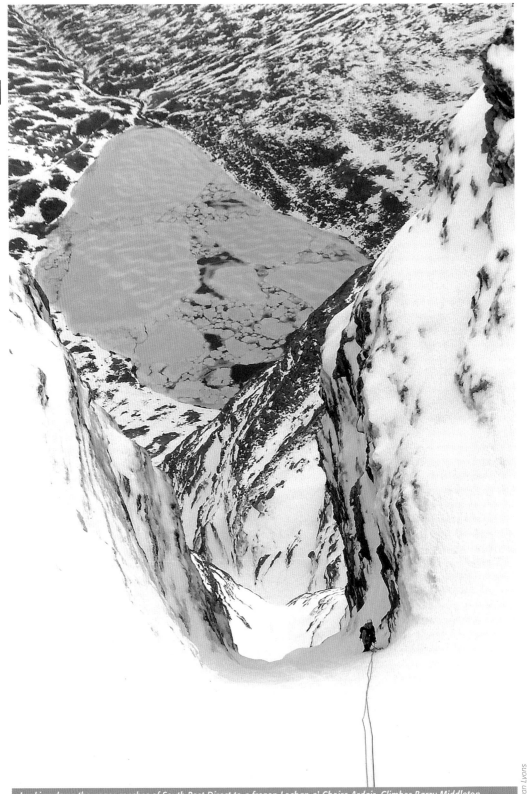

Looking down the upper reaches of South Post Direct to a frozen Lochan a' Choire Ardair. Climber Barry Middleton

Ewan Lyons

SOUTH POST DIRECT

Grade: 400m, V,4
Location: Coire Ardair, Creag Meagaidh
Route Base, Aspect & Rock Type: 750m, East facing, Mica Schist
First Ascent: Norman Tennent & Malcolm Slessor, 10 February 1956
Complete Ascent: Ian MacEacheran & Jock Knight, March 1964

Andy Inglis

James Sutton moving confidently up the first pitch of South Post Direct

*T*he alpine-scale Post Face in Creag Meagaidh's Coire Ardair is one of the largest mountain cliffs in the British Isles. The Victorians recognised its potential and in April 1896, the formidable team of Harold Raeburn, William Tough and Willie Douglas attempted Centre Post. In thawing conditions they reached the base of the impressive icefall halfway up the gully, but then made a swift retreat when the cornice collapsed!

The corrie was neglected in winter until April 1934 when Jim Bell made a matter-of-fact ascent of Staghorn Gully (III), then South Pipe (III) the following January. His finest ascent however, was Centre Post (III) with Colin Allan in March 1937. Although pitches of comparable difficulty had already been climbed on Ben Nevis (Raeburn had led Green Gully some 30 years earlier), Bell's concept of what was possible was visionary. He returned to Centre Post two winters later with an anxious Bill Murray to attempt the great icefall direct. Murray later recounted that Bell "arrived armed with a big bagful of sawn-off brass curtain rods... Tubular pitons, he had correctly discovered, gave better grip in water ice. He had ringed their tops and filed their bottoms... My inward dismay at the thought he may want me to lead... was relieved next day when we found insufficient ice in the gully. I had grim forebodings for next winter, when the attempt must be renewed, but was saved by that eleventh hour outbreak of war".

After another gap of nearly 20 years, interest was resumed in the Post Face when Malcolm Slesser and Norman Tennent climbed South Post in February 1956. A three-day wait camping below the cliff was rewarded by good freeze conditions allowing them to avoid the steep initial ice section by traversing in from the right. Six years later, Tom Patey added the first pitch and the first complete ascent fell to MacEacheran and Knight in March 1964, when they straightened out the third pitch. Today, South Post Direct is recognised as the finest of the Post Face ice routes.

33

Jenny Jarvis

Last Post lies to the left of South Post Direct. It provides a popular alternative that is often in condition. Climber Rob Jarvis

Approach

Start from the Creag Meagaidh National Nature Reserve car park on the A86 (NN483873). Follow a signposted footpath, passing to the north of Aberarder farm and continue by a path on the north side of the Allt Coire Ardair. The path stays well above and parallel to the burn, as the glen swings to the west, at which point the cliffs come into view. The path eventually descends to the floor of the glen, about 1km before Lochan a' Choire Ardair and continues to the north-east corner of the lochan (**1hr 30mins** to **2hrs**). In heavy snow, the path may be buried and progress then becomes very laborious and time-consuming.

Descent

The summit plateau of Creag Meagaidh is flat and featureless and great care is necessary when navigating in poor visibility. Several climbers have been benighted, or have inadvertently descended north to Glen Roy. Keep well away from the edge as massive cornices build up, especially above the Inner Corrie. In good conditions, it is possible to descend **Easy Gully** (I), otherwise it is best to descend via the deep col of the Window (NN426886), which leads to the Inner Corrie and so to the lochan. There is a line of old fence posts running down to the Window and a small rock outcrop has to be bypassed on the left.

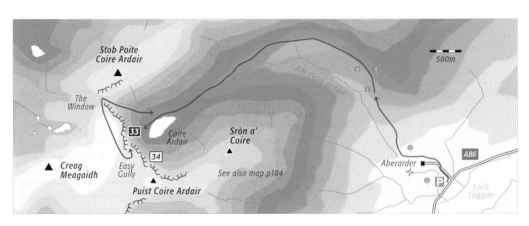

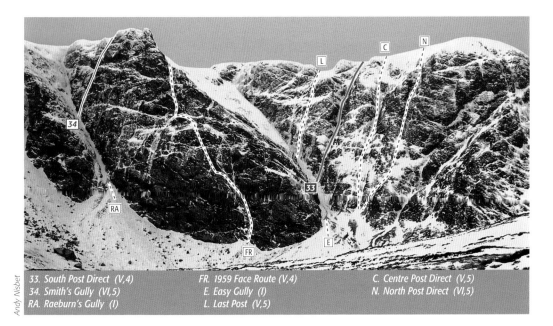

Andy Nisbet

33. South Post Direct (V,4)	FR. 1959 Face Route (V,4)	C. Centre Post Direct (V,5)
34. Smith's Gully (VI,5)	E. Easy Gully (I)	N. North Post Direct (VI,5)
RA. Raeburn's Gully (I)	L. Last Post (V,5)	

Conditions

The cliff holds plenty of snow and the majority of the routes are climbable in most winters. Although water-courses such as South Post can provide excellent, steep water-ice climbs during an early season period of cold weather, the best conditions are likely to be found during a cold and sunny spell in February or early March, a few weeks after heavy snowfall. The corrie is particularly prone to severe avalanches and should be avoided during a thaw or immediately after a heavy fall of snow.

Top Tips

The shattered nature of Creag Meagaidh's mica schist allows both pegs and nuts to be placed for runners and belays, but they can be well spaced. Ice screws are essential for the steeper ice routes and ice hooks can also be placed with surprising security in the huge areas of vegetation draped all over the cliff.

Route Description

A tremendous ice route, often climbable and low in the grade. The Post Face stretches from Easy Gully on the left to Staghorn Gully, where the cliffs turn in to the Inner Corrie. Its most prominent features are the four parallel slits of the Posts, separated by well defined buttresses. South Post is the second gully from the left and comprises two steep ice sections separated by easier-angled ground. Climb the initial tapering icefall in one long pitch and continue up the icy gully-line above to the second ice section, which normally provides the crux. Climb it from left to right in another long pitch and follow the couloir above, with one more ice section, to gain the plateau.

Alternative Routes

South Post is Grade III if the initial steep icefall is avoided by traversing up and left from the foot of Centre Post. The crux pitch can also be bypassed on the left and the gully-line regained above. **Last Post** (V,5) is another popular ice climb. It starts halfway up Easy Gully and climbs a series of three impressive icefalls. **Centre Post** (III) provides a magnificent route of alpine proportions. The lower 250m is a steep snowfield which leads, with one ice pitch, to the foot of the impressive icefall taken by **Centre Post Direct** (V,5). The easier version turns this on the right, before continuing up the gully. **North Post Direct** (VI,5), the rightmost and narrowest of the Posts is an excellent climb, but the ice takes a while to fully form and it is not often in perfect condition.

Guidebooks

Ben Nevis (SMC), *Scottish Winter Climbs* (SMC), *Winter Climbs in the Cairngorms* (Cicerone).

Good snow and ice conditions on the second pitch of Smith's Gully. Together with Point Five, Smith's is one of the most prized gully climbs in Scotland. Climber Helen Rennard

Henning Wackerhage

SMITH'S GULLY

Grade: 180m, VI,5
Location: Pinnacle Buttress, Creag Meagaidh
Route Base, Aspect & Rock Type: 850m, East facing, Mica Schist
First Ascent: Jimmy Marshall & Graham Tiso, 8 February 1959

Henning Wackerhage

Approaching Coire Ardair with the classic Meagaidh gullies in perfect condition

*J*immy Marshall was the step-cutting master throughout the 1950s. Marshall first visited Creag Meagaidh in 1951 and noted the winter possibilities of the gully-lines on the front face of Pinnacle Buttress. He returned with George Ritchie on a fine but windy day in February 1957, to find Robin Smith already at work on what was to become Smith's Gully. "We sat and jeered, watched him for a spell, comforted by the cataracts of powder thundering on his head, then moved on to traverse into the left-hand gully above the icefall." Marshall made a shrewd decision; although they also had a difficult battle with deep powder, they were eventually successful on their route which they named Ritchie's Gully, whilst Smith was forced to retreat in the snowy conditions.

Marshall returned to Meagaidh in February 1959 with the strong team of Jimmy Stenhouse, Dougal Haston and Graham Tiso. After a heavy snowfall followed by a period of freeze-thaw, conditions were perfect and the gullies were choked with ice. Whilst Haston and Stenhouse attempted what was later to become Centre Post Direct, Marshall and Tiso cut their way up Smith's Gully. This was a step-cutting tour de force, but the strain began to show on the final pitch "...the familiar flapping axe, spent arms, and frantic, stomping front-points were all in evidence...". The name of course, was a gibe at Robin Smith's failure on the route two years earlier. The following day, Marshall joined forces with Haston and Stenhouse to climb the long and open 1959 Face Route.

Smith's Gully was an outstanding ascent and comparable in difficulty with Minus Two Gully (V,5) on Ben Nevis which the same trio climbed two days later. They were considered the hardest gully climbs in Scotland until 1972, when the front pointing revolution took hold and Labyrinth Direct (VII,6) was climbed on Creag an Dubh Loch.

34

Henning Wackerhage

Helen Rennard cruising up the fourth pitch of Smith's Gully. This section is normally considered the crux

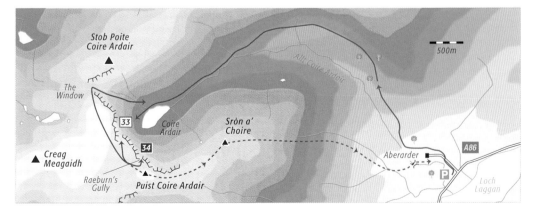

Approach

Follow the approach for South Post Direct (p180) to the lochan, then climb Raeburn's Gully to the foot of Smith's Gully, the central of the three parallel gullies cutting the huge triangular front face of Pinnacle Buttress (**1hr 30mins to 2hrs**).

Descent

The simplest descent is **Raeburn's Gully** (I), which does not often form a cornice. **Easy Gully** (I), (topo p181), is another alternative, but if snow conditions are poor it is safest to descend via the deep col of the Window as described for South Post Direct (p180). Alternatively in wild weather, it is possible to descend east over Puist Coire Ardair and down the ridge of Sròn a' Choire back to Aberarder.

Conditions

Pinnacle Buttress is not as exposed to a large snow-collecting plateau area as the Post Face, so the routes take longer to form. Smith's Gully is steep and sustained and will be extremely challenging if the ice is too soft for placing screws. The fourth pitch can be particularly difficult if unconsolidated. The best conditions are likely to be found during a cold spell between late January and early March, several days after a heavy snowfall. With solid ice and first time placements Smith's Gully can be a straight-forward Grade V, but normally it is considered a more difficult undertaking than Point Five Gully on Ben Nevis.

Top Tips

Take a selection of ice screws and half a dozen pegs. Some of the belay pegs are rather old and may need replacing (although other gear is also available).

Route Description

An outstanding climb taking a prominent line through the imposing front face of Pinnacle Buttress, Smith's

Henning Wackerhage

34. Smith's Gully (VI,5) F. The Fly Direct (VII,6)
RA. Raeburn's Gully (I) RI. Ritchie's Gully (IV,4)

Gully is one of the finest gullies in Scotland, with steep and interesting climbing all the way.
1. 35m Climb the gully exiting left at the top chock-stone and belay on the left at the top of a snow bay.
2. 20m Continue up a short steep ice wall to a second snow bay.
3. 45m Climb up the steep groove above to a broad terrace crossing the gully.
4. 45m Continue up the vertical ice wall above to easier ground.
5. 35m Finish up snow slopes. The cornice is normally bypassed on the right.

Alternative Routes

The gullies either side of Smith's Gully are Ritchie's Gully and The Fly Direct. **Ritchie's Gully** (IV,4) is the shortest of the three and provides a possible back up if Smith's Gully is not in prime condition, although the cornice can sometimes be difficult. **The Fly Direct** (VII,6) is one of Scotland's most prized ice climbs, but unfortunately it is not often fully formed. The route is serious and sustained, and the third pitch, which can be very intimidating if thinly iced, is normally considered to be the crux. The 450m-long **1959 Face Route** (V,4) takes the line of least resistance up the slightly easier-angled right side of Pinnacle Buttress. A classic route, it starts nearly 200m lower than Smith's Gully, so is far less often in condition (*see topo p181*).

Guidebooks

Ben Nevis (SMC), *Scottish Winter Climbs* (SMC), *Winter Climbs in the Cairngorms* (Cicerone).

The deep atmospheric cleft of Crowberry Gully makes it a classic route in the traditional mold. Climber Robert McMurray

Colin McGregor

CROWBERRY GULLY

Grade: 300m, IV,4
Location: North-East Face, Buachaille Etive Mòr
Route Base, Aspect & Rock Type: 750m, North-East facing, Rhyolite
First Ascent: Harold Raeburn, William Brigg & Scott Tucker, April 1909

Cubby Images

Crowberry Gully follows the deep slit running up to the left side of the summit of Buachaille Etive Mòr, one of Scotland's most iconic mountains. The long central gully-line is Great Gully

*I*n February 1983, Crowberry Gully was in excellent condition and I was the proud owner of a brand new sky blue Gore-Tex jacket. This new magic material had only recently been introduced, and I received numerous admiring glances as I soloed past several teams climbing Crowberry that day. The atmosphere was relaxed and friendly and the gully was a mix of hard snow and soft squeaky ice; even the Junction Pitch was in benign Grade III shape. I'm not normally known for the smartness of my attire, but I received several compliments on my jacket and somebody even asked if I was famous!

My friend Roger Webb also soloed Crowberry Gully that day. He was not wearing a fancy new Gore-Tex jacket and on the crux someone even offered him a top rope. Afterwards, Roger observed wryly that the different reactions to our ascents were a direct response to what we were wearing. But in fairness, Roger was particularly unkempt that day. He had driven up to the Coe with Gavin Mitchell, but when they arrived Roger realised that he'd forgotten his boots. Rather than write off the day, Gavin set off up the hill to solo a route and returned at midday to let Roger borrow his boots for the afternoon shift.

A superb raconteur, Gavin has never been one to let the truth get in the way of a good story. He explained in great detail to a crowd of bemused onlookers who had watched the rapid transition in the car park, that Roger and he were poor students and could only afford one set of winter climbing gear between them. This meant they had to climb alone – one in the morning and the other in the afternoon. Looking back, our day seems to capture the whole spirit of Crowberry Gully – a classic climb to be enjoyed in good conditions on a fine winter day.

35

Chris McDaid leading the Cave Pitch on Crowberry Gully. Conditions can vary, but this pitch often provides the crux

Tony Stone

Approach

Leave the A82 Glen Coe road at Altnafeadh (NN221563) and follow the track south, crossing a bridge over the River Coupall and passing to the left of the SMC's Lagangarbh Hut.

Take the left branch where the path splits at NN221558 and follow it around towards the cliffs on the north-east face of Stob Dearg, to where it crosses the lower reaches of Great Gully. From here it is possible to scramble up the easy-angled lower part of North Buttress and head left into Crowberry Basin, the prominent depression below Crowberry Ridge.

Alternatively, continue along the path below North Buttress to reach the well named Waterslide Slab and ascend steep slopes on the left, before making an exposed traverse right to enter Crowberry Basin (**1hr 30mins**).

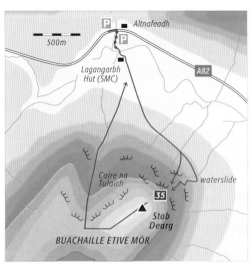

Descent

From the summit follow the south-west ridge (400m on bearing 250⁰ Grid, then 300m on 270⁰ Grid) to gain the level col at NN216542, at the head of Coire Tulaich. In poor visibility careful navigation is required and many parties remain roped. It is essential to avoid descending to the right (north) too early. From the col descend northwards down Coire na Tulaich, crossing a possible cornice at the top, to reach easier slopes leading back to Lagangarbh. The upper slopes can be very icy (leave crampons on) and the area is also avalanche-prone.

Conditions

Crowberry Gully varies greatly from year to year and with perfect build up it will be a straightforward snow climb with short steeper ice sections. When leaner it will provide significantly more challenge, and the Junction and Cave pitches may be very technical if they are just verglassed. Good cover on the traverse right from the Junction is desirable. The best conditions are likely to be found during a cold spell in the middle of a season that has had significant snowfall earlier in the winter to fill the gully, followed by adequate time to allow consolidation.

Top Tips

Despite its proximity to the road, Buachaille Etive Mòr can be a dangerous mountain. Avalanches occur regularly in the Great Gully and Crowberry Basin areas and the only practicable descent via Corrie na Tulaich is notorious. There have been both fatal falls down the headwall of the corrie when icy, and lethal wind-slab avalanches after heavy snowfall. All in all, it is worth saving Crowberry Gully for a good day, rather than pushing it when conditions are marginal.

Route Description

The major gully system between Crowberry Ridge and North Buttress, leading to the summit of an iconic mountain, is one of Scotland's most classic winter

35. Crowberry Gully (IV,4)
L. Crowberry Gully, Left Fork (IV,5)
N. Naismith's Route (IV,5)
NZ. North-East Zig-Zag (III,4)

Rab Anderson

climbs. The gully is typically climbed in five pitches, but the difficulty of these varies considerably with the depth of snow. From Crowberry Basin, climb easy snow to where the gully narrows and surmount a chockstone. Continue up more snow to the Thincrack Chimney, which provides 10m of icy slabs or steep steps. Above is the Junction with the impressive **Left Fork** continuing directly ahead. Instead, follow the Right Fork by making a delicate traverse across slabs. An easier pitch of snow leads to the Cave Pitch, which is normally the crux. Climb this via a screen of ice on its right wall and continue up snow to exit close to the summit.

Alternative Routes

The Left Fork (IV,5) provides an exciting alternative finish. It is a good climb, but different in character to the original route as it involves back and footing up the verglassed walls of a deep enclosed chimney to surmount an overhanging capstone. **North-East Zig-Zag** (III,4) climbs the right flank of Crowberry Gully, and is a useful back up if there is a risk of avalanche in the gully itself. The other great winter climb from Crowberry Basin is Crowberry Ridge via **Naismith's Route** (IV,5). This starts from the narrows of Crowberry Gully and follows the left-hand of two chimneys to reach the crest.

Guidebooks

Glen Coe (SMC), *Scottish Winter Climbs* (SMC), *Winter Climbs Ben Nevis and Glen Coe* (Cicerone).

Ross Hewitt climbing the gully leading up to the fork of Hanging Garden Route in superb snow and ice conditions

Henning Wackerhage

HANGING GARDEN ROUTE

Grade: 300m, V,4
Location: Creag an Dubh Loch
Route Base, Aspect & Rock Type: 750m, North-East facing, Granite
First Ascent: Andy Nisbet & Alf Robertson, 6 January 1977

Neil Morrison

Looking across to the great cliffs of Creag an Dubh Loch from the approach

*W*ith more than a kilometre of 300m-high cliffs, Creag an Dubh Loch is rightly recognised as one of the finest rock climbing venues in the British Isles. This reputation transfers to winter, but only in a qualified way. Success on one of the great lines on Central Gully Wall would crown any Scottish winter career, but conditions are so rare that they reside in a highly specialised category. The four winter climbs on this face have only had six ascents between them over a period of 30 years.

Fortunately the huge depression left of the Central Slabs holds more snow and has a more northerly orientation, so it ices readily on a consistent basis. The big tick here is Labyrinth Direct (VII,6), the most difficult pure ice gully in Scotland, but more amenable in nature is Hanging Garden Route.

For many years the route was graded IV and when Dave Hesleden and I started up it as a fall-back option one New Year, we quickly realised we had severely underestimated it. We had come prepared for mixed climbing so our axes and crampons were blunt and we carried no ice screws, but once we were above the Hanging Garden, the big depression in the centre of the face, the Left Fork was a continuous ribbon of brittle ice. Cracks are sparse on this section of cliff and the few protection possibilities were obscured by a bullet-hard glaze of ice. We climbed three long and sustained pitches with only our ice tools for belays and no runners. I was immensely grateful that I was climbing with Dave, one of Britain's finest all rounders.

A couple of years later when Andy Nisbet asked me to review the script for the first edition of the SMC's Scottish Winter Climbs, I suggested Hanging Garden Route should be upgraded to V,4. Andy agreed, and it has kept that grade ever since in recognition of a long, superb, committing and ultimately very satisfying ice climb.

36

Labyrinth Couloir on the approach to the Hanging Garden. Climber Ross Hewitt

Henning Wackerhage

Approach

From the Spittal of Glenmuick car park (Pay & Display) follow the vehicle track southwards to near the north end of Lock Muick. Bear right along a path passing a boathouse to gain the vehicle track on the west side of the loch and follow it to its end at the shooting lodge of Glas-allt-Shiel. From here, a good path leads through trees and then up the north side of the Allt an

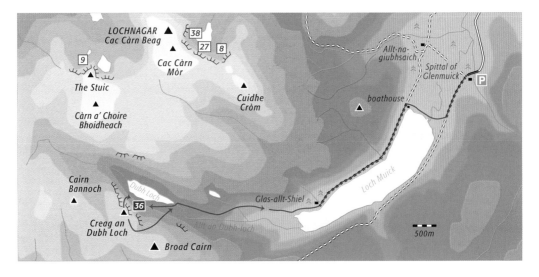

Simon Richardson

36. Hanging Garden Route, Left Fork (V,4)
R. Hanging Garden Route, Right Fork (V,4)
LD. Labyrinth Direct (VII,6)

LE. Labyrinth Edge (IV,5)
C. Central Gully (I)

Dubh-loch to gain the east end of the Dubh Loch. Cross the river and skirt around the western side of the loch (or walk across it if well frozen) to reach the foot of the prominent Labyrinth Couloir (**2hrs** to **2hrs 30mins**).

Descent
Either descend Central Gully (straightforward Grade I) or walk south-east from the top of the climb to the open col between Creag an Dubh Loch and Broad Cairn and follow the depression leading down to the east end of the Dubh Loch.

Conditions
A sustained period of cold weather is required to make climbing on Creag an Dubh Loch a viable proposition, however with a north-east aspect, the Hanging Garden routes form more readily. Unlike the rest of the cliff, which tends to build ice mid-season, Hanging Garden Route can be climbable as early as December and a wet autumn will help ice formation. However the cliff is very susceptible to thaw and will strip quickly, even after only a few hours of warm air.

Top Tips
Protection is hard to find, so take ice screws, pegs and ice hooks and make sure your axes and crampons are sharp!

Route Description
Creag an Dubh Loch is divided into two main sections by Central Gully. The left-hand section is cut by the prominent Labyrinth Couloir that leads to a high snowfield known as the Hanging Garden. Above, the couloir splits into two forks. Either can be climbed, but the Left Fork is the more obvious line with ever increasing exposure. Start up the couloir, move left to gain the Hanging Garden and continue up the gully above to reach an inverted triangular buttress that separates the two forks. Move left to belay on a pedestal a little way up the left fork, then continue up a steep icy groove until the way is blocked by a steep wall. Traverse left across an awkward slab and ascend easing ground to the cornice that is normally passed on the left.

Alternative Routes
The icy stepped fault of the **Right Fork** (V,4) is an obvious alternative line, but it can lead to a difficult cornice. If the ice in the Hanging Garden area is poor, **Labyrinth Edge** (IV,5) provides a good alternative mixed route of equivalent stature. It takes a vegetated line on the left side of the Central Slabs with a high-light pitch up a vegetated crack cutting through the left edge of the exposed Sea of Slabs.

Guidebooks
The Cairngorms (SMC), *Scottish Winter Climbs* (SMC), *Winter Climbs in the Cairngorms* (Cicerone).

37

Roger Webb fully engaged on the crux pitch of Royal Pardon during the first ascent

Simon Richardson

ROYAL PARDON

Grade: 220m, VI,5
Location: North Face, Aonach Beag
Route Base, Aspect & Rock Type: 950m, North facing, Mica Schist
First Ascent: Roger Webb & Simon Richardson, 18 February 1987

Guy Steven

Nearing the top of the first pitch of Royal Pardon. Climber Paul Swail

*D*uring the winter of 1983 Roger Webb spotted large areas of ice on the north face of Aonach Beag and in November 1985 he persuaded me to take a look. This was pre-Aonach Mòr Gondola days and after battling drifting snow and poor visibility, it took us more than six hours to gain the Aonach Mòr-Aonach Beag col. Unsure of exactly where we were, we settled on the easiest looking line on the face up a snowy couloir, which resulted in a Grade II we called Whiteout. Through the mist and murk we could make out many impressive ice features and vowed to return.

Our chance came the following season, one perfect February day. As we dropped down from the col we marvelled at the number of unclimbed ice-lines, but were struck by the compelling central icefall. We didn't have the nerve to attempt it that day, so instead we climbed King's Ransom – a narrow gully with steep mixed ground to finish. On the summit we met Geoff Cohen, Des Rubens, Dave Broadhead and Rob Collister who had just climbed the North-East Ridge. We knew they must have seen the icefall too, so with potential competition in the offing, we took a day off work and were back in position three days later.

After a long first pitch I was surprised to find two old pegs and an abseil sling at the foot of the main icefall. (I have never discovered who left them and would love to find out some day). Roger started up the icefall, but after climbing ten metres the split pins in his Chacal sheared and the pick bent flat against the ice. A delicate manoeuvre followed as he lowered a rope to change his hammer with mine... and we both breathed again. Above, a series of icefalls led to the top. Continuing the royal theme we called the route Royal Pardon, in recognition of Roger's lucky escape and our ascent of a quintessentially perfect Scottish ice route.

Paul Swail reaching for an ice screw on Stand And Deliver. The route continues up the spectacular vertical ice pillar above

Guy Steven

Approach

The Aonach Mòr Gondola provides the easiest access to Aonach Mòr (see Grooved Arete p64). The Aonach Mòr-Aonach Beag col (NN194719) is the key to approaching the routes on the north side of Aonach Beag and can easily be reached by descending from the summit of Aonach Mòr in about 15mins. From the col, descend close under the north face (steep and possible cornice) for 100m, to reach the start of the route (**1hr 30mins** from the Top Station).

If an early start is required, then the col is best reached on foot from Glen Nevis. From the car park at the head of the glen, follow the path through the gorge to the ruins at Old Steall. Leave the main glen here and head north up the hillside on the west side of the Allt Coire Guibhsachan. After 250m of ascent the angle eases and a vague path leads towards the unnamed bealach between Càrn Mòr Dearg and Aonach Mòr.

Near the head of the glen, at approximately NN186716, strike up the steep slope to the north-east which eventually leads to the col between Aonach Mòr and Aonach Beag, after a tough climb of 550m (**3hrs to 3hrs 30mins**). About 30 mins can be saved by taking the brutally steep shortcut over the Bealach Cumhann (NN178700). This is best approached by ascending the west side of the small burn which descends from the bealach, starting from where it cuts the upper minor path through the Glen Nevis gorge.

Descent

As for the North-East Ridge of Aonach Beag (p172).

Conditions

The North Face of Aonach Beag is a serious cliff and good ice conditions are a prerequisite for an enjoyable experience. Unfortunately, predicting their occurrence has perplexed many observers over the years. The North Face is not a cliff that holds the cold and the surrounding topography means cold air sinks and drains away north towards Leanachan Forest. Fortunately, the face is visible from the summit slopes of Aonach Mòr, so keeping an eye on conditions via the avalanche blogs, or making a reconnaissance after climbing on Aonach Mòr will pay dividends.

Top Tips

There is a good belay at the top of the first pitch, but typically rock anchors are well spaced. In good conditions it is possible to belay on ice screws throughout, and sacks can be left at the col if the weather is fine. Most parties approach from the Aonach Mòr Gondola, but Royal Pardon is a route that will repay a very early start from Glen Nevis. It certainly beats the crowds!

Route Description

The icefall that hangs down from the shallow depression in the centre of the buttress is a compelling line and has become a modern classic.

1. 50m Start directly below the icefall and climb a series of icy steps to a flake belay at the bottom right side of the main icefall.

2. 40m Climb the icefall to a belay on the right.

3. 20m Continue up the final ice wall to a broad snow

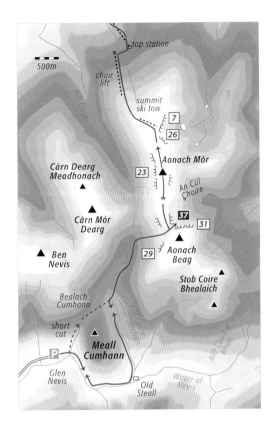

couloir.

4 to 6. 110m Follow the couloir for 50m to where it steepens into an icy gully and follow this, trending up and left for two pitches to the top.

Alternative Routes

King's Ransom (VI,6), which starts up the narrow gully bounding the left side of the steep section of Aonach Beag's North Face, is the most reliable technical route on this part of the mountain. **Stand And Deliver** (V,6), the imposing icefall directly above the initial gully of Whiteout provides a long and sustained ice pitch which also readily comes into condition. To the right of Royal Pardon is **Camilla** (V,5), a good sustained ice route based on the twin icicles which hang down the right side of the barrier wall. If all else fails, **Whiteout** (II) should still be possible. It follows the right branch of the broad Y-shaped feature on the right side of the face.

Guidebooks

Ben Nevis (SMC), *Scottish Winter Climbs* (SMC), *Winter Climbs Ben Nevis and Glen Coe* (Cicerone).

see also
topo p173

Aonach Mòr
Aonach Beag Col

37. *Royal Pardon* (VI,5)
31 *North-East Ridge* (III)

K. *King's Ransom* (VI,6)
C. *Camilla* (V,5)

S. *Stand And Deliver* (V,6)
W. *Whiteout* (II)

Murdoch Jamieson

197

The two-tiered Black Spout Buttress looking splendid under a mantle of deep mid-winter snow

Simon Richardson

BLACK SPOUT BUTTRESS

Grade: 250m, III,5
Location: North-East Coire, Lochnagar
Route Base, Aspect & Rock Type: 900m, East facing, Granite
First Winter Ascent: John Tewnion, Charlie Hutcheon, Doug Sutherland & Kenny Winram, 9 January 1949

Greg Strange

Ian Sommerville, Tom Anderson and Kevin Tremain tackle the lower section of Black Spout Buttress in good conditions of consolidated snow and frozen turf

The great North East Corrie of Lochnagar is a superb winter playground, but apart from the two branches of the Black Spout its routes are long and challenging. Even the easier gullies such as Raeburn's and Parallel A, require some ice and a little build up to make them climbable, so traditionally the buttress routes are climbed as often as the gullies.

With a cliff height of 250m, mixed routes on Lochnagar are not quick affairs, but the most popular ones are Shadow Buttress A and Black Spout Buttress. Of the two, I think Black Spout Buttress is the better climb; it is superbly positioned on the right flank of the great rift of the Black Spout and stares you right in the face from the other side of the corrie, when you reach the Meikle Col on the approach.

Black Spout Buttress is divided into two halves. The lower section is typical Cairngorm vegetated grooves and can be unpleasant if not properly frozen. Above a midway terrace, the route is better defined and takes a series of steep steps on superb rough granite in a great position. The rock is less vegetated here and the climbing positive and well supplied with large holds. Some think it hard for the grade, especially on the crux chimney. To recognise this, the technical grade was increased to 5 in the latest SMC Cairngorms guidebook, but even so, the Grade III tag is possibly a little mean for such a long route.

When you top out on the plateau, you have to walk around the corrie rim to reach the descent to the Meikle Col. If it is dark or the weather is poor, this will add to an already long day. However, this can only enhance the feeling that you've climbed a real Cairngorms winter classic.

38

Dave Riley moving along the narrow level section of Black Spout Buttress

Alan Crichton

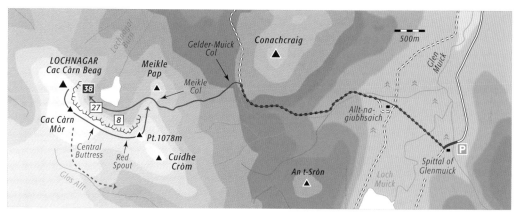

38. Black Spout Buttress (III,5) **BV. Black Velvet (V,7)**
D. Direct Variation (V,6) **W. Western Slant (III)**
BS. Black Spout (I)

Simon Richardson

is a popular gearing up spot. From here, Black Spout Buttress can be seen just right of the prominent gully of the Black Spout. It is easily approached by crossing the corrie on a bearing of 286° Grid (**2hrs**).

Descent
As for Raeburn's Gully (p152).

Conditions
Black Spout Buttress is climbable from the first snows and a good choice under powder. Later in the season the whole of West Buttress catches the sun and strips fast, however Black Spout Buttress lies more in shadow and is climbable until early March.

Top Tips
Early in the season, the lower section of Black Spout Buttress may lack snow cover or not be properly frozen. In this situation the upper half can be reached by climbing 30m of broken ground up the right wall of the Black Spout to belay by a small pinnacle. The upper section of the buttress can then be climbed as a Snowed-Up Rock route, as it does not rely on frozen turf.

Route Description
An excellent winter route with several technical sections. Start below a gully about 10m right of the Black Spout. Climb the gully and continue more easily for about 60m to a level crest marking the end of the lower section. The upper section begins with a blocky ridge that leads to a short chimney, which is more difficult than it looks. Continue more easily to a short wall, which is climbed with a tricky exit up the corner on the right. Above, a steep 10m-high wall is bypassed by traversing right into the top of Western Slant, the fault-line bounding the buttress on the right. Regain the crest on the left as soon as possible, and finish up easier ground to the plateau.

Approach
From Spittal of Glenmuick car park (Pay & Display), follow the approach to the Meikle Col as for Magic Pillar (p68). From the col, drop down and cross the broad corrie of the Southern Sector, then ascend a little to gain rocks at the foot of Central Buttress which divides the Southern Sector from the North-East Coire. The large metal first aid box at NO251857, situated on a platform approximately 100m from the foot of Central Buttress,

Alternative Routes
Shadow Buttress A is the obvious sister route to Black Spout Buttress. It is similar in length, but a recent rock-fall has increased it from Grade III to IV,5. Black Spout Buttress has three harder starts – **Black Velvet** (V,7) takes a direct line up the steep lower crest and **Queue Jump** (IV,5) follows a ramp on the lower right wall of the Black Spout. The **Direct Variation** (V,6) takes the curving groove between Black Velvet and the original route. The upper section of Black Spout Buttress can also be climbed direct over the two towers above the chimney pitch at Tech 6 to provide a more sustained route. Black Spout Buttress is defined on its right side by **Western Slant** – a good Grade III.

Guidebooks
The Cairngorms (SMC), *Scottish Winter Climbs* (SMC), *Winter Climbs in the Cairngorms* (Cicerone), <www.scottishwinter.com>

Excellent mixed climbing conditions on the upper section of Raeburn's Route

Cubby Images

RAEBURN'S ROUTE

Grade: 150m, IV,4
Location: Stob Coire nan Lochan
Route Base, Aspect & Rock Type: 900m, North-East facing, Rhyolite
First Ascent: Harold Raeburn, Charles Inglis Clark & Jane Inglis Clark, April 1907

Mike Pescod

Sarah Lewis enjoying the lower section of Raeburn's Route

Tall and columnar buttresses separated by deep gullies make Stob Coire nan Lochan the most majestic of Glen Coe's corries. The cliff is famous for its modern mixed test-pieces such as Central Grooves and Unicorn, but the main gullies are so striking that they demand to be climbed. SC Gully (III), which cuts straight up between the South and Central Buttresses, was first ascended in the 1930s, and is one of the most popular climbs in the Coe. Twisting Gully (III,4), another well known classic, wriggles up to the left of South Buttress. An easy pitch leads to a deep recess where the gully forks. On the first ascent in the 1940s, Bill Murray took the left branch, but Jimmy Marshall's Right Fork (IV,5) is the more aesthetic way to go.

The gullies are classic, but if you descend by following the cliff rim round to the north and cut back down easy ground to the corrie, the line of Raeburn's Route on Central Buttress stands out as the route to do. The guidebook gives it IV,4, but it was first climbed by Harold Raeburn and the Inglis Clarks way back in 1907, so can it really be that difficult?

A ramp leads up to the crest in a long mixed pitch from the left. A move right at its top takes you to an exposed stance overlooking NC Gully on the right. You follow the edge to a tower and bypass it on the right. Above is a short vertical wall. Could this really have been climbed back in 1907? Perhaps it is Grade IV after all? A good nut placement (Raeburn wouldn't have had that), a long reach and your picks thud into the hidden but reassuring turf above. A sharp pull and you're up!

Rob Milne climbing the initial chimney of Raeburn's Route. The climb moves right below the steep impasse above

Rob Anderson

Approach

From the large car park (NN168569) on the south side of the A82, cross the River Coe by the bridge at NN167566 and ascend the deep glen between Gearr Aonach and Aonach Dubh. After a steady climb, surmount a final steepening to gain the corrie floor (**1hr 30mins** to **2hrs**). From here it is another 30 minutes to the foot of the route, but the exact time will depend on what the snow is like underfoot. If it is deep this section can take a surprisingly long time, and even more so if there is no trail in place (**2hrs** to **2hrs 30mins**).

Descent

The safest route is to follow the edge of the corrie north towards Aonach Dubh and descend a short, easy-angled snow slope to the corrie floor. Another popular descent is to head down the centrally situated **Broad Gully** (I). This provides a faster descent, but any potential avalanche hazard should be assessed first.

Conditions

Stob Coire nan Lochan is the most reliable winter cliff in Glen Coe and is often possible to climb here when

other venues in the area are not in condition. The route has a surprising amount of turf, but parties often struggle after venturing onto the route with the first pitch not fully frozen. Conversely, overly wintry conditions can be a problem, as the slabby wall above the Tower

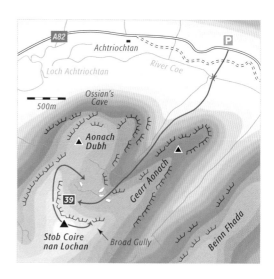

is awkward under deep snow and protection can be buried. Good conditions for Raeburn's Route are well frozen turf, some useful névé, clear cracks and a layer of rime ice on the rocks. In ideal conditions, the upper two pitches can be perfect névé.

Top Tips

Many parties inadvertently climb the initial chimney in its entirety and do not break out right at the impasse. This way is steep and sustained and will add a technical grade to the ascent. If the route is very busy, or you are starting late in the day, it is possible to avoid the long crux first pitch by traversing in from the lower section of NC Gully. Similarly, if time is running short after the first two pitches, it is possible to escape right into NC Gully and finish up that.

Route Description

An excellent route with exciting positions taking the right edge of the prominent Central Buttress. Start 10m right of the steep front face of the buttress (cut by the distinctive line of Central Grooves) beneath a chimney that narrows with height. Climb this to an impasse and break out right up easier ground to gain a short groove leading to the buttress crest (a long pitch). Move up to the Tower and climb it from the right via a short chimney that divides it from the main face. Climb the slabby wall above and continue to a steep section that can be taken direct, or avoided on

Alternative Routes

Stob Coire nan Lochan is well known for its Mixed climbs, but most are significantly harder than Raeburn's Route. The gullies are highly sought after too and make good alternative options. **SC Gully** (III,4) is one of the classic winter climbs in Glen Coe taking the deep cleft between the towering South and Central buttresses. **Twisting Gully** (III,4) is a superb and continuously interesting climb up the left flank of South Buttress. Its **Right Fork** (IV,5) is just as good but a little steeper and requires ice. **Moonshadow** (IV,5) breaks out right in a superb position from halfway up Twisting Gully Right Fork and ascends the front face of South Buttress. The classic triptych here is SC Gully, Twisting Gully and Raeburn's Route, and if you are going well, all three are perfectly possible in a day.

Guidebooks

Glen Coe (SMC), *Scottish Winter Climbs* (SMC), *Winter Climbs Ben Nevis and Glen Coe* (Cicerone).

the right. Go back left to the crest and finish more easily to the top.

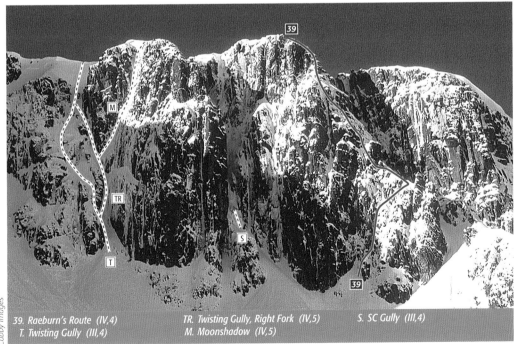

39. Raeburn's Route (IV,4)
T. Twisting Gully (III,4)

TR. Twisting Gully, Right Fork (IV,5)
M. Moonshadow (IV,5)

S. SC Gully (III,4)

Cubby Images

The corner-groove on the second pitch of Tower Face Of The Comb is one of the finest mixed pitches on Ben Nevis. Climber Henning Wackerhage

Henning Wackerhage

TOWER FACE OF THE COMB

Grade: 250m, VI,6
Location: Coire na Ciste, Ben Nevis
Route Base, Aspect & Rock Type: 1000m, North facing, Andesite
First Ascent: Robin Smith & Dick Holt, 1 January 1959

Henning Wackerhage

Robbie Miller on the first pitch of Tower Face Of The Comb

*W*hen Harold Raeburn made the first ascent of Green Gully in 1906 his initial intention was to climb a line up the crest of The Comb, the impressive buttress dividing the back wall of Coire na Ciste. Half a century later, his vision was realised by Robin Smith and Dick Holt when they climbed Tower Face Of The Comb.

I still find it incredible that Smith and Holt had the audacity to attempt this route on New Year's Day back in 1959. To choose a day with only seven hours daylight for a 250m-long mixed route that would take technical Nevis climbing forward by a full grade is astonishing. Tower Face Of The Comb was the first new route Smith added to Ben Nevis and no doubt the confidence gained from this ascent prompted the pair to return at the end of the month, venture onto the awe-inspiring Orion Face for the first time in winter, and climb the Smith-Holt Route.

The winter of 1959 was a great season on the Ben with first ascents of Point Five and Minus Two gullies, but it is Tower Face Of The Comb that has retained its cachet. In the 1980s, when ascents of the great Ben ice routes were becoming commonplace, it acquired a somewhat enigmatic reputation. Despite several attempts, I don't know of any repeats until that by Stephen Venables and Victor Saunders in February 1986.

Since then it has been climbed many times and several variations have been added. It is now regarded as one of the greatest mixed routes on the mountain. Choose icy conditions to enjoy the route to the full and marvel at the skill and tenacity of Smith and Holt more than 50 years before.

Looking down the second pitch of Tower Face Of The Comb. Climber Shauna Clark

Dan Moore

Approach

From the CIC Hut, head over the domed rock west of the Hut, then negotiate a short vegetated wall at the foot of Coire na Ciste before heading up into the corrie bowl, passing to the right of a small lochan. Climb snow slopes to reach the foot of Comb Gully on the left flank of The Comb, the prominent feature dividing the back wall of the corrie into two (about 1hr from the Hut, see p30-31).

Descent

See Ben Nevis Approaches & Descents (p30-33).

Top Tips

Several teams have had difficulty locating the start of the route. Spend some time studying the guidebook beforehand and take care to identify the ledge system that cuts across the buttress at one-third height. A few minutes spent avoiding a false start will pay dividends later.

Conditions

Tower Face Of The Comb can be climbed under powder, but it is at its best when the crux corner-groove is icy. This is likely to occur from mid-January

Sitting astride the large flake on the third pitch

Dan Moore

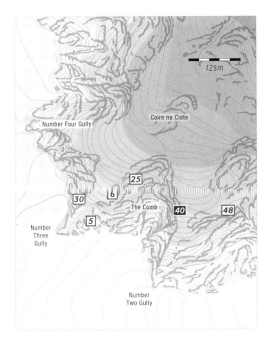

3. 45m Traverse left past a series of flakes and blocks, then climb straight up turfy mixed ground to below a steep wall. Traverse right along a ledge and belay by a large flake, which forms a 'window' on the right.

4. 35m Move right to the end of the ledge, then climb a steep wall on the left before breaking out right to the crest.

5 & 6. 80m Continue easily up the exposed final crest to the plateau.

40. *Tower Face Of The Comb* (VI,6)
C. *Comb Gully* (IV,4)
Q. *Quisling Wall* (VI,6)
H. *Hesperides Ledge* (III)

Simon Richardson

to early March. Be wary of attempting the route in heavy conditions as too much snow can make the top section slow and laborious.

Route Description

A futuristic route for its day that is nowadays recognised as one of the finest mixed climbs on Ben Nevis. Start near the foot of Comb Gully where a distinct snow terrace cuts diagonally across the buttress at one-third height.

1. 40m From the left end of the terrace, climb a left facing corner to reach a parallel terrace 10m higher. Move right until halfway along the terrace, then climb a short, steep wall and mixed ground to a belay below the prominent left facing corner-groove that cuts through the lower section of the face.

2. 50m Climb the corner-groove (crux) and continue up easier ground to belay below an impending wall.

Alternative Routes

Stringfellow (VI,6) on the Pinnacle Buttress of the Tower is a similar undertaking to Tower Face Of The Comb in terms of length and difficulty and a worthwhile alternative. It starts slightly higher up the mountain at an altitude of 1100m and faces north-west, so it may be climbable a little later in the season. There are several variations to Tower Face Of The Comb, but the only independent route in the vicinity is **Quisling Wall** (VI,6). If time is short, an easier but worthwhile alternative is **Hesperides Ledge** (III), which takes an exposed traverse from higher up Comb Gully and finishes up the superb final crest of the buttress.

Guidebooks

Ben Nevis (SMC), *Scottish Winter Climbs* (SMC), *Winter Climbs Ben Nevis and Glen Coe* (Cicerone).

Steve Helmore climbing the prominent corner on the fifth pitch of Postern. Well featured square-cut granite makes climbing on the Shelter Stone a mixed climber's dream

Simon Richardson

POSTERN

Grade: 240m, VI,6
Location: Shelter Stone Crag, Loch Avon Basin
Route Base, Aspect & Rock Type: 850m, North-East facing, Granite
First Winter Ascent: Kenny Spence, Murray Hamilton & Alan Taylor, 5-6 January 1980

Henning Wackerhage

Approaching via Coire Domhain with Càrn Etchachan and the Shelter Stone straight ahead

*T*hroughout the early 1970s, the curved axe revolution concentrated Scottish winter development on climbing ice, mainly on Ben Nevis, but towards the end of the decade the focus began to turn back towards climbing long Cairngorms mountain rock climbs in winter. The Cumming-Crofton Route (VI,6) on Beinn a' Bhuird by Greg Strange and Dick Renshaw in 1977 and The Link Face (VII,7) on Lochnagar by John Anderson and Andy Nisbet in 1979, heralded the new wave and the winter of 1980 saw a race between rival Edinburgh and Aberdeen teams to pick the major Cairngorms mixed plums.

Kenny Spence and Murray Hamilton scored a notable coup with the first winter ascents of Postern and The Citadel – the two big lines of weakness running up the impregnable looking front face of the Shelter Stone Crag. After two failed attempts on Postern, they roped in Alan Taylor and deliberately set out to make a two-day ascent with a bivouac and the seconds jumaring. The tactic worked and Postern and The Citadel were both graded VI, the highest grade of the day.

When Steve Helmore and I made an ascent of Postern in April 1992 it had seen a handful of repeats, but nobody had gone exactly the same way. We decided to avoid the initial summer pitches (which require ice) by using the winter start to The Needle, which takes a sloping shelf leading up from the right. Soon we were engrossed in superb climbing with immense exposure below our feet and the grandeur of the Loch Avon Basin all around. The granite was steep yet well featured with square-cut footholds and good hooks. Eager for more, we took the sustained groove of the Direct Finish to Clach Dhian Chimney at the top.

Starting up a variant of the winter start to The Needle has now become the standard way of climbing the route, and unlike The Citadel which is a full-on VII,8, Postern is a more amenable VI,6. However, it retains its cachet as a big and impressive route and is a highly coveted tick.

41

41. Postern (VI,6)
S. Sticil Face (V,6)

C. The Citadel (VII,8)
CD. Clach Dhian Chimney (IV,4)

W. Western Union (IV,6)
P. Pinnacle Gully (I)

Henning Wackerhage

For those with time and energy to spare, the Direct Finish to Clach Dhian Chimney provides a sustained and exciting finishing pitch. Climber Steve Helmore

Simon Richardson

Approach

From the Coire Cas car park at the top of the ski road, follow the approach to Coire an t-Sneachda as for The Message (p48). From the inner lochan, head south past the broad Fluted Buttress and ascend the Goat Track to its top at NH992028. From here, descend the easy-angled Coire Domhain until level with the base of Hell's Lum Crag, then make a slightly descending traverse crossing the burns of Feith Bhuidhe and Garh Uisge to gain the foot of the cliff. This approach can be avalanche-prone in north-westerly winds so careful judgment is required (**2hrs 30mins**).

Descent

It is best to return by traversing the plateau around the head of the Loch Avon Basin back to the Goat Track. This can feel a long way at the end of the day and requires careful navigation.

Conditions

Unlike the original line, the route as described does not require any ice and can be climbed as a Mixed route. Postern sees ascents from December onwards and it is also possible late in the season during cold weather and after a heavy fall of snow. The Loch Avon Basin holds cold air longer than the more exposed Northern Corries, so routes on the Shelter Stone can remain in condition longer than one might think.

Top Tips

This is a long and sustained route, so choose a good day, start early and take spare headtorch batteries. Pre-planning the navigation across the plateau for the return will remove some of the stress towards the end of the day.

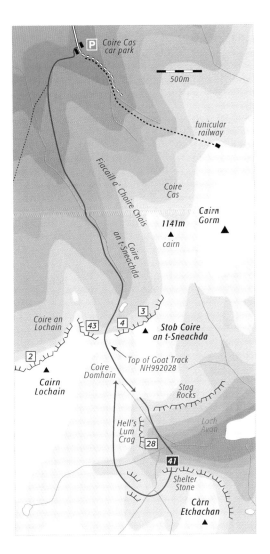

Alternative Routes

Sticil Face (V,6) is the most popular winter route on the Shelter Stone. However it requires ice, so may not be a good back up if you're at the crag early in the season. **Western Union** (IV,6) takes surprisingly amenable terrain to the right of Clach Dhian Chimney and requires similar conditions to Postern. **The Citadel** (VII,8) is another outstanding route, but it is near the top of its grade and a considerably harder proposition than Postern.

Guidebooks

The Cairngorms (SMC), *Scottish Winter Climbs* (SMC), *Winter Climbs in the Cairngorms* (Cicerone).

Route Description

Start just left of Clach Dhian Chimney and climb a prominent left-facing groove past a jammed block to gain a left-slanting ramp that leads to a terrace (the Gallery). Climb the Slanting Crack above for 60m. It is straightforward at first and runs diagonally right to where it becomes a steep chimney. Climb the chimney until unlikely moves left gain a corner. Climb the corner, traverse left along a narrow ledge and step down into a gully. Continue left until it is possible to gain a higher ledge system and follow the obvious right-trending line to the Second Step, the large platform on the skyline. Finish diagonally out right overlooking Pinnacle Gully.

Alternatively, the V-groove taken by the Direct Finish to Clach Dhian Chimney (VI,6), which lies directly above the Second Step, provides a fine finish.

42

Roger Everett passing through the giant arch during the first ascent of Archway

Simon Richardson

ARCHWAY

Grade: 250m, IV,4
Location: Gleann na Sguaib, Beinn Dearg
Route Base, Aspect & Rock Type: 650m, North-East facing, Mica Schist
First Ascent: Roger Everett & Simon Richardson, 7 February 1988

Scott Muir

Following the stone wall during the descent of Diollaid a' Mhill Bhric as the sun sets over An Teallach

*B*ack in the late 1980s, with a great weekend forecast for the North-West, Roger Everett and I made the long trek up the A9. It was soon clear that the Met Office had got it badly wrong. That night there was a raging blizzard, and if a plough hadn't cleared the road mid-morning we would have been stranded. We limped into Ullapool and saved the day by walking up Cùl Beag in knee-deep snow.

Next day with plans in disarray, we decided to play safe and visit the Gleann na Sguaib cliffs on Beinn Dearg. As we emerged from the forest, the cliff was hidden in cloud and the path was deep in snow. We headed towards Emerald Gully, but it was hopeless – thin ice and bottomless powder. Our weekend was falling apart fast, so in a last ditch attempt to climb something we headed left into an unseen snow couloir.

We were vaguely aware that the gully terminated in a steep rock wall and as we gained height, we could see through the blowing snow that a series of impenetrable-looking roofs barred the way. I'm not sure why we continued. I'd like to say it was a sixth sense, some innate route-finding genius, but in truth it was simply because we'd run out of options.

At the end of the third pitch I reached a shallow cave below the roofs expecting to set up an abseil, only to make an astounding discovery. There was a hidden way through the roofs via a giant arch! I whooped as Roger led an intriguing icy mixed pitch up through the arch onto a series of ice smears above. We could relax now – the mood had changed and we revelled in the final two rope lengths of squeaky plastic ice. It was dark and stormy on the way off, but the weather gods were now behind us and even when the descent slope avalanched, we were able to climb safely down to one side.

Penguin Gully, which lies high on the mountain and leads directly to the summit, makes an excellent back up option to the routes lower down Gleann na Sguaib. Climber Ian Hey

Ruth Taylor

Approach

Park about 10km south of Ullapool at the Inverlael car park (NH182853), just off the A835 . Follow the forestry tracks up Gleann na Sguaib through Inverlael Forest and continue on a path up the open glen on the north side of the River Lael. Cross the river at approx NH246823 and ascend to the cliffs below Diollaid a' Mhill Bhric, which are cut by six distinct gullies. Archway lies just left of Emerald Gully, which is the fourth gully from the right (**2hrs** to **2hrs 30mins**).

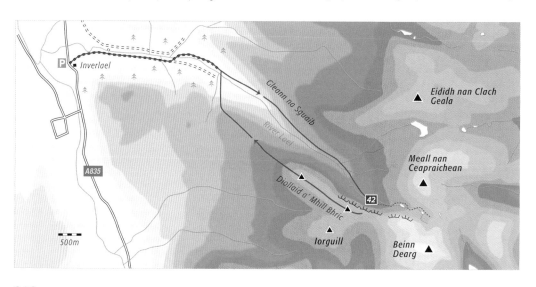

Tom Prentice

42. Archway (IV,4)
T. Tower Of Babel (IV,6)

F. Fenian Gully (IV,4)
W. Wee Freeze Gully (IV,4)

J. Jewel In The Crown (VI,5)
E. Emerald Gully (IV,4)

Descent
The simplest descent is to follow the Diollaid a' Mhill Bhric spur (which is topped by a stone wall) north-west until it opens out into easy slopes. Descend these into Gleann na Sguaib, then cross the River Lael to gain the access path. In heavy snow conditions it may be worth descending nearly as far as Inverlael Forest to reduce the avalanche risk.

Conditions
Beinn Dearg is a big bulky mountain and first in line to catch snow from north-westerlies running in from the North Atlantic. Its more northerly latitude means that it stays a little colder than mountains of similar height further south. Archway is not a high elevation climb so it needs several days of cold weather. Nevertheless, it is often climbed instead of its more famous neighbour Emerald Gully as it is less reliant on ice. Following heavy snowfall the approach path can be drifted over and give hard going beyond the shelter of Inverlael Forest.

Top Tips
For many years it was possible to drive through Inverlael Forest and park at its end, but this is no longer possible. If the snowline allows, the best option is to cycle through the forest, which will save an hour from the day.

Route Description
An entertaining route that weaves through some very impressive rock architecture. Start at the lowest point of the buttress left of Emerald Gully.

1 to 3. 150m Follow open snow grooves just left of the steepest rocks to reach a prominent cave-like depression beneath huge roofs.
4. 40m Climb up through the arch in the roof of the cave.
5 and 6. 60m Follow the continuation gully and groove system up right to finish.

Alternative Routes
Emerald Gully (IV,4) is the classic of the crag, but it takes a while to consolidate and is not often in condition. **Fenian Gully** (IV,4) is the most reliable gully on the Gleann na Sguaib cliffs and gives a good sustained climb. The nearby **Wee Freeze Gully** (IV,4) is a worthwhile outing too. Icy streaks taken by **Jewel In The Crown** (VI,5) run down the left wall of Emerald Gully, but unfortunately they are rarely formed. If this area of cliff is not in condition, it is best to head further up the glen and climb **Penguin Gully** (III,4), an excellent route leading to the summit of the mountain. Its more northerly aspect and higher starting altitude mean that it is more reliably in condition. Another option is the excellent **Tower Of Babel** (IV,6), the finest Mixed climb on the Gleann na Sguaib cliffs, which relies on frozen turf rather than ice.

Guidebooks
Northern Highlands North (SMC), *Scottish Winter Climbs* (SMC).

217

CHAPTER 5 ▶ LATE SEASON

The spring brings longer days and opportunities to climb Scotland's great ice routes

Indicator Wall, Ben Nevis; Henning Wackerhage

Some of the finest climbing of the winter takes place late in the season, but typically it is restricted to the cliffs of the Cairngorms and Ben Nevis. In April the days are long and the sun rises high in the sky, quickly stripping crags with a southerly or easterly aspect. West facing cliffs suffer too, although they can remain frozen in the morning before the sun reaches them later in the afternoon.

In general, high altitude north and north-west facing cliffs hold the best objectives, although climbing in cloudy weather immediately after a storm is a possible tactic to constrain the power of the sun.

Conditions change rapidly late in the season, and

Helen Rennard climbing on Goodeve's Buttress on Ben Nevis. As a general rule, north and north-west facing cliffs provide the best Late Season venues

Simon Richardson

fresh snow that would lie as powder for weeks mid-winter, rapidly consolidates and turns to névé.

Air temperatures in weather forecasts can some-times be a little misleading as routes can remain frozen even when the freezing level is above the summits. This is due to the Wet Bulb Effect, which typically occurs in very dry air when snow is kept cool due to energy loss from rapid evaporation. Such conditions are most common during 'bluebird' spring days of stable high pressure and temperature inver-sion. Even if the forecast air temperature at 1000m is a few degrees above zero, shaded north facing slopes are likely to remain frozen.

The Northern Corries of Cairn Gorm are not as

frequented late on as they are earlier in the winter, but their north-west facing aspect ensures they hold on to winter late into the season. Some Mixed routes become half buried from an accumulation of the winter's snow so they are not particularly attractive, and others can be threatened by large cornices. However, Fiacaill Buttress in Coire an t-Sneachda tends to avoid these problems, and **Invernookie** and its adjacent routes make fine late season objectives.

Deeper in the Cairngorms, early April is an excellent time to tackle **Mitre Ridge** on Beinn a' Bhuird. This is one of the great Cairngorms classics, famed as much for its remoteness as for its climbing. Long April days take the sting out of the lengthy approach, and the route is often climbed just after the 'lambing snows', an early spring snowfall and cold snap that occurs almost every year.

The high altitude of Ben Nevis means that it is home to the majority of late season objectives. Whilst routes like **Point Five Gully** and **Orion Direct** are often in condition as early as February, they are often at their very best in early April. This is a superb time to climb on the Ben, as the mid-winter crowds have largely disappeared.

It can take a full four months of snow, freeze and thaw to bring routes like **Albatross** on Indicator Wall into condition. This is an archetypal Thin Face route, an almost uniquely Scottish style of climbing, where the cliff is coated in a thin layer of snow-ice. At first sight it looks as though it should be possible to climb almost anywhere, but it takes considerable skill and courage to commit to blind leads with spaced protection and long runouts. Thin Face routes take a long time to form, but they are also very fragile. A day's thaw can destroy them, undoing months of good work, so take every opportunity to climb them when they are in condition.

The steep Mixed routes on the Ben are unlikely to be climbable late in the season unless they have been refreshed by a late season storm. The lower-angled Mixed routes on Goodeve's Buttress hold snow and ice well however, and can be reached by following the first half of **The White Line**. Facing north-west they are exposed to the afternoon sun, but are in the shade in the cool of the morning.

As temperatures rise through April, it is the great mountain Icefalls such as **Hadrian's Wall Direct** and **Smith's Route** that are the longest surviving. As the days lengthen, the increasing contrast between day and night temperatures encourages greater ice formation, but an early start will be required to avoid the heat of the day. An alpine mentality is required; rising in the early hours of the morning, starting the route at dawn and finishing on the summit plateau by mid-morning. Cornice collapse is an ever-present risk

Duncan Curry

Many classic Ben Nevis ice routes such as Point Five Gully are at their best in April when the ice has formed fat and thick

and considerable care should be taken to select objectively safe routes.

Late season is a highly enjoyable time to be winter climbing in the Scottish mountains. The routes tend to be longer and icier than the shorter and more technical Snowed-Up Rock and Mixed routes at the start of the winter. More daylight and better weather reduce the overall feeling of seriousness, and best of all, the cliffs become increasingly quiet as many climbers move into rock climbing mode. Winter opportunities are plentiful, so make sure you don't miss out on one of the finest parts of the season!

Roger Webb enjoying helpful conditions of consolidated snow and soft ice during an April ascent of Invernookie

Simon Richardson

INVERNOOKIE

Grade: 120m, III,4
Location: Fiacaill Buttress, Coire an t-Sneachda, Cairn Gorm
Route Base, Aspect & Rock Type: 1050m, North-East facing, Granite
First Ascent: Kenny Spence & John Porteous, 4 January 1969

Henning Wackerhage

Fiacaill Buttress looking splendid after a late season storm

*F*iacaill Buttress is the attractive cliff that flanks the right side of Coire an t-Sneachda. It's an intriguing and complex-looking feature, and at first it's not easy to understand how it all fits together. The slanting Fiacaill Couloir, which is hidden on the approach, is key to unlocking the architecture of the cliff and separates the compact wedge-shaped lower tier on the left from the more featured upper wall on the right. The two classic climbs on Fiacaill Buttress are Belhaven and Invernookie. The former takes the no-compromise direct corner up the centre of the back wall, whilst Invernookie follows a more amenable line weaving through less steep terrain up ramps and corners to the right.

Invernookie is one of the great mixed climbs of the Cairngorms and its popularity is well deserved; the higher you climb, the more interesting the moves and protection is always available where it matters. The highlights are in the upper half of the route where a technical corner leads to an atmospheric cave, and a spectacular final pitch with an exposed and airy traverse. And if you ever tire of the grandstand view of the ever-busy Coire an t-Sneachda below, the outlook across upper Speyside along the flank of Fiacaill Ridge is superb.

Due to its high altitude and location on the northern side of the Cairngorms, Invernookie comes into condition early in the winter and remains so throughout the season. Under powder however, some of the steep steps, especially on the last two pitches, can be hard for the grade and the route can feel more like IV,5. It is probably best climbed after a thaw and re-freeze, as it only takes a small build up of consolidated snow or ice to make it a III,4. Later in the season it can become quite icy, which makes for easier climbing but with less protection. As Roger Webb told me after a recent ascent in optimal icy nick, "You know Simon, that felt more like IV,3 than III,4."

43

George Cave

Climbing the lower slopes of Invernookie in perfect late season conditions

Approach
From the Coire Cas car park at the top of the Cairn Gorm ski road, follow the approach into Coire an t-Sneachda as for The Message (p48). From the two small lochans head south-west, picking the optimum way through the boulders, to gain the foot of the buttress (**1hr**).

Descent
It is simplest to continue up the easier upper section of Fiacaill Ridge to reach the plateau, and then descend the Goat Track, the steep strip of snow that rises up to the col between Fluted Buttress and Fiacaill Buttress at the south-west corner of the corrie at NH992028. Take care in conditions of heavy snow, or in strong westerly winds, as it can be avalanche-prone (there are accidents here most years). Alternatively, climb down Fiacaill Ridge (easiest on the western Coire an Lochain side, rather than the crest) and drop down into Coire an t-Sneachda below the ridge's steep rocky section.

Conditions
Fiacaill Buttress faces north-east, and lies at an altitude of 1050m, so it comes into condition fast. This makes Invernookie an ideal choice for a quick ascent when temperatures start falling immediately following a thaw. It is sheltered from south-westerly winds

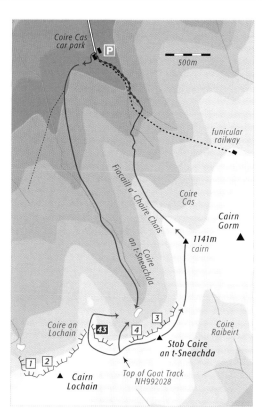

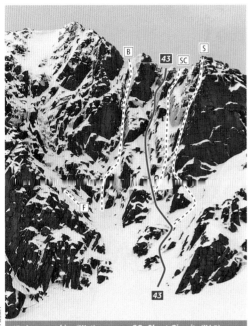

43. Invernookie (III,4)
F. Fiacaill Couloir (II)
B. Belhaven (V,6)
SC. Short Circuit (IV,5)
S. The Seam (IV,5)

Simon Richardson

to gain the ramps and a stance below the steep right facing corner.

2. 20m Climb the corner and step left at its top (crux) to easier ground leading to a cave.

3. 20m Traverse 5m right in a spectacular position along a narrow ledge and finish up the hanging groove on the right to reach the crest of Fiacaill Ridge.

Top Tips

Invernookie is a popular route, but this is not a remote outing with a long approach, so in late season a lunchtime start can be a good way of avoiding the morning shift. Alternatively, if you finish early, a 60m abseil down the line of Short Circuit will allow you to climb the top pitch of The Seam (which shares its lower pitch with Invernookie).

Henning Wackerhage

Absorbing mixed climbing on the final pitch of The Seam

although probably not the associated spindrift! The route finishes on Fiacaill Ridge, the pronounced divide between Coire an t-Sneachda and Coire an Lochain, which rarely cornices, as there is little snow catchment directly above. This made Invernookie a good option during the very snowy 2014 season when many routes across the Highlands were out of bounds from early March due to the size of the cornices.

Route Description

An excellent mixed route and Cairngorms favourite, based on the line of ramps and corner above the start of Fiacaill Couloir.

1 and 2. 80m From the foot of the Couloir climb up right, then trend left over a short wall (possible belay)

Alternative Routes

Short Circuit (IV,5) makes an enjoyable alternative when there is good snow and ice build up. It starts as for Invernookie but takes the ramp to its right and finishes up a steep corner. Further right is **The Seam** (IV,5) which also starts as for Invernookie and provides a brilliant mixed top pitch. It does not require ice and is a good choice at both the beginning and the end of the season. The prominent corner of **Belhaven** on the other hand, has lost much of its vegetation since the first ascent in 1979 (when it was graded IV) and is now a substantial V,6 that is best climbed with some helpful ice.

Guidebooks

The Cairngorms (SMC), *Scottish Winter Climbs* (SMC), *Winter Climbs in The Cairngorms* (Cicerone)

The 200m-high Mitre Ridge lies deep in the Cairngorms and any winter ascent demands respect

Simon Richardson

MITRE RIDGE

Grade: 250m, V,6
Location: Garbh Choire, Beinn a' Bhuird
Route Base, Aspect & Rock Type: 950m, North facing, Granite
First Winter Ascent: Bill Brooker & Tom Patey, 12 April 1953

Henning Wackerhage

Moving up to the foot of the Second Tower during an ascent of Mitre Ridge. Climber Henning Wackerhage

One thing you'll remember about Mitre Ridge is that it is a long way from the road. This just adds to its allure; the journey is as much an attraction as the route itself. And the route itself climbs the finest rock feature in the Cairngorms – the beautifully proportioned Mitre Ridge that proudly thrusts out into Garbh Choire. Clean-cut, deeply fractured and more than 200m high, it just has to be climbed.

The development of Mitre Ridge encapsulates the history of Cairngorm climbing. First ascended in summer 1933 via two separate routes by a Cambridge University team, these climbs were the most difficult in the area at the time. The first winter ascent by Tom Patey and Bill Brooker brought the spectacular 1953 winter to a close. This season was one of the most productive in the golden days of Cairngorm winter development and saw the first winter ascents of The Stack, Eagle Ridge, Scorpion and Polyphemus Gully. In recent times, the first winter ascents of Slochd Wall and The Primate on the west flank of Mitre Ridge stand alongside the most impressive achievements elsewhere in the massif.

Patey and Brooker neatly short-cut the long approach by riding Brooker's BSA motorbike to Slugain Lodge at the head of the Fairy Glen. They also climbed the route in April to maximise the available daylight. Not that they needed to however, because they made a swift four and a half hour ascent and graded the route IV, which some believe is a more accurate assessment of the difficulty than the current rating of V,6. The two-tier system is meant to be independent of approach and seriousness, but the route has earned a slightly enhanced grade because of its location. Somehow this seems entirely appropriate, as climbing Mitre Ridge in winter is as much about the approach as the climbing itself. And as I said, it is a long, long way from the road.

Robbie Miller on the Original Start to Mitre Ridge. This straightforward mixed pitch is frequently climbed as an alternative to the initial groove on the front face which requires consolidated snow or ice

Henning Wackerhage

Approach

From the Pay and Display car park (NO188912) at Keiloch, 3km east of Braemar and just north of the A93, follow the tarmac road past Invercauld House to where the track divides before the farmstead of Altdourie. Turn right and follow the upper track above Altdourie to a junction at NO166932. Turn left, descend back to the lower track and follow it through forestry to a turning at NO160933, before it descends to cross the Allt an t-Slugain. Turn right here onto a grassy track up Gleann an t-Slugain, which is romantically known as the Fairy Glen. Take the left fork at NO129950, cross over the Allt an t-Slugain and follow the track to near the ruins of Slugain Lodge where it turns into a path and leads steeply up to the open moorland below the east side of Beinn a' Bhuird.

Follow a good path north for 3km and cross a burn just before the prominent boulder of Clach a' Clèirich. Continue up the left side of Glas Allt Mòr to reach The Sneck, the high col between Beinn a' Bhuird and Ben Avon. Cut down and west from here into Garbh Choire and traverse approximately 800m to reach the base of the prominent Mitre Ridge (**4hrs** to **5hrs**).

Descent

Walk south for a kilometre keeping east of Cnap a' Clèirich, then descend steep slopes south-eastwards to the Clach a' Clèirich boulder, and reverse the long approach.

Conditions

Beinn a' Bhuird is one of the highest mountains in the Cairngorms and Garbh Choire faces north and collects large amounts of snow. Mitre Ridge comes into condition early, and remains so through much of the season. However, it is best avoided in heavy snow or very cold conditions. The approach has to be considered as much as the climb itself, which is why Mitre Ridge is at its best either early in the season, or at its end. Later in the season the approach is more likely to be clear of snow and the daylight hours are longer.

Top Tips

A bicycle will take at least an hour off the approach and two hours on the return. In good cycling conditions it is possible to ride as far as Slugain Lodge, allowing Mitre Ridge to be climbed in a round trip

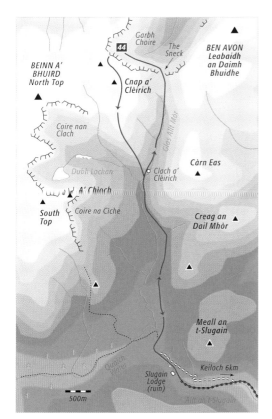

short gully to exit onto the crest of the ridge at a shoulder. Above is a short steep wall that normally provides the crux. Climb it by making steep moves up and right, then move left across a slab and climb the 'splintered chimney' to a large ledge. Surmount the wall above and climb up to the gap between the First and Second Towers. Turn the tower on the left and continue to a spectacular finish along the final arete.

44. Mitre Ridge (V,6)   O. Mitre Ridge, Original Start (III)

Simon Richardson

from the road, but many parties choose to make an overnight stop and camp at the head of the Fairy Glen.

Route Description
Start up the prominent right facing groove that runs up the right side of the lower front face. Surmount an awkward wall on the left after 30m and continue up an easy ramp that leads to a deep-cut chimney on the west face. Wriggle up the chimney and continue up a

Alternative Routes
If the initial groove of Mitre Ridge is not iced or full of consolidated snow, it is best avoided by taking the **Original Start** (III). This follows an amenable left facing corner on the west face that leads to the base of the deep-cut chimney. If you have time to spare, **Bell's Variation** (V,7) which traverses right from the col and climbs a steep crack on the west face of The Second Tower, provides an exciting finish. The natural companion to Mitre Ridge is the **Cumming-Crofton Route** (VI,6) which takes the prominent corner on the right side of the crest of the First Tower. It is a grade harder and a good target for a second visit. There are limited easier mixed options in the corrie. **Mandarin Buttress** (III) is occasionally climbed but it is a poor choice in thaw conditions as the route is often threatened by a large cornice. If conditions are poor on the approach it may make sense to divert into the more accessible Coire na Ciche. **Hourglass Buttress** (VI,6) is the stand-out route, but **Slugain Buttress** (III) is a good fall-back that is possible in most conditions.

Guidebooks
The Cairngorms (SMC), *Scottish Winter Climbs* (SMC), *Winter Climbs in The Cairngorms* (Cicerone).

Point Five Gully is the most famous gully in Scotland, and one of the world's most sought-after winter climbs. Climber Steve Holmes

Duncan Curry

POINT FIVE GULLY

Grade: 325m, V,5
Location: Observatory Gully, Ben Nevis
Route Base, Aspect & Rock Type: 1000m, North-West facing, Andesite
First Winter Ascent: John Alexander, Ian Clough, Don Pipes & Robin Shaw, 16 January 1959

Rob Dyer cruising the Rogue Pitch on Point Five Gully

John Roberts

*I*n March 1980, fellow student Pat Bailey and I set off up Point Five Gully. Conditions were lean that year, and it took us a long time to reach the foot of the infamous Rogue Pitch. Caught in the deep confines of the gully we hadn't noticed that the weather had changed and we were soon engulfed in clouds of spindrift pouring from above. We choked in the freezing torrent of ice particles, and whenever we looked up our faces were stung raw. I started up the next pitch, but it was hopeless. The spindrift came down harder and then the powder avalanches started. I huddled next to Pat as we were pummelled by wave after wave. We couldn't talk, we couldn't breathe, we couldn't move. The situation was desperate. We couldn't go up and we couldn't go down. Abseiling off would have been suicidal.

Somehow we had to get out of the gully. On impulse I moved right up a short verglassed wall and emerged on a ledge. I had escaped the avalanches but a full-on storm was now raging. I blindly continued traversing along the ledge conscious of a huge drop below me. Eventually it opened out onto a steep terrace. We had no idea where we were, but at least we were moving away from the gully. We traversed for pitch after pitch until suddenly the ground eased. Completely lost, we headed down into the gloom and eventually stumbled into the CIC Hut, somewhat surprised and very relieved to be alive.

Thawing out in the hut, we felt a profound sense of satisfaction that we had survived, but looking back we were just plain lucky. It was only years later that I realised that we had followed the line of the Girdle Traverse into Observatory Gully. Our experience showed that although Point Five has been tamed by modern equipment, it is still a long route on a big, serious mountain and is best not attempted in poor conditions.

James Ellson on beautiful late season plastic ice at the start of the Rogue Pitch on Point Five Gully

Robert McMurray

Approach
From the CIC Hut, head diagonally up the hillside, passing below the Douglas Boulder to gain Observatory Gully, the great corrie defined by North-East Buttress and Tower Ridge. Climb increasingly steepening snow slopes between Observatory Ridge and Observatory Buttress to gain the start of the route (about **1hr** from the Hut, see p30-31).

Descent
See Ben Nevis Approaches & Descents (p30-33).

Conditions
Point Five Gully typically forms in January and remains in place until the end of the season. It is more difficult early on, when the ice can be brittle and chandeliered, but as the winter progresses the gully fills and the ice becomes more aerated and plastic. The first

three pitches are the most challenging and opinions vary as to which of these are the most difficult. Common consensus is that the first pitch can be steep (although it banks out a little as the season progresses), the second pitch is bold and the third pitch is the crux. The final three or four pitches climb the upper funnel. This is technically straightforward but can be a little intimidating as the belays are difficult to find and runners infrequent. In windy conditions the route is best avoided, as the upper funnel collects vast quantities of spindrift, which causes mini-avalanches to cascade down the lower narrow section. This is particularly noticeable on the (third) Rogue Pitch, which is how this pitch earned its name.

Top Tips
This is one of the most desired winter climbs in Scotland, so it is rare to be alone. Multiple parties can

result in falling ice, so choosing when you start is important. Either begin climbing at first light, or if you're feeling confident, start in the afternoon when earlier teams have completed the first three pitches. An alternative strategy is to wait until later in the season when the mountain will be considerably quieter. Point Five Gully is often climbable until late April when the weather is more benign and the days are longer. One aspect of climbing the route later in the season is that is more likely to be stepped out – this is either an advantage or a disadvantage, depending on your point of view!

Route Description

An iconic route and arguably the most celebrated ice gully on the planet. Belays are good and the route is an excellent introduction to the Grade V classics.

1. 40m Start up icy slabs to reach a steep wall, which is typically climbed on the left, to gain a snow bay.

45. Point Five Gully (V,5)   L. Left-Hand Finish (IV,4)

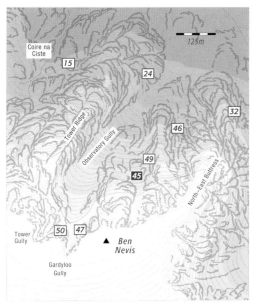

2. 45m Climb the narrow icy chimney to a stance.

3. 30m Continue up the gully and climb the bulging wall above to gain the easier upper section (the Rogue Pitch).

4 to 7. 210m Follow the gully, which opens out into a wide funnel, to gain the plateau. This section often contains several short, steep steps and the cornice is normally passed on the right.

Alternative Routes

Point Five's **Left-Hand Finish** (IV,4) breaks out from the top of the fourth pitch and follows a left-trending line of grooves and short ice walls. It is not often climbed, but it makes a good alternative to finishing up the final funnel. **Zero Gully** (V,4), (*see topo p237*), is similar in stature to Point Five Gully, although arguably it is more serious and not quite as good. The technical climbing is concentrated in the first two pitches, which are never very steep, but they are hard to protect and belays can be difficult to find. Similar to Point Five, Zero comes into condition in January and remains climbable throughout most of the winter.

Guidebooks

Ben Nevis (SMC), *Scottish Winter Climbs* (SMC), *Winter Climbs Ben Nevis and Glen Coe* (Cicerone).

Climbers moving up to the final tower of Orion Direct in perfect Thin Face conditions. The 400m-high Orion Face on Ben Nevis is the most alpine of all British cliffs

Henning Wackerhage

ORION DIRECT

Grade: 400m, V,5
Location: Orion Face, Ben Nevis
Route Base, Aspect & Rock Type: 1000m, North-West facing
First Ascent: Jimmy Marshall & Robin Smith, 13 February 1960

Davie Scott

David Anderson moving around the exposed Second Slab Rib during an ascent of Orion Direct

*C*hris Cartwright and I were a little curious when we pushed open the heavy front door of the CIC Hut on Ben Nevis one January night. Well known French climber Catherine Destivelle was staying in the hut, but a week of poor weather had prevented her from doing a single route. Catherine joined in the general banter with grace and charm, but you could sense she was disappointed. She visibly brightened when hut custodian Robin Clothier suggested Catherine and her partner follow him and Harvey Mullen up Orion Direct the following day.

It was a preposterous suggestion. The mountain was very snowy and it was too early in the season for the Thin Face routes to have formed. Next morning was dark and grey with low cloud and blowing spindrift and most climbers chose routes low down on the mountain. Robin was undeterred however, and soon after breakfast the party set off for the Orion Face. Chris and I climbed on Càrn Dearg and it was dark by the time we returned to the busy hut. Everyone was recounting the day's adventures over steaming mugs of tea, and Catherine's eyes danced with delight as she described their climb.

They had followed Robin and Harvey up into the murky gloom of Observatory Gully and when the slope steepened they roped up as two pairs and started climbing. There was no ice, just a six-inch layer of barely consolidated snow covering smooth slabs with no runners or belays. Blindly they followed Robin and Harvey across the delicate traverse that leads right from The Basin to the maze of exit gullies above. Every so often they could hear avalanches hissing down Zero Gully somewhere to their right. When they reached the summit, Robin pointed instinctively through the swirling snow with his axes and they plunged down through the whiteout towards the Càrn Mòr Dearg Arete. "It was like nothing I've ever done before," Catherine told me. "It's a climb I'll never forget."

46

Henning Wackerhage

Superb ice climbing in the lower gully below The Basin on Orion Direct. Climber Henning Wackerhage

Approach

From the CIC Hut, head diagonally up the hillside, passing below the Douglas Boulder to gain Observatory Gully, the great corrie defined by North-East Buttress and Tower Ridge. Climb steepening snow slopes left of Observatory Ridge to gain the start of the route just left of Zero Gully (about **1hr** from the Hut, see p30-31).

Descent

See Ben Nevis Approaches & Descents (p30-33).

Conditions

Orion Direct is the archetypal Thin Face route, which relies on the build-up of plastic ice on steep smooth slabs – an almost uniquely Scottish phenomenon and a result of our variable climate and innumerable freeze-thaws. Unlike Catherine Destivelle's ascent, the route is best climbed later in the season once it has come properly into condition. In some years there is insufficient build up, but once formed the route is

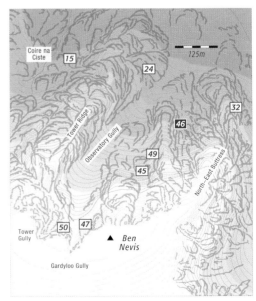

Coire na Ciste

15

125m

24

Tower Ridge

Observatory Gully

46

32

49

45

North-East Buttress

Tower Gully

50

47

▲ Ben Nevis

Gardyloo Gully

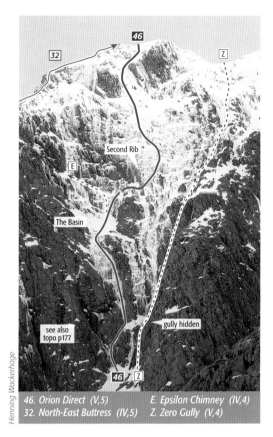

Henning Wackerhage

46. **Orion Direct** (V,5)   E. *Epsilon Chimney* (IV,4)
32. *North-East Buttress* (IV,5)   Z. *Zero Gully* (V,4)

considerably in the intervening 50 years, but Orion Direct will always have a special place in Scottish climbing. In good conditions, which tend to occur mid to late season, it is a reasonable V,5 and well within the reach of many climbers. Choose a fine day to savour the exposure and position and treat yourself to one of Scotland's finest mountain adventures.

Route Description

The V-shaped Orion Face fans out from Minus One Gully on the left to Zero Gully on the right. Start left of Zero Gully and gain a terrace that leads left to the foot of an open ice gully. Climb the gully for 90m and exit left into the Basin, the prominent snowfield in the centre of the face. Move up and right across the Basin to the foot of the Second Slab Rib, a prominent feature defining its right side. Descend a couple of metres, move round the right side of the rib, then climb up and right across a steep icy wall (crux). From here, trend left up icy grooves to the snow slope under the final tower. Turn this by climbing the furthest left of three groove-lines to reach easier snow slopes that lead up and right to the top of North-East Buttress.

Mike Pescod

Nick Lawry high on Orion Direct

resilient to minor thaws and can remain in condition for several weeks.

Top Tips

Orion Direct takes a superb natural line up one of the largest faces in the British Isles with 400m of sustained climbing leading to the summit of our highest peak. The first ascent in February 1960 by Jimmy Marshall and Robin Smith is regarded as the pinnacle of the step-cutting era. Not only was Orion Direct the biggest ice undertaking in Scotland at the time, no other ice climb in the world could match it for sustained difficulty. Winter climbing has moved on

Alternative Routes

If time is pressing there are a number of escapes, and **Epsilon Chimney** (IV,4) – the line of the **Smith-Holt Route** (V,5) – is the quickest exit from The Basin. It is also possible to traverse easily left from the foot of the Second Slab Rib to reach North-East Buttress. If conditions are poor on the upper section, it may be necessary to make a long traverse to the right below the final tower to find an exit just left of Zero Gully.

Guidebooks

Ben Nevis (SMC), *Scottish Winter Climbs* (SMC), *Winter Climbs Ben Nevis and Glen Coe* (Cicerone).

Moving past the overlap on the second pitch of Albatross. Situated directly underneath the summit of Ben Nevis, Indicator Wall is home to many of the finest Thin Face routes in the country

Cubby Images

ALBATROSS

Grade: 140m, VI,5
Location: Indicator Wall, Ben Nevis
Route Base, Aspect & Rock Type: 1200m, North-West facing, Andesite
First Ascent: Mick Geddes & Con Higgins, 21 January 1978

Brian Whitworth

Heike Puchan starting up the second pitch of Albatross

I have always found Indicator Wall a spooky place. Sometime in the late 1980s, Robin Clothier and I wandered up there one wild and windy March day. It was thawing at the CIC Hut, but we'd climbed Psychedelic Wall a couple of weeks before and were hopeful that winter was still hanging on high up. As we approached the foot of the wall through knee-deep wet snow we spotted an icy groove looming out of the mist. We had no idea what it was, but it looked good, so I climbed the groove and Robin led through on the second pitch. The ice was an unusual translucent grey, and was so thin in places that it was difficult to tell it apart from the rock.

Robin placed a poor runner and pulled over a roof. He was out of sight and all I could hear was the screeching of crampons, and the dull thud of picks hitting rock. Slowly the rope ran out; 20 metres, 40 metres and still no runner. The screeching continued and I became very nervous. Robin is a big man and I didn't dare think about a direct fall onto the belay. Eventually he found a single nut anchor on the rope stretch. I followed and finished up thankfully thicker ice to the plateau. It was two very relieved climbers who descended to the CIC Hut later that afternoon, where we realised that we'd climbed Albatross.

Robin and I have climbed on Indicator Wall many times since, and it remains a very special part of the Ben for me, but it is not a place to be taken lightly. The routes are excellent, but their exacting nature demands absolute commitment. Even with today's high standards and modern equipment, routes such as Albatross are amongst the most respected climbs on the mountain.

Perfect Thin Face conditions on the first pitch of Albatross

Simon Richardson

Approach

From the CIC Hut, head diagonally up the hillside, passing below the Douglas Boulder to gain Observatory Gully, the great corrie defined by North-East Buttress and Tower Ridge. Climb steepening snow slopes to gain the foot of Indicator Wall a little before the start of Gardyloo Gully (about **1hr 30mins** from the Hut, see p30-31).

Descent

See Ben Nevis Approaches & Descents (p30-33). Tower Gully is the quickest descent to the CIC Hut from the top of Indicator Wall, but it requires good snow conditions and a passable cornice.

Conditions

It is not wise to venture onto Indicator Wall unless it is in good condition. Lying at the very top of the Ben, the wall is snow-covered for most of the winter, and it takes a series of freeze-thaws at summit level to transition the lying snow into ice. This typically only occurs late March into early April.

Top Tips

Finding protection on Indicator Wall can be difficult and often the routes are a cerebral experience! Take a good selection of ice screws and pegs and supplement your rack with a couple of 'stubbie' ice screws. Although these can be as short as 10cm, when placed in good ice they can provide just enough confidence to make the next tenuous move.

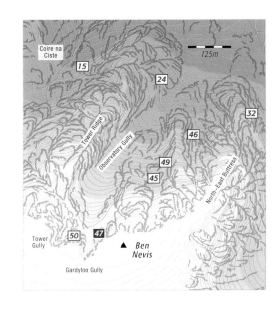

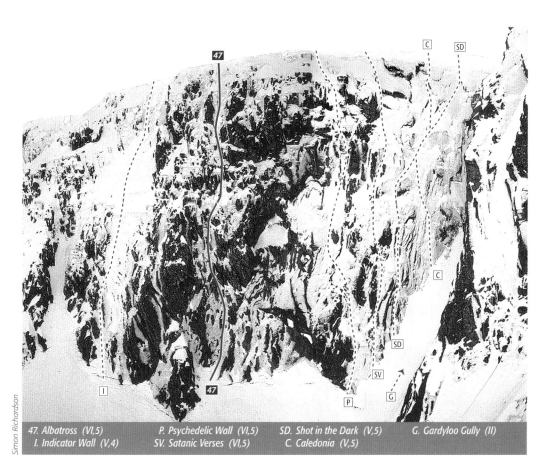

Simon Richardson

47. Albatross (VI,5)   P. Psychedelic Wall (VI,5)   SD. Shot in the Dark (V,5)   G. Gardyloo Gully (II)
I. Indicator Wall (V,4)   SV. Satanic Verses (VI,5)   C. Caledonia (V,5)

Route Description

A strong line taking the prominent shallow corner in the centre of the wall that runs the full height of the cliff. Start in a small snow bay, about 25m right of the toe of the buttress, which borders the right side of the broad ice sheet of Indicator Wall.

1. 30m Start up a shallow icy groove that leads up and right before moving up to a rock spike in a corner leading up to an overlap.

2. 50m Continue up twin icy grooves and make an awkward move left over the overlap. Climb the groove above, and continue up icy slabs passing to the right of a second overlap to gain a snow bay.

3. 50m Leave the top of the bay by following a short slanting groove, then step left into a shallow left facing corner. This leads to a steep icy bulge and a small snowfield below the cornice.

4. 10m Climb easily up to the cornice and gain the plateau very close to the summit triangulation pillar.

Alternative Routes

The eponymous **Indicator Wall** (V,4) is the most popular climb on the wall and provides an outstanding Mountain Icefall route on thick ice at the lower end of its grade. It is often in condition until the very end of the season and will outlast thaws longer than most other climbs on the mountain. **Psychedelic Wall** (VI,5) is the other great classic, and provides memorable Thin Face climbing on ground that is not quite as steep as Albatross. It is a slightly easier undertaking, but still guaranteed to provide an exciting excursion! **Satanic Verses** (VI,5) is another excellent route, and lying higher up Gardyloo Gully it stays in condition a little later in the season.

Guidebooks

Ben Nevis (SMC), Scottish Winter Climbs (SMC), Winter Climbs Ben Nevis and Glen Coe (Cicerone).

The White Line has several alternatives in its upper section. Here, Helen Rennard tackles the rarely climbed Sirius Finish

Simon Richardson

THE WHITE LINE

Grade: 350m, IV,4
Location: Goodeve's Buttress, Ben Nevis
Route Base, Aspect & Rock Type: 1100m, North-West facing, Andesite
First Ascent: Mick Geddes & Harold Gillespie, 18 March 1971

Dave Riley

Approaching the start of The White Line. The two alternative starts to The White Line follow the icefalls above the climber, while Glover's Chimney takes the gully to their left. Climber Debbie Lee

To the right of the upper half of Glover's Chimney is a broad triangular buttress that reaches the plateau at the same point as Tower Ridge. The buttress is named after Major Thomas Goodeve who led a party up this section of cliff in December 1907 after a failed retreat from Tower Ridge. Whilst it is tempting to credit Goodeve with the first ascent of Goodeve's Buttress itself, it is likely that he climbed the upper part of Raeburn's Easy Route during his epic night time escape.

The true first ascent of the buttress fell to Nevis pioneer Mick Geddes with Harold Gillespie in 1971 when they climbed The White Line. This route starts up the icefall just right of Glover's Chimney and climbs the full height of the cliff, finishing up a prominent groove cutting through the centre of the buttress. Its high altitude and north-west facing aspect means that it is often in condition late in the season, but don't be fooled by the Grade III rating given by the first ascensionists. The initial icefall pitches are steep and sustained, and the route fully deserves its contemporary grade of IV,4. Overall The White Line's length and exposure make it feel like a mini-alpine north face, and it has been described as 'a soft climber's Orion Direct'.

Further exploration of Goodeve's Buttress waited until 1987 when Bob Reid and Ian Crofton found Beam Me Up Scotty, the series of icy grooves on the right side of the buttress. This route threaded its way through some interesting ground and pointed to the new route potential on this fine feature. Nine years later Reid returned and added Hale Bopp Groove with Bob Appleyard, a fine companion route to the left of the buttress crest. Eventually others began to take notice, and in recent seasons Goodeve's Buttress has become established as one of the Ben's finest mixed climbing venues with a number of excellent middle grade routes.

243

48

Andy Cave on the first ascent of Techno Wall. The routes on Goodeve's Buttress can be approached via the lower pitches of The White Line and provide excellent mixed climbing until late in the season

Simon Richardson

Approach

From the CIC Hut, head over the domed rock west of the Hut, then negotiate a short vegetated wall at the foot of Coire na Ciste before heading up into the bowl of the corrie to the right of a small lochan. Climb snow slopes up and left around the top of Garadh na Ciste to reach the foot of the icefall below Glover's Chimney (about **1hr 15min** from the Hut, see p30-31). The mixed routes on Goodeve's Buttress can be approached by climbing either **Raeburn's Easy Route** (II) and traversing left, or by following the lower part of The White Line.

Descent

See Ben Nevis Approaches & Descents (p30-33).

Conditions

The White Line typically becomes climbable during February and remains so until late in the season. The mixed routes on Goodeve's Buttress quickly come into condition throughout the season and have the advantage of not being threatened by a cornice. Lying high on the mountain they are resistant to thaw, but in April their westerly aspect means they catch the afternoon sun, so are best climbed in the morning after an early start.

Top Tips

Take at least six ice screws. The icefall pitches on The White Line are long and sustained and are steeper than they look.

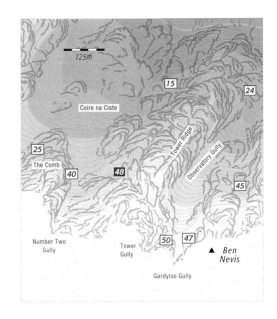

Henning Wackerhage

right-slanting snow terrace. A third icefall (sometimes awkward to start) leads to a snowfield; the mixed routes on Goodeve's Buttress start from here. From the top of the snowfield, climb a short icy chimney on the left, then follow a shallow gully to a bifurcation. Take the steep left branch (Hale Bopp Groove takes the right) to gain an exposed open snowfield. This leads to short icy runnels that finish near the top of Tower Ridge.

Simon Richardson

48. The White Line (IV,4)
O. The White Line,
    Original Start (III)
G. Glover's Chimney (III,4)
B. Beam Me Up Scotty (III)
U. The Upper Cascade (V,5)

Route Description

An excellent ice climb typically climbed in six long pitches on 60m ropes. Start up a short icefall 20m right of Glover's Chimney, cross a snow terrace and continue up a steeper second icefall to gain a second

48. The White Line (IV,4)
H. Hale Bopp Groove (III,4)
S. Sirius (V,6)
G. Goodytwoshoes (V,6)
T. Techno Wall (V,6)
BC. The Borg Collective (V,6)
B. Beam Me Up Scotty (III)
U. The Upper Cascade (V,5)

Alternative Routes

The **Original Start** (III) to The White Line avoids the first two ice pitches by starting up the initial icefall of Glover's Chimney and continuing up icy mixed ground just right of Glover's Chimney to gain the second snow terrace that leads up and right to the start of the third icefall. Most unusually for the Ben, the rock on Goodeve's Buttress is cracked and friendly and the protection is good, making it an ideal playground for those looking for the less demanding end of the mixed climbing spectrum. **Hale Bopp Groove** (III,4) follows the prominent slanting couloir right of The White Line, and **Sirius** (V,6) climbs the buttress between the two gully-lines. **Goodytwoshoes** (V,6) takes a more mixed line up chimneys and cracks near the buttress crest. Further right the terrain is steeper and breached by **Techno Wall** (V,6) and the prominent chimney of **The Borg Collective** (V,6). The excellent **Beam Me Up Scotty** (III) follows icy grooves on the right flank of the buttress just to the left of **The Upper Cascade** (V,5).

Guidebooks

Ben Nevis (SMC), *Scottish Winter Climbs* (SMC), *Winter Climbs Ben Nevis and Glen Coe* (Cicerone), *Scottish Mountaineering Club Journal 2003, 2008 & 2015*. For *SMC Journal* new routes see <*www.smc.org.uk/new-routes*>.

Superb ice conditions on the flanks of Observatory Gully with teams established on the great Nevis classics of Hadrian's Wall Direct and Point Five Gully

Henning Wackerhage

HADRIAN'S WALL DIRECT

Grade: 350m, V,5
Location: Observatory Ridge West Flank, Ben Nevis
Route Base, Aspect & Rock Type: 1000m, North-West facing, Andesite
First Ascent: Mick Geddes & Graham Little, April 1971

Henning Wackerhage

The steep second pitch of Hadrian's Wall Direct. Climber Robbie Miller

*T*he curved axe revolution took off in the early 1970s after the leading climbers of the day had been experimenting with ice daggers. These were plunged into the ice above the head allowing the climber to move up very quickly for a couple of moves. In 1970, John Cunningham and Bill March used the technique to climb The Chancer (V,6) on Hell's Lum Crag, which has a short section of vertical ice, but using ice daggers turned out to be stressful and strenuous and too precarious for sustained high-angle climbing.

The technological advance came later that season when Yvon Chouinard visited from the USA. Chouinard had been experimenting with a curved pick tool, to allow fast movement across long ice slopes in California's Sierra Nevada. He showed his tools to Cunningham at Glenmore Lodge and Hamish MacInnes in Glen Coe, and then proved their effectiveness by climbing the difficult Direct Finish (VI,6) to Raven's Gully with Doug Tompkins. MacInnes had also been experimenting with dropped pick tools, but without success, but after talking to Chouinard he increased the angle of his pick and created the Terrordactyl. Mick Geddes, a Scot studying at Cambridge University, was the first to apply the curved axe technique to Ben Nevis, with quick repeats of Smith's Route and Point Five Gully in March 1971. The following month Geddes climbed the prominent icefall of Hadrian's Wall Direct (V,5), the first major ice route to be climbed on Ben Nevis without step-cutting.

With long sections of high-angle ice and 350m overall length, Hadrian's Wall Direct was a major climb to trial the new technique, and there was no stopping Geddes after that. The following winter he made the long-awaited second ascents of Minus Two Gully and Orion Direct with fellow student Al Rouse. They climbed Orion with sacks full of their weekend gear so they could rush back down the Mountain Track and start the long hitch back to Cambridge that night!

Robbie Miller at the ice screw belay at the top of the second pitch of Hadrian's Wall Direct. Above, a party can be seen climbing the deep icy chimney on the third pitch

Henning Wackerhage

Approach

From the CIC Hut, head diagonally up the hillside, passing below the Douglas Boulder, to gain Observatory Gully, the great corrie defined by North-East Buttress and Tower Ridge. Climb steepening snow slopes right of Observatory Ridge to gain the start of the route just left of Point Five Gully (about **1hr** from the Hut, see p30-31).

Descent

See Ben Nevis Approaches & Descents (p30-33).

Conditions

Hadrian's Wall Direct typically comes into condition in January and remains climbable until the end of the winter. It is a safe climb late in the season as it is not threatened by a cornice, and it is one of the last routes on the mountain to collapse once the spring thaw sets in. Hardened Nevis regulars use the collapse of Hadrian's Wall as the signal that the season is finally coming to an end. The first three pitches provide excellent ice climbing, and the interest continues all the way to the top. Watch out for windy weather when there can be considerable spindrift on the chimney pitch.

Top Tips

Hadrian's Wall Direct is normally climbed in seven pitches and climbing with 60m ropes will provide more opportunity to find belays, especially on the first pitch and in the upper section. Ice screws are essential for both belays and protection on the lower three pitches.

Route Description

The prominent icefall on the west flank of Observatory Ridge provides three steep pitches followed by

49. Hadrian's Wall Direct (V,5)   S. Sickle (V,5)
45. Point Five Gully (V,5)

Simon Richardson

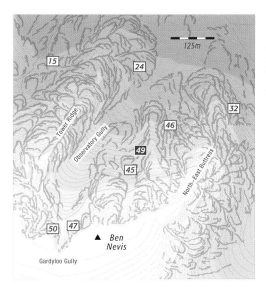

continually interesting climbing in its second half. Climb the icefall to a belay near steep rocks on the left (**60m**). Continue up slightly easier-angled ice to a second ice screw belay (**50m**). Trend slightly right to a deep icy chimney, which leads with interest to a large snowfield (**40m**). From here it is possible to climb up and left to reach the crest of Observatory Ridge in two pitches, but it is better to follow the snowfield up and right for 100m to below a shallow icy scoop between two buttresses. Climb the scoop and slabby walls above in two pitches (**100m**) to gain the plateau a little to the right of Observatory Ridge.

Alternative Routes

Sickle (V,5) is a steeper companion route to Hadrian's Wall Direct, taking the curving slabby groove to the right. It is more sustained with thinner ice and it does not survive as late into the season. Further left is **Vade Mecum** (V,5) which takes a steep ice groove and vertical ice pillar to reach the crest of Observatory Ridge. It is not often in condition but worth doing when it is. To the right of Hadrian's Wall Direct is an area of very steep icy slabs. There are several serious routes up this wall, but the finest and the established classic is **Galactic Hitchhiker** (VI,5). This is a step up from Hadrian's Wall Direct in technical difficulty and seriousness, and provides one of the finest Thin Face climbing experiences on Ben Nevis.

Guidebooks

Ben Nevis (SMC), *Scottish Winter Climbs* (SMC), *Winter Climbs Ben Nevis and Glen Coe* (Cicerone).

Approaching the cave belay at the end of the first pitch of Smith's Route in excellent late season conditions

Cubby Images

SMITH'S ROUTE

Grade: 130m, V,5
Location: Gardyloo Buttress, Ben Nevis
Route Base, Aspect & Rock Type: 1200m, North facing, Andesite
First Ascent: Robin Smith & Jimmy Marshall, 8 February 1960
Icicle Variation: Ken Crocket & Chris Gilmore, February 1975

Henning Wackerhage

A foreshortened view of Gardyloo Buttress from Gardyloo Gully. The climber is on the Icicle Variation

*I*n February 1960, Jimmy Marshall and Robin Smith enjoyed a momentous week of climbing on Ben Nevis. Their much-celebrated collection of routes included the first winter ascent of Observatory Buttress and the second ascent of Point Five Gully. However, the technical highlight was the first ascent of Smith's Route on Gardyloo Buttress. Smith's lead of the very steep second pitch was nothing short of extraordinary when you realise he was climbing with ten point crampons and a single axe. Together with Orion Direct climbed later that week, this was the highpoint of the step-cutting era, and it took a revolution in equipment design (front point crampons and curved picks) before it was repeated in 1971. Four years later, Ken Crocket and Chris Gilmore added the more direct Icicle Variation, which has now become the standard route.

Smith's Route was one of my first Grade Vs. Climbing in early January with Roger Everett, the Icicle Variation had yet to form, so I was naturally drawn towards Smith's original line. As I climbed higher, the ice became thinner and thinner until I reached a point where it suddenly all plated away. I was left eye-balling bare rock with my front points teetering on the top of the remaining ice. Necessity is the mother of invention in situations like this, and after 20 minutes of searching I found a 1cm deep vertical corner-slit where I could place a kingpin with its eye camming against a sidewall. I tied this off and heart in mouth, made a long move right to gain thicker ice that led to the top of the pitch.

Climb Smith's Route later in the season via the Icicle Variation and you should experience no collapsing ice problems, as the icicle forms fat and solid from the snow scoop above. As you enjoy the brilliant exposed climbing, spare a thought for Smith on his long and lonely lead more than 50 years before.

Looking up the first pitch of Smith's Route to the cave belay and Icicle Variation. On this occasion in late March, the icicle has merged into a curtain of ice to the left of the cave. Climbers Alastair Robertson and Stuart Allinson

Henning Wackerhage

Approach

From the CIC Hut, head diagonally up the hillside, passing below the Douglas Boulder to gain Observatory Gully, the great corrie defined by North-East Buttress and Tower Ridge. Climb steepening snow slopes to near the foot of Gardyloo Gully and traverse rightwards to gain the foot of Gardyloo Buttress. These slopes can be avalanche-prone, and a fall on the traverse would take you over the steep buttress containing Tower Scoop (about **1hr 30mins** from the Hut, see p30-31).

Descent

See Ben Nevis Approaches & Descents (p30-33).

Tower Gully is the fastest descent to the CIC Hut from the top of Gardyloo Buttress, but it requires good snow conditions and a passable cornice.

Conditions

The Icicle Variation and the Original Line of Smith's Route are both rated V,5. The Original Line is less steep and forms earlier in the season, but tends to have thinner ice and is harder to protect. The Icicle Variation comes into condition later, but is steeper and has thicker ice. Once formed, Smith's Route is one of the most resistant routes in the country to thaw and will often stay in condition until the end of April.

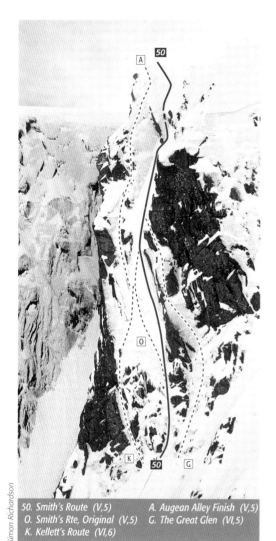

Simon Richardson

50. Smith's Route (V,5)   A. Augean Alley Finish (V,5)
O. Smith's Rte, Original (V,5)   G. The Great Glen (VI,5)
K. Kellett's Route (VI,6)

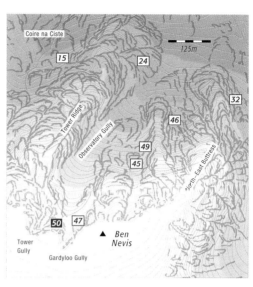

Top Tips

Take ice screws to protect the route and for belays. A 'Deadman' may be useful to belay in the snow scoop in the final funnel.

Route Description

The steep and compact Gardyloo Buttress lies at the head of Observatory Gully. Its upper half consists of twin ridges either side of a shallow depression that opens out into a wide funnel. In winter the funnel forms a snow chute, which drains into an icefall and a left-slanting ice groove. Start directly below the lower end of the slanting grooves on the front face of the buttress.

1. 40m Climb the ice groove to a good belay in an ice cave, flanked by a thick icicle on its left side. In late season, the icicle may merge into a steep curtain of ice. A rock belay can also be taken 10m below the cave, but this can be obscured later in the season.

2. 35m The Icicle Variation: Climb the icicle on its left side, then continue up the ramp above into the funnel. Peg belay on the right wall.

3 and **4. 55m** Continue easily up the snow funnel, and avoid the cornice (which can be huge) by finishing up the arete on the left.

Alternative Routes

The **Original Line** (V,5) moves left from the first belay up a steep groove, before breaking out right on steep ice to gain the left side of the funnel. **Kellett's Route** with **Augean Alley Finish** is an outstanding VI,6 outing taking a direct line up the centre of Gardyloo Buttress. It forms most winters, although not as readily as Smith's Route. **The Great Glen** (VI,5) takes the parallel ramp to the right of Smith's Route and requires a good ice plating to make it climbable. Unfortunately this rarely happens, but it is a much-prized route so climb it when you can! The routes on the right side of Indicator Wall are in the shadow of Gardyloo Buttress and stay in condition late in the season. **Shot in the Dark** (V,5) is the easiest climb in the area and **Caledonia** (V,5) is also very good.

Guidebooks

Ben Nevis (SMC), *Scottish Winter Climbs* (SMC), *Winter Climbs Ben Nevis and Glen Coe* (Cicerone).